Mostly Manga

Recent Titles in
Genreflecting Advisory Series

Diana Tixier Herald, Series Editor

Mostly Manga

A Genre Guide to Popular Manga, Manhwa, Manhua, and Anime

Elizabeth F. S. Kalen

Genreflecting Advisory Series

Diana Tixier Herald, Series Editor

LIBRARIES UNLIMITED

AN IMPRINT OF ABC-CLIO, LLC
Santa Barbara, California • Denver, Colorado • Oxford, England

Library of Congress Cataloging-in-Publication Data

Kalen, Elizabeth.
  Mostly manga : a genre guide to popular manga, manhwa, manhua, and anime / Elizabeth Kalen.
    p. cm.—(Genreflecting advisory series)
  Includes bibliographical references and index.
  ISBN 978-1-59884-938-7 (acid-free paper)
1. Graphic novels—Translations into English—Bibliography. 2. Comic books, strips, etc.—Asia—History and criticism.   3. Animated films—Japan—Catalogs.
4. Libraries—Special collections—Graphic novels.   5. Readers' advisory services—United States.   I. Title.
  Z5956.C6K35   2012
  [PN6710]
  016.7415'95—dc23   2011028456

ISBN: 978-1-59884-938-7

16 15 14 13 12   1 2 3 4 5

Libraries Unlimited
An Imprint of ABC-CLIO, LLC

ABC-CLIO, LLC
130 Cremona Drive, P.O. Box 1911
Santa Barbara, California 93116-1911

This book is printed on acid-free paper ∞

Manufactured in the United States of America

To the University of Western Ontario Winter 2009 M.L.I.S. Cohort—
The Best Cohort Ever. Thanks for all the support, guys.

Contents

Acknowledgments

I would like to acknowledge the help and support of Peter Kalen and Linda Stewart-Kalen, Seth Kalen, Paulette Rothbauer, Lynne McKechnie, Susan Getchell, Paula Kobos, Susan Reese, Megan Hine, Helen Gianoulis, Multnomah County Library—especially the Belmont Branch and its staff, Seattle Public Library, Powell's Books, Borders Books and Music, Movie Madness, Starbucks, Seattle's Best Coffee, Barbara Ittner, Robin Brenner, Adam Arnold at Seven Seas Entertainment, and Corine Hare.

Introduction

I discovered anime and manga when I was in middle school. At that point, the first English translations of manga were being pioneered, but that wasn't really how my friends and I read manga. Those translations were hard to find at times and, quite honestly, not especially good. Most libraries didn't even know what manga were. My friends and I were lucky enough to be in the San Francisco Bay area. We would buy manga in Japanese and take them to the one girl in our group who could read Japanese, and she would provide us with what amounted to a summary. Things have changed.

Now manga can be found almost everywhere. Libraries commonly have manga in their graphic novel collections. Furthermore, manga are no longer the only graphic novel import from Asia. While perhaps not quite as popular as manga, Korean manhwa are now commonly found as well, and Chinese manhua are beginning to appear on store shelves and in libraries. Still, for people unfamiliar with or new to manga, manhwa, manhua, and anime, it can be hard to know where to start or how to find titles they'll enjoy. That's where this guide comes in.

Whether you are looking for a place to start reading Asian graphic novels or looking for more titles to try, this book should prove to be a useful resource. *Mostly Manga* collects titles for manga, manhwa, manhua, and anime, providing information on whether a series is ongoing, how many volumes are in the series, and other useful information. It also provides genre information and will let people find read-alike titles. No matter who uses this book, I hope that they will find it useful in finding titles they enjoy reading.

Purpose and Audience

While there are genre guides for graphic novels in general, there has not been an in-depth reader's advisory guide for the Asian graphic novels. This guide is intended to help readers and reader's advisors find titles of interest to them. Titles for children, teens, and adults are included. It organizes and describes titles available for their reading pleasure. This book provides a guide and resource for reader's advisory in regards to manga, manhwa, manhua, and anime. It mainly covers material for adults and teens with some titles that are appropriate for children. It also provides information on resources should a person be interested in further study on or just looking for a basic guide on the subject.

Scope, Selection Criteria, and Methodology

This publication lists the three major types of Asian graphic novels as well as Japanese anime released in North America from the 1990s until present day. Most of these titles were published in North America within the last 20 years, with a few exceptions. Series that were discontinued by the publisher have not been included except when the titles were especially popular or considered to be classics or groundbreaking. All of the titles in this book were reviewed by the author, with the first volume and at times further volumes examined for multiple volume series. The anime selected for this book were looked at with a focus on series that would be easy for a library to collect in a cost-effective way. Because of this, many of the anime included were those released in box sets. As with other literature, it is recommended that one read a graphic novel or watched an anime before recommending it to young readers.

The book deals with four major formats:

- Manga—Japanese graphic novels

- Anime—Japanese animation

- Manhwa—Korean graphic novels

- Manhua—Chinese graphic novels

This book does not include:

- Animanga—graphic novels created from still shots of an animated work

- Original English-language graphic novels

- Art books—collections and showcases of an artist's work or a series' art

- Series and character guides

- How-to-draw manga books

- Types of animation other than Japanese anime

- Live-action movies based on anime or manga titles

Organization and Features

Mostly Manga organizes title by format and demographic. Some chapters are also subdivided by genre. This book lists all of the major demographics of Japanese manga as well as listing anime titles, Korean manhwa, and Chinese manhua. Each format of graphic novel tends to be a cultural product of its country of origin. Some fans prefer one format over others, and these fans can be very specific about what they are looking for.

The manga are categorized by their main demographic and subdivided by their main genre. This is followed by a section on anime. The manga industry markets its works mainly on the intended audience of a work, and many fans will go looking for that before they look for a specific genre. The manhwa are organized by genre while the manhua are listed alphabetically by title. In chapters where genre is used to organize titles, titles have been put under what I considered the main genre of a work to be. However, it should be noted that genre blending is very common in Asian graphic novels, so many titles fit into multiple genres, and those subsequent genres have also been listed in the entry. There is also a genre index included in the book. Another thing to note is that there are some genres that are not often found outside of the Asian graphic novels. I have provided a brief description of these genres below.

Genres Specific to Asian Graphic Novels

- Harem—Harem stories typically feature a main character surrounded by a cast of supporting characters, most of which are romantically interested in the main character. Most of these stories feature male main characters surrounded by women, but they are a few like *Ouran High School Host Club* that feature female main characters. These stories often include quite a bit of comedy, and the focus of the story, whether it be romance, action, or comedy, varies greatly.

- Magical Girl—Magical girl stories typically focus on either an ordinary girl who is given some sort of power to transform or a girl with some sort of special powers who has come to Earth to fulfill a mission. Her powers can come from magic, supernatural abilities, or even technology. These stories often have a strong focus on friendship and romance. Magical girls are extremely common in Shojo manga, but they can be found in the other demographics as well.

- Mecha—Mecha is a term used to describe giant robots of some sort, usually piloted by a human. As a genre, these stories tend to explore relationships between a robot and its pilots as well as many other science fiction themes. They also often include battles between mechs. With manga, this genre is in many ways similar to the superhero genre in American comic books and has a long tradition in the Japanese comic industry. Mecha are often found in science fiction and action stories, but they can also show up in other genres.

- Slice of Life—Slice of life stories often focus either on a particular setting or character. They tend to depict things out of daily life such as school or family life, and while there may be plot arcs, those are not necessarily required. In many ways, slice of life stories are similar to sitcoms in tone and style, though the manga often have a wide range in subject matter and tone. Some slice of life stories tend to be somewhat realistic while others veer off in other directions, and they can be found blended with a number of different genres.

- Yaoi—Yaoi is also sometimes called Shonen-Ai or Boy's Love and features romances between two male characters. They range in content from mild and extremely fluffy to explicit. Yaoi stories tend to be written by women and are mostly aimed at a female audience, and they do not typically reflect realistic representations of homosexual life in Japan. While it was originally a term used for manga, Yaoi is also used as a genre for manhwa as well.

- Yuri—Yuri is similar to Yaoi, but depicts relationships between women. Yuri titles tend to be most common in demographics targeted to men, but they are found in other demographics as well. They do not typically reflect realistic representations of homosexual life in Japan.

Other Genres Covered

- Action—These stories focus on the action sequences and often involve martial arts or adventures.

- Adventure—Adventure stories often center around a quest or a journey of some sort. The main character is usually working toward some goal or trying to complete a mission.

- Comedy—These stories center around humor. They can range from slapstick to satire to black humor.

- Crime—This genre focuses on crimes and the criminal world. It is sometimes related to mysteries, but the two genres are not necessarily linked in all cases.

- Detective—Detective stories follow a detective and the process of solving a mystery or a crime. They tend to have a focus on problem and puzzle solving. Often related to the crime and mystery genres.

- Drama—In drama, the focus is people experiencing emotional themes and issues. Dramas are often realistic in nature. This genre is often blended with others.

- Historical Fiction—Usually the historical fiction graphic novel uses a setting that occurred before the mid-1980s.

- Horror—Intended to invoke feelings of fear and horror in the reader, horror stories often have dark subject matter and are related to the supernatural genre.

- Fantasy—A setting with magic is typical in fantasy. The setting can be contemporary, historical, or a completely original world, but magic is present in some way.

- Military—Military stories center around members of a military or take place in a military setting.

- Mystery—These stories revolve around the solving of a mystery either by a professional or an amateur detective.

- Romance—Romances center on the romantic relationships of the characters.

- Romantic Comedy—These are romances that center equally on romantic relationships and comedy.

- Science Fiction—Scientific advancements or futuristic settings form the focus of science fiction. They often are set in space or alternate realities.

- Supernatural—Supernatural concepts and creatures such as vampires, werewolves, and witches are the central elements of these stories. They have a slightly different tone than horror as they are less focused on inspiring fear and terror.

- Suspense—These stories are fast-paced and often have a tense atmosphere. A suspense story will usually follow characters through a series of events where they try to unravel or explain something. This genre is related to mysteries and thrillers.

- Thriller—Thrillers are centered around a profession and contain action and suspense. They are often related to suspense and mysteries.

- Western—As might be expected, Westerns are set in the American West during the later half of the 19th century. However, stories that are considered Westerns have also taken the trappings and ideas of the American West and applied them to another setting.

Within each section, entries are organized by alphabetical order by series title. Titles can also be accessed through author, subject, and genre indexes. Entries for all graphic novel titles in this book include the title of the book or series, writer and illustrator, publisher, publication year, if the series is ongoing or not, number of volumes currently in the series, rating, genre, and if there are any related anime as well as a brief description. If the publication year is left open-ended, the series is either still ongoing in Japan or has not been completely translated into English yet. The number of volumes represents the number of volumes in existence for the series, not the number of volumes translated into English. The annotation also notes whether a series has been discontinued by a North American publisher and how many volumes of the series have been published in North America.

The anime annotations include the length of the programs and how many episodes there are if it is a television series. The anime entries do not list related manga if they exist. Most of the anime listed are complete, but a few are included that are still ongoing series in Japan.

The rating designations used are:

A = All Ages

Y = Youth Ages 10 and Above

T = Teens Ages 13 to 15

O = Older Teens Ages 16 and 17

M = Mature Readers Ages 18 and Older

Ratings are, of course, subjective. The ones used in this book are based on ratings by the publishers, librarians and readers, and my own reviews of the material. Readers should read the material they are comfortable with it and enjoy it regardless of the designated age range. Some of the graphic novels that have been marked for mature readers in response to certain content can very well be read and enjoyed by younger readers. The idea of what a mature reader is can be subjective and not limited to a strict interpretation based on age.

The annotations are designed more to give the reader an idea of what to expect from a title than to be a critical review. The focus of the annotation is on the main characters and plot, which is why content such as sex or violence is not specifically indicated.

Some Notes about Anime

Popular manga often have anime adaptations and vice versa. However, just because an anime and a manga share the same title and characters does not mean that their content is exactly the same. Many anime adaptations take different story directions than the manga they may be based on, especially if the manga may not be complete by the time the anime needs to be. In such cases, the ending or overall plot of the anime may be completely different from the manga. Sometimes, another version series will be made to more closely match the manga.

Anime typically fit into one of three categories: films, television shows, or original video animation (OVA). There can be both OVA versions and television versions of some series with exactly the same title. Generally, OVAs either consist of a few episodes or one long episode. They can also be more explicit than other anime because they are released directly to DVD or video.

How to Use This Guide

This guide can be used in several ways. It can be used as a reader's advisory aide and to help find read-alike options. Many sections of the book are broken down by genre, and they can be used to help a patron find read-alikes or simply new titles. The book can also be used for those new to these formats, but not sure where to start reading. It also can be used to build core collections of manga, manhwa, manhua, and anime as well as to add to existing collections of those formats.

This book does not cover all of the wealth that is out there when it comes to both Asian comics and Japanese anime. An attempt has been made to cover a wide range of the materials that are available and to include some classic titles. Some of the titles included have recently gone out of print, while others have been republished in omnibus format. Also, as of May 31, 2011, Tokyopop has ceased production of all of its North American publications. While many of its manga and manhwa are still available in stores at the present, they are now effectively out of print. Some of this titles may be picked up by other publishers eventually. However, this book does provide a broad sampling of what is available and, hopefully, it will provide readers with a useful resource whether they are longtime fans or new to these formats.

Chapter 1

Shonen Manga and Anime

Shonen manga and anime were originally marketed toward boys ages 10 to 18, though they often appeal to other audiences as well. These manga have a range of genre and styles, but they generally have several traits in common. Known for their action sequences and comedy, common genres among Shonen manga are action, adventure, and science fiction. Stories focusing on sports and other hobbies are also common. Shonen manga tend to focus on friendships between characters and camaraderie. Often the heroes have goals that involve bettering themselves and becoming the best or some other sort of quest.

Shonen manga make up one of the largest groups of manga published in both Japan and North America and have an extensive range of subjects and titles. While they may have had a targeted audience, they often to appeal to both adults and young women as well as teenage boys. Many of the most well-known manga and anime like *Naruto, One Piece, Bleach, Dragon Ball Z, InuYasha, Death Note*, and *Fullmetal Alchemist* are all shonen titles. The titles in this section are organized by their main genre, though all of the genre that a title fits into are included.

Shonen Manga

- From Japan

- Marketed toward boys ages 10 to 18

- Read right to left

- Often focus on friendship and camaraderie

- Adventure and quest stories very common

Shonen Manga

Action

Black Cat. Written and Illustrated by Kentaro Yabuki. VIZ Media, LLC, 2006–2009. 20 Vol. **O** Genre: Action, Adventure, Comedy, Fantasy, Science Fiction. Related Anime: *Black Cat*.

> Chronos Numbers are assassins for the Chronos organization. But when Chronos Thirteen, a young man named Train Heartnet, runs across a bounty hunter one day, he decides to leave the organization. Now a bounty hunter, he's pretty happy with his life. But his past may not be as far behind him as he thinks.

Cat Paradise. Written and Illustrated by Yuji Iwahara. Yen Press, 2009–2010. 5 Vol. **O** Genre: Action, Supernatural.

> Yumi thought that Matabi Academy was the perfect fit for her since students were allowed to have their cats in the dorms. That meant she wouldn't have to be separated from her cat and best friend, Kansuke. But when they are attacked by a demon almost immediately after arriving on campus, the two will find themselves drawn into a battle to protect their school from a demon's quest for vengeance.

Chrono Crusade. Written and Illustrated by Daisuke Moriyama. ADV, 2004–2006. 6 Vol. **T** Genre: Action, Adventure, Drama, Romance. Related Anime: *Chrono Crusade*.

> In the shadows of the Roaring Twenties, the Order of Magdalene fights against a demon threat. Sister Rosette Christopher and Chrono, her demon partner, are two of their agents fighting to protect humanity and solve mysteries in their own pasts that are linked to the threat.

Claymore. Written and Illustrated by Norihiro Yagi. VIZ Media, LLC, 2006–. Ongoing Series. 19 Vol. **O** Genre: Action, Fantasy, Supernatural. Related Anime: *Claymore*.

> Humans are terrorized by Yoma and have little chance fighting against them. The worst part is that Yoma can disguise themselves as humans, and no one would know the difference until it is too late. Humanity's only hope are the warriors called Claymore. They are hybrids, part monster, part human. And while a Claymore can defeat a Yoma, Claymores have their own dangers as well.

Fate Stay Night. Written and Illustrated by Dat Nishiwaki. Tokyopop, 2008–. Ongoing Series. 12 Vol. **T** Genre: Action, Romance, Supernatural, Thriller. Related Anime: *Fate Stay Night*.

> Shiro Miya dreams of becoming a hero of justice like his stepfather. However, what he doesn't know is that he is about to be swept up in a magical war. Now despite the fact that he's not sure what's going on, he will find himself fighting for survival with the help of a mysterious young woman named Saber.

Firefighter!: Daigo of Fire Company M. Written and Illustrated by Masahito Soda. VIZ Media, LLC, 2003–2007. 20 Vol. **T** Genre: Action, Adventure.

> Daigo was rescued by a firefighter when he was a child and ever since has been determined to become one himself. As he enters the firehouse, Daigo is going to learn that he has a long way to go, but with courage and determination he can make it. Winner of the Shogakukun Award.

GTO: Great Teacher Onizuka. Written and Illustrated by Tohru Fujisawa. Tokyopop, 2002–2005. 25 Vol. **O** Genre: Action, Comedy, Drama. Related Anime: *GTO: Great Teacher Onizuka.*

> Eikichi Onizuka isn't exactly what you would expect for a high school teacher. He's rude, crude, short-tempered, and an ex-biker. However, his goal is to be the greatest teacher in the world, and he might actually manage it. Onizuka's got more than just schoolwork to teach, and his students will definitely find him a change of pace. Winner of the Kodansha Award.

Gunslinger Girl. Written and Illustrated by Yu Aida. Seven Seas, 2011–. Ongoing Series. 13 Vol. **O** Genre: Action, Science Fiction. Related Anime: *Gunslinger Girl, Gunslinger Girl II.*

> The Social Welfare Society rescues young girls in desperate situations and turns them into assassins for the Italian government. Henrietta is one such girl. Her injuries repaired with cybernetics and her memories wiped away, she is now quite lethal. But she still has some fragmented memories, and they just may cause some problems. Six volumes of the series were published by ADV, which then discontinued the series. It is currently published in omnibus format for the first 6 volumes and will afterward be published in single volumes.

Hayate Cross Blade. Written and Illustrated by Shiziru Hayashiya. Seven Seas, 2008–. Ongoing Series. 13 Vol. 2 Omnibus Vol. **O** Genre: Action, Comedy, Yuri.

> Tenchi Academy is known for training sword fighters. For students in the Sword Bearer program, it means they compete in a school-wide battle in order to win money and fame. Hayate is one such student. She wants to win in order to help pay off her orphanage's debts. It might not be an easy task, but Hayate is determined.

Jing: King of Bandits. Written and Illustrated by Yuichi Kumakura. Tokyopop, 2003–2004. 7 Vol. **T** Genre: Action, Adventure, Comedy, Fantasy, Science Fiction. Related Anime: *Jing: King of Bandits; Jing, King of Bandits: Seventh Heaven.*

> Jing may be young, but his reputation as the bandit king has spread far and wide. Of course, some people don't believe that he's the bandit king when they first meet him, but they often change their minds once they see him in action. One thing is for sure, though: with Jing the adventures never end.

Jing: King of Bandits: Twilight Tales. Written and Illustrated by Yuichi Kumakura. Tokyopop, 2004–2007. 7 Vol. ▨ Genre: Action, Adventure, Comedy, Fantasy, Science Fiction.

> *Twilight Tales* follows Jing's continuing adventures as the king of bandits.

Law of Ueki. Written and Illustrated by Tsubusa Fukuchi. VIZ Media, LLC, 2006–2009. 16 Vol. ▨ Genre: Action, Comedy. Related Anime: *Law of Ueki*.

> There is a contest to determine who will get to be the next Celestial King. Each candidate gives a power to a junior high school student, and then the students battle it out. Kosuke Ueki is one such student. He has the power to turn to trash into trees, and the battle is about to start—even if he's doesn't know he's in the tournament just yet.

Muhyo & Roji's Bureau of Supernatural Investigation. Written and Illustrated by Yoshiyuki Nishi. VIZ Media, LLC, 2007–2010. 18 Vol. ▨ Genre: Action.

> If you have a problem with a ghost, Muhyo and Roji are your guys. The two of them will deal with the ghost, sending it to its just reward according to magical law—that is, if Muhyo can stay awake long enough to deal with them and if the two can keep their partnership from breaking apart.

Nabari No Ou. Written and Illustrated by Yuhki Kamatani. Yen Press, 2009–. 14 Vol. ◙ Genre: Action, Comedy, Drama, Supernatural. Related Anime: *Nabari No Ou*.

> Miharu was perfectly willing to make his way through high school apathetically without caring about much. Then a group of ninja try to kidnap him in broad daylight. He soon learns that he carries the most powerful secret ninja art sealed within his body. And if he wants to survive, he will have to learn to be a ninja himself.

Project Arms. Written by Kyoichi Nanatsuki. Illustrated by Ryoji Minegawa. VIZ Media, LLC, 2003–2009. 22 Vol. ◙ Genre: Action, Science Fiction, Supernatural. Related Anime: *Project Arms*.

> Ryo thought he was just a normal teenager, but when people start trying to kill him and government agents start hunting him, he realizes that something is going on. As his own body begins to transform, Ryo finds himself thrust into a world full of secrets including some about his own past. Winner of the Shogakukun Award.

The Qwaser of Stigmata. Written by Hiroyuki Yoshino. Illustrated by Kenetsu Sato. Tokyopop, 2010–. Ongoing Series. 11 Vol. ▧ Genre: Action, Adventure, Romance, Supernatural.

> Mafuyu and her cousin Tomo find themselves swept up when a Russian boy named Sasha arrives at their school. Sasha is a Qwaser, a person with supernatural powers, and with his arrival, their school becomes a battleground. Things may never be the same for the two cousins.

Saiyuki. Written and Illustrated by Kazuya Minekura. Tokyopop, 2004–2005. 9 Vol. **O** Genre: Action, Fantasy. Related Anime: *Saiyuki*.

Sanzo, Goku, Gojyo, and Hakkai have been sent to India in order to stop the possible resurrection of Gyumaoh. It won't be an easy journey. Between traveling conditions, assassins, and the four men themselves, there is plenty to throw them off track.

Switch. Written by Otoh Saki. Illustrated by Tomomi Nakamura. VIZ Media, LLC, 2008–2010. **O** Genre: Action, Detective, Yaoi.

Two new detectives in the narcotics division, Kai and Hal soon find themselves struggling to do their job and keep the streets safe from drugs. This is complicated by the fact that under certain situations, Kai seems to have a complete change of personality and become a killing machine. The two partners work to do their job and piece together the mysteries in Kai's past.

Toriko. Written and Illustrated by Mitsutoshi Shimabuku. VIZ Media, LLC, 2010–. Ongoing Series. 11 Vol. **T** Genre: Action, Comedy.

Toriko is a Gourmet Hunter. His job is to find the rarest and most precious ingredients for meals. It's a dangerous job, and there's at least one organization that would like to monopolize the world's food sources for itself. But that won't stop Toriko, who is determined to make the ultimate dinner.

Adventure

BakeGyamon: Backwards Game. Written and Illustrated by Mitsuhisa Tamura. VIZ Media, LLC, 2009. 5 Vol. **A** Genre: Adventure.

Sanshiro's tiny island doesn't offer him much of a chance for adventure. However, when a stranger invites him to play a game, he finds himself pulled into another world. The game he's been invited to play consists of fighting with monsters. But Sanshiro's not so sure just how this adventure will turn out when his monsters are just a bunch of mud balls.

The Best of Pokemon Adventures: Red. Written by Hidenori Kusaka. Illustrated by Mato. VIZ Media, LLC, 2006. 1 Vol. **A** Genre: Action, Adventure, Fantasy.

Join Red on his adventures to become a great Pokemon trainer. He will make friends and enemies along the way, and he may even stumble upon a plot or two by the evil Team Rocket.

The Best of Pokemon Adventures: Yellow. Written by Hidenori Kusaka. Illustrated by Mato. VIZ Media, LLC, 2006. 1 Vol. **A** Genre: Action, Adventure, Fantasy.

When Yellow comes to Pallet Town searching for Pikachu, he soon finds himself on a quest to find Red. But this quest may be harder than it seems, and Red's disappearance may be part of some bigger plan.

Beyblade. Written and Illustrated by Takao Aoki. VIZ Media, LLC, 2004–2006. 14 Vol. **A** Genre: Action, Adventure. Related Anime: *Beyblade, Beyblade: V Force, Beyblade: V Revolution.*

> Tyson is passionate about Beyblading. He wants to be the best, and unlike some of his opponents, he refuses to cheat in order to win. However, as Tyson prepares for a tournament he will find himself tested as he makes both friends and enemies.

A Certain Scientific Railgun. Written by Kazuma Kamachi. Illustrated by Motoi Fuyukawa. Seven Seas, 2011–. Ongoing Series. 6 Vol. **T** Genre: Action, Adventure, Fantasy, Science Fiction. Related Anime: *A Certain Scientific Railgun.*

> In Academy City, both magic and scientifically advanced superpowers exist. Most of the city's inhabitants are students learning to control their powers. Mikoto Misaka is one of those students. She also happens to be the third most powerful Level Five Esper in the city. With other members of the student-run law enforcement agency, Judgment, Mikoto works to keep the city safe, but during the course of her job she may just run across some secrets that could threaten all she knows.

Dragon Drive. Written and Illustrated by Ken-ichi Sakura. VIZ Media, LLC, 2007–2009. 14 Vol. **A** Genre: Adventure, Comedy, Science Fiction. Related Anime: *Dragon Drive.*

> Reiji doesn't think he's much good at anything and tends to give up on most things before long. However, his friend Maiko introduces him to the game Dragon Drive. Reiji's dragon, Chibi, doesn't look impressive and seems to sleep all the time, but when push comes to shove, Chibi is more than meets the eye.

Et Cetera. Written and Illustrated by Tow Nakazaki. Tokyopop, 2004–2007. 9 Vol. **Y** Genre: Action, Adventure, Comedy.

> Mingchao is determined to become a Hollywood star. However, to do so, she'll have to get there first. She sets off across the Wild West alone with her grandfather's gun. Along the way she picks up a companion in Baskerville, a priest. Together they'll continue on a journey that may become the adventure of a lifetime.

Fullmetal Alchemist. Written and Illustrated by Hiromu Arakawa. VIZ Media, LLC, 2005–. 27 Vol. **T** Genre: Adventure, Fantasy, Science Fiction. Related Anime: *Fullmetal Alchemist, Fullmetal Alchemist: Brotherhood, Fullmetal Alchemist the Movie: Conqueror of Shamballa.*

> Alchemy gives its users the ability to change the world around them, but it comes with a price. When Edward and Alphonse Elric attempt to resurrect their dead mother using it, Edward loses an arm and a leg, and Alphonse's soul is trapped in a metal suit of armor. In order to reclaim what they have lost, Edward sets out to become a State Alchemist and find the Philosopher's Stone. But the brothers have a long journey ahead of them, and it won't be easy. Winner of the Shogakukun Award.

Hunter x Hunter. Written and Illustrated by Yoshihiro Togashi. VIZ Media, LLC, 2005–. Ongoing Series. 27 Vol. **O** Genre: Action, Adventure, Drama, Supernatural. Related Anime: *Hunter x Hunter.*

> Gon hopes to be able to earn the title of Hunter like his father before him. Hunters are special. They are able to track magical beasts, other men, and treasures. But in order to become a Hunter, Gon will have to earn his license, and the challenges he will face will be nothing like he's ever encountered before.

Kaze No Hana. Written by Ushio Mizta. Illustrated by Akiyoshi Ohta. Yen Press, 2008. 3 Vol. **T** Genre: Action, Adventure, Comedy.

> Momoko lost both her parents and her memory four years ago. Her father's relatives took her in, and now Momoko finds herself caught up in a battle where she may hold the key. With a spiritual sword she doesn't quite understand, Momoka will have to face her destiny.

Legendz. Written by Rin Hirai. Illustrated by Makoto Haruno. VIZ Media, LLC, 2005–2006. 4 Vol. **A** Genre: Action, Adventure, Fantasy, Science Fiction.

> In a world where mythical creatures exist, children train with them in order to compete in Legendz tournaments. Ken is one such kid. He and his Windragon are out to win their school's tournament, and they aren't going to let anything stop them.

Naruto. Written and Illustrated by Masahi Kishimoto. VIZ Media, LLC, 2003–. Ongoing Series. 52 Vol. **T** Genre: Action, Adventure, Drama. Related Anime: *Naruto, Naruto: Shippuden, Naruto: Mission: Protect the Waterfall Village!, Naruto The Movie: Ninja Clash in the Land of Snow, Naruto The Movie 2: Legend of the Stone of Gelel, Naruto The Movie 3: Guardians of the Crescent Moon Kingdom, Naruto: Shippuden: the Movie.*

> Naruto Uzumaki is determined to succeed as a ninja and become of the next Hokage of his village. Not even the fact that he's dead last at the ninja academy is going to stop him. But more than just missions and adventures exist in Naruto's future. Secrets of the past and dangerous enemies also lurk there, but no matter what happens, Naruto isn't one to give up on his dream.

Nausicaä of the Valley of the Wind. Written and Illustrated by Hayao Miyazaki. VIZ Media, 2004. 7 Vol. **T** Genre: Adventure, Drama, Fantasy, Science Fiction. Related Anime: *Nausicaä of the Valley of the Wind.*

> After a devastating war, the world has fractured. Humanity exists in small isolated enclaves while nature itself has become toxic. In the Valley of the Wind, a small kingdom lies protected from the worst of the dangers of the world, and it is here that Nausicaä lives. She has a unique connection to the giant insects of the toxic forest and may even hold the key to finding both peace and healing for the world. Winner of the Seiun Award.

Negima!: Magister Negi Magi. Written and Illustrated by Ken Akamatsu. Del Rey, 2004–2010. Kodansha, 2011–. Ongoing Series. 33 Vol. **O** Genre: Action, Adventure, Comedy, Harem, Magical Girl, Romance. Related Anime: *Negima!: Magister Negi Magi, Negima!: Spring, Negima!: Summer.*

Negi Springfield is a 10-year-old wizard who dreams of becoming a Magister Magi. However, after graduating from his school of magic he gets given the job of teaching English at a girls school in Japan. It's not going to be easy, especially since his new students don't seem to take him very seriously. The first 28 volumes were published by Del Rey. Kodansha comics has taken over publishing the series as of 2011 and will release further volumes as well as also publishing previously released volumes in a omnibus format.

Negima!? Neo. Written by Ken Akamatsu. Illustrated by Takuya Fujima. Del Rey, 2009–2010. Kondasha Comics, 2011–. Ongoing Series. 10 Vol. **O** Genre: Action, Adventure, Comedy, Harem, Magical Girl, Romance. Related Anime: *Negima!?.*

A retelling of *Negima! Magister Negi Magi*, *Negima!? Neo* tells the story in a different direction. Negi Springfield is a very powerful wizard. He also happens to be 10 years old. After graduating from a magic school in England, he somehow ends up being assigned to teach English at an all-girls school in Japan. Negi finds his class of 31 girls a handful, especially since some of them aren't what he expected. But when the Star Crystal disappears, Negi and his class will have more than just schoolwork to deal with.

One Piece. Written and Illustrated by Eiichiro Oda. VIZ Media, LLC, 2003–. Ongoing Series. 59 Vol. **T** Genre: Action, Adventure, Comedy, Drama. Related Anime: *One Piece.*

Monkey D. Luffy has been determined to find the legendary One Piece treasure and become the Pirate King since childhood. Now that he has the power to stretch like rubber (acquired when he accidentally ate the fruit of the Gum Gum), Luffy is off to find the treasure. Along the way he'll acquire a crew and a ship, and together they'll make a name for themselves as pirates.

Pokemon: Arceus and the Jewel of Life. Written and Illustrated by Mokoto Mizobuchi. VIZ Media, LLC, 2011. 1 Vol. **A** Genre: Adventure, Fantasy.

Years ago, the Pokemon Arceus was betrayed by a human. Now it is back and wanting revenge. Ash is joined by new friends and the Pokemon Dialga, Palkia, and Giratina in order to try and save humans from Arceus' wrath.

Pokemon: Diamond and Pearl Adventure!. Written and Illustrated by Shigekatsu Ihara. VIZ Media LLC, 2008–2010. 8 Vol. **A** Genre: Action, Adventure, Fantasy.

Hareta has been living wild in the forest with Pokemon for years until he meets Mitsuki, his grandfather's assistant. She helps him choose his first Pokemon, Piplup, and the two of them soon set off on a journey to find the legendary Pokemon, Dialga. But they aren't the only ones searching for Dialga, and the big question is who will find it first?

Pokemon: Giratina and the Sky Warrior!. Written and Illustrated by Makoto Hijioka. VIZ Media, LLC, 2009. 1 Vol. **A** Genre: Adventure, Fantasy.

> The Pokemon Shaymin was caught in the midst of a battle between two powerful Pokemon and found itself lost. When it is found by Ash and his friends, they quickly learn that many people are interested in the Pokemon and that it might have a connection to Giratina and the Reverse Dimension.

Pokemon: The Rise of Darkrai. Written and Illustrated by Ryo Takamisaki. VIZ Media, LLC, 2008. 1 Vol. **A** Genre: Action, Adventure, Fantasy. Related Anime: *Pokemon: The Rise of Darkrai.*

> Ash is in for an adventure when he arrives in Alamos Town. When trouble begins to happen, a mysterious Pokemon named Darkrai is blamed. But is all of the trouble Darkrai's fault, or is there something more going on?

Pokemon Adventures. Written by Hidenori Kusaka. Illustrated by Mato. VIZ Media, LLC, 2009–. Ongoing Series. 13 Vol. **A** Genre: Adventure, Fantasy.

> Join Red, Yellow, and many other trainers as they pursue their Pokemon journeys. Some of the material in this series has been previously released in "Best of" compilations.

Pokemon Mystery Dungeon: Ginji's Rescue Team. Written and Illustrated by Makoto Mizobuchi. VIZ Media, LLC, 2007. 1 Vol. **A** Genre: Action, Adventure, Fantasy.

> Ginji was a pretty normal boy until the day he woke up as a Pokemon. Together with some new Pokemon friends, Ginji sets out to rescue other Pokemon and maybe try and get back to being human too.

Pokemon Ranger and the Temple of the Sea. Written and Illustrated by Makoto Mizobuchi. VIZ Media, LLC, 2008. **A** Genre: Action, Adventure, Fantasy. Related Anime: *Pokémon Ranger and the Temple of the Sea.*

> When Ash and Pikachu meet Jackie, a Pokemon Ranger with the mission to protect a rare Pokemon, they are in for an adventure. There's a pirate out to steal the Pokemon and collect a mysterious treasure. Ash, Pikachu, and Jackie are going to have their work cut out for them, and there are a number of mysteries they must unravel before Jackie's mission comes to an end.

Rave Master. Written and Illustrated by Hiro Mashima. Tokyopop, 2003–2009. Kondansha Comics, 2011. 35 Vol. **Y** Genre: Adventure, Comedy, Fantasy.

> When Demon Card, an evil organization, threatens his friends and his life on Garage Island, Haru finds himself thrust into a search for the five missing RAVE stones. With a transforming sword and a strange guide named Plue, he's off on an adventure that might just involve saving the world. Tokyopop published volumes 1 through 32. The final three volumes were published by Kondansha Comics in an omnibus format.

Sand Land. Written and Illustrated by Akira Toriyama. VIZ Media, LLC, 2003. 1 Vol. **A** Genre: Action, Adventure, Supernatural.

> In a land where there is little water and the king hoards most of it, Sheriff Rao is fed up. He is off to search for a long-lost lake. When Rao asks the demon king for help, he gets Beelzebub, the king's son, and Thief, Beelzebub's assistant. The three of them set off in a tank across the desert, determined to find water.

Tegami Bachi: Letter Bee. Written and Illustrated by Hiroyuki Asada. VIZ Media, LLC, 2009–. Ongoing Series. 11 Vol. **T** Genre: Adventure, Comedy, Drama, Steampunk, Supernatural.

> AmberGround is a world in darkness. The only light comes from a man-made sun, and that isn't much. There are all sorts of dangers lurking about as well. However, there are those who will brave those dangers in order to deliver mail. They are the Letter Bees. And for one young boy, all it takes is meeting one to make him wish to join their ranks.

Toto!: The Wonderful Adventure. Written and Illustrated by Yuko Osada. Del Rey, 2008–2009. 5 Vol. **T** Genre: Action, Adventure, Comedy, Fantasy.

> Kakashi has always wanted to travel the world like his father. When he receives his father's journal, Kakashi is determined to do so. He stows away on a zeppelin that just happens to have been hijacked by criminals. There he meets a little dog named ToTo, and together the two of them will face any adventures that this journey throws at them.

Yu-Gi-Oh!. Written and Illustrated by Kazuki Takahashi. VIZ Media, LLC, 2003–2004. 7 Vol. **T** Genre: Action, Adventure, Fantasy. Related Anime: *Yu-Gi-Oh!: Duel Monsters, Yu-Gi-Oh! Capsule Monsters, Yu-Gi-Oh! The Movie: Pyramid of Light, Yu-Gi-Oh! 3D: Bonds Beyond Time*.

> Yugi Muto typically spends his time on one game or another. He might get bullied and made fun of, but at least with games and puzzles Yugi has an escape. When he finally completes the Millennium Puzzle, an ancient Egyptian puzzle, Yugi finds that inside is the spirit of the King of Games. He has no qualms possessing Yugi and challenging bullies to some rather interesting games in order to teach them a lesson. But this may be only the beginning for the pair.

Yu-Gi-Oh!: Duelist. Written and Illustrated by Kazuki Takahashi. VIZ Media, LLC, 2005–2007. 24 Vol. **T** Genre: Genre: Action, Adventure, Fantasy.

> Yugi is finding that Duel Monsters may be a more dangerous game than he's ever played before. When he gets blackmailed into a tournament run by the wealthy Maximillion Pegasus, Yugi and his friends head off to face the challenge. But more than just a card game hangs in the balance at this tournament, and Yugi is in for one of his greatest challenges yet.

Yu-Gi-Oh!: GX. Written and Illustrated by Naoyuki Kageyama. VIZ Media, LLC, 2007–. Ongoing Series. 8 Vol. **A** Genre: Action, Adventure, Comedy, Fantasy. Related Anime: *Yu-Gi-Oh! GX*.

Jaden is a student at Duel Academy and in one of the lowest classes. He wants to make his mark on the world, but will he be able to rise to the top?

Yu-Gi-Oh!: Millennium World. Written and Illustrated by Kazuki Takahashi. VIZ Media, LLC, 2005–2008. 7 Vol. **T** Genre: Action, Adventure, Fantasy.

Yugi now has all of the Egyptian God cards and the ability to find out about the Pharaoh's past. Together with their friends they will explore the forgotten past and encounter an enemy that may have been forgotten as well.

Yu-Gi-Oh!: R. Written and Illustrated by Akira Ito. VIZ Media, LLC, 2009–2010. 5 Vol. **T** Genre: Action, Adventure, Fantasy.

Yugi finds himself in a race to save one of his friends. Yako Tenma, Pegasus's protégé, has kidnapped Anzu and is guarding her with some of the world's best duelists. Now Yugi and his other friends will have to duel their way to her and hopefully reach her before it is too late.

Comedy

Alice on Deadlines. Written and Illustrated by Shiro Ihara. Yen Press, 2007–2008. 4 Vol. **O** Genre: Comedy, Fantasy.

The shinigami Lapan is sent to the human realm in the body of a skeleton as a punishment for slacking. However, due to a slight mix-up, he's now in the body of Alice, a student at an all-girls school, and she's the one in the skeleton. Now that Lapan's in her body, he's leaving quite a mess in his wake, and what is poor Alice to do about all this?

B. Ichi. Written and Illustrated by Atsushi Ohkubo. Yen Press, 2008–2009. 4 Vol. **O** Genre: Action, Comedy.

Shotaro is a dokeshi. He can use a greater percentage of brain in order to unleash special powers. However, there is one condition. He has to do one good deed every day. When his path crosses that with Mana, the two of them don't exactly get along at first. But together the two of them end up setting off searching for Shotaro's missing friend, and it may turn into the adventure of their lives.

Dr. Slump. Written and Illustrated by Akira Toriyama. VIZ Media, LLC, 2005–2009. 18 Vol. **T** Genre: Comedy, Drama, Science Fiction.

When Senbei, an inventor, comes with a robot who looks like a young girl, he finds his latest invention might be more than he can handle. Curious and without much knowledge of the world, Arale will need some help if Penguin Village is to be kept in the dark about the fact that she's not really human. Winner of the Shogakukun Award.

Gin Tama. Written and Illustrated by Hideaki Sorachi. VIZ Media, LLC, 2007–. Ongoing Series. 36 Vol. **O** Genre: Comedy, Parody, Science Fiction. Related Anime: *Gin Tama*.

Aliens invaded Japan and conquered it. Then they took all of the jobs and took the swords away from the samurai. It's a tough world to make a living in, but Sakata "Gin" Gintoki is doing the best he can. And that means doing whatever job comes his way no matter how odd. Just don't mess with the man's need for sweets because when his blood sugar level drops, everyone's in trouble.

Girls Bravo. Written and Illustrated by Mario Kaneda. Tokyopop, 2005–2007. 10 Vol. T Genre: Comedy, Harem. Related Anime: *Girls Bravo.*

Yukinari has been so bullied by girls by the time he reaches high school that he actually breaks out in hives if he touches one. When he accidentally gets transported to an alien world populated mainly by women, Yukinari meets Miharu, who amazingly doesn't cause an allergic reaction. She follows him home, and things would have been all right, except for the fact that she's not the only one. Yukinari's life has just gotten a whole lot more complicated.

Hetalia: Axis Powers. Written and Illustrated by Hidekaz Himaruya. Tokyopop, 2010–. Ongoing Series. 3 Vol. O Genre: Comedy, Historical Fiction. Related Anime: *Hetalia: Axis Powers, Hetalia: World Series, Hetalia: Axis Powers: Paint It, White.*

World history has never been so interesting as it is in *Hetalia*, an allegorical tale where the countries of the world are now the main characters. Join Germany, Italy, and Japan as they begin to form a partnership and set events in motion that will lead to some of the most famous periods of history.

Midori Days. Written and Illustrated by Kazurou Inoue. VIZ Media, LLC, 2005–2006. 8 Vol. O Genre: Comedy, Drama, Romance. Related Anime: *Midori Days.*

Seiji is a teenage delinquent with bad grades and no prospects for a girlfriend. Or at least that's what he thinks. However, Midori happens to worship him from afar. Then one day, she ends up somehow miniaturized and attached to Seiji where his right hand was. Now he has to try and keep it a secret and perhaps figure out how to fix things, and he might just end up with a girlfriend after all.

Sayonara, Zetsubou-Sensei. Written and Illustrated by Koji Kumeta. Del Rey, 2009–2010. Kodansha, 2011–. Ongoing Series. 22 Vol. O Genre: Comedy, Satire. Related Anime: *Sayonara, Zetsubou-Sensei.*

Nozomu Itoshiki tried to kill himself. He failed because one of his new homeroom students rescued him. To make matters worse, he finds that every single one of his new students has some sort of quirk that needs to be dealt with. This isn't easy when the man takes everything in the most negative light possible. And it makes for a rather interesting life for everyone involved. Winner of the Kodansha Award.

SGT. Frog. Written and Illustrated by Mine Yoshizaki. Tokyopop, 2004–. Ongoing Series. 20 Vol. T Genre: Comedy, Science Fiction. Related Anime: *SGT. Frog.*

Sgt. Keroro was in charge of an invasion of Earth by his people. At least he was until he accidentally got captured by a pair of middle school students. Now he's stuck living with a human family, but that doesn't mean he's given up on taking over the world, though it seems to have made things much harder for him. Winner of the Shogakukun Award.

Welcome to N.H.K. Written by Tatsuhiko Takimoto. Illustrated by Kendi Oiwa. Tokyopop, 2006–2008. 8 Vol. **M** Genre: Comedy, Drama, Romance. Related Anime: *Welcome to N.H.K.*

Satou, a 20-something college dropout, thinks he might have discovered a secret conspiracy designed by the Japanese Broadcasting Company NHK. Of course, this also has the result of him becoming a reclusive shut-in. When a girl named Misaki arrives in his life, however, Satou will find himself coming out of his reclusive state only to get caught up in a journey that might just get a little crazy.

Yakitate!! Japan. Written and Illustrated by Takashi Hashiguchi. VIZ Media, LLC, 2006–2011. 26 Vol. **O** Genre: Comedy, Cooking.

Kazuma Azuma is determined to come up with Japan's national bread: a bread that tastes better than rice. To further his baking skills, he moves to Tokyo and is determined to get a job at Pantasia, a famous baking chain. But first Kazuma will have to pass their entrance exam, and he's not the only one who wants a job there. Kazuma is up for a challenge, but he isn't going to give up on his dreams. Winner of the Shogakukun Award.

Your & My Secret. Written and Illustrated by Ai Morigana. Tokyopop, 2008–2010. 7 Vol. **T** Genre: Comedy, Romance.

Akira is the guy that no one notices, and Nanako is the girl that everyone notices until she opens her mouth and scares them away. When a freak accident involving one of Nanako's grandfather's inventions switches their bodies, both of them experience a number of changes and new freedoms. And the question becomes not only, "Will they be able to switch back?" but also, "Will they want to?"

Cyberpunk

Black Magic. Written and Illustrated by Shirow Masamune. Dark Horse, 2008. 1 Vol. **O** Genre: Cyberpunk, Science Fiction. Related Anime: *Black Magic M-66.*

In its ancient past, Venus once teemed with life. A supercomputer controls the government with bioroids to enforce its edicts. However, even on Venus there are factions and power struggles. So Duna Typhon is created. A super-bioroid independent from the supercomputer, she has been raised among humans and will use her powers to protect them if need be.

Detective

Spiral: The Bonds of Reasoning. Written by Kyo Shirodaira. Illustrated by Eita Mizuno. Yen Press, 2007–2011. 11 Vol. **T** Genre: Comedy,

Detective, Mystery, Romance, Thriller. Related Anime: *Spiral: The Bonds of Reasoning.*

> When his brother, a detective, disappears, Ayumu becomes determined to find him. He has only one clue, the words "Blade Children," which were the only words he could make out from his brother's final phone call. With the help of a journalist from his school and his sister-in-law, a detective, Ayumu sets out to unravel the mystery of the Blade Children, but it may involve more than he ever expected.

Steam Detectives. **Written and Illustrated by Kia Asamiya. VIZ Media, LLC, 1999–2004. 8 Vol. T Genre: Detective, Noir. Related Anime:** *Steam Detectives.*

> In Steam City, coal is the only source of fuel, and steam engines power most things. With the air thick with steam and fog, criminals lurk everywhere. But Narutaki, a young detective, fights to make the city a safe place. With the help of the nurse Ling Ling, Narutaki is going to help protect Steam City, no matter how dangerous it is.

Drama

Black Jack. **Written and Illustrated by Osamu Tezuka. Vertical, 2008–2011. 17 Vol. O Genre: Drama, Medical.**

> He is known as Black Jack, and he is a medical mercenary. An extremely talented surgeon, Black Jack will perform just about any operation for you, for a price. However, he has been known to perform acts of kindness and charity as well. Whatever else he might be, Black Jack is something of a mystery. Winner of the Kodansha Award.

Highschool of the Dead. **Written by Daisuke Sato. Illustrated by Shouji Sato. Yen Press, 2011–. Ongoing Series. 6 Vol. M Genre: Drama, Horror, Supernatural, Romance. Related Anime:** *Highschool of the Dead.*

> When a pandemic sweeps the world, leaving zombies in its wake, six high school students band together in order to survive. Takashi and his friend are two of them. Takashi finds himself in the position of leader, but he doesn't know how long he can keep them all alive or if there's any hope for survival at all.

I"s. **Written and Illustrated by Masakazu Katsura. VIZ Media, LLC, 2005–2007. 15 Vol. T Genre: Drama, Romance. Related Anime:** *From I"s, I"s Pure.*

> Itchitaka has a crush on his classmate Iori. However, he's too shy to say much, and she just happens to be sick of fending off jerks, thanks to a modeling job. Things get even more complicated when Ichitaka's female childhood friend Ituski moves back to Japan and into his house, and she just happens to be interested in him. Itchitaka is torn between the two women, and he will find that love and relationships don't come easy.

Someday's Dreamers. **Written and Illustrated by Norie Yamada. Tokyopop, 2006. 2 Vol. T Genre: Drama, Fantasy, Romance. Related Anime:** *Someday's Dreamers.*

> Yume has moved to Tokyo for the summer in order to continue her training as a mage. Mages can only use their powers with special permission. Trainee mages

must complete an apprenticeship under another mage, and Yume's apprenticeship has just begun.

Someday's Dreamers: Spellbound. Written by Norie Yamada. Illustrated by Kumichi Yoshizuki. Tokyopop, 2006–2008. 5 Vol. T Genre: Drama, Fantasy, Romance.

Nami is a magic user who doesn't exactly have the best of luck with life at times. When Ryutaro, a new student, arrives at her school, Nami finds herself drawn to him. But with her luck, will she be able to get to know him or will her bad luck strike again?

Fantasy

+Anima. Written and Illustrated by Natsumi Mukai. Tokyopop, 2006–2008. 10 Vol. T Genre: Adventure, Fantasy.

There are those who have strange abilities. They are able to change parts of their bodies into animals and have other animal-like powers. These people are called +Anima. Cooro is one of them, as is Husky. When the two boys meet, they soon set off on a quest to find others like themselves.

Arata: The Legend. Written and Illustrated by Yuu Watase. VIZ Media, LLC, 2009–. Ongoing Series. 8 Vol. T Genre: Adventure, Fantasy.

Arata is the successor to the Hime Clan. The only problem is that he's a boy, not a girl, so Arata spends most of his time cross-dressing. However, somehow he manages to switch places with another boy named Arata, this one from modern Japan. In a world totally unfamiliar to them, both Aratas will have an adventure on their hands. But will they ever get switched back, and will they want to be?

D. Gray-Man. Written and Illustrated by Katsura Hoshino. VIZ Media, LLC, 2004–. Ongoing Series. 21 Vol. O Genre: Action, Fantasy. Related Anime: *D. Grey-Man.*

Allen Walker is a 15-year-old exorcist fighting against demons known as akuma and searching for Innocence, the substance used to make anti-akuma weapons. Along with other members of his order, Allen fights against the Millennium Earl, who wishes to destroy humanity, and it may just be Allen who holds the key to defeating him.

Desert Coral. Written and Illustrated by Wataru Murayama. ADV, 2004–2006. 5 Vol. A Genre: Fantasy.

Naoto has been daydreaming about a fantasy world for quite a while. However, he never expected it to be real or to find himself summoned there. The sorceress, Lusia, who has summoned him, has plans for him, and this may be one dream that Naoto can't wake up from.

Elemental Gelade. Written and Illustrated by Mayumi Azuma. Tokyopop, 2006–. 18 Vol. **T** Genre: Action, Adventure, Fantasy, Romance. Related Anime: *Elemental Gelade.*

> In Guardia, humans coexist with Edel Raids. The Edel Raids can fuse with a human to become a living weapon. When sky pirate Coud Van Giruet captures an Edel Raid named Ren on a raid, he finds himself drawn into an adventure he never expected. As they journey to find a legendary land of gold, they'll have to defeat enemies and maybe find something besides gold.

Enchanter. Written and Illustrated by Izumi Kawachi. DMP, 2006–. 19 Vol. **O** Genre: Action, Fantasy, Romance.

> Haruhiko has a crush on his next-door neighbor, Yuka, now a teacher at his school. However, his life gets completely disrupted when her exact lookalike shows up. Eukanaria may look like Yuka, but she happens to be a demon and will stop at nothing to get Haruhiko's body so she can restore the enchanter Fulcanelli, her love. Nothing is going to be the same in Haruhiko's life again.

Fairy Tail. Written and Illustrated by Hiro Mashima. Del Rey, 2008–. Kodansha, 2011–. Ongoing Series. 25 Vol. **T** Genre: Action, Adventure, Comedy, Fantasy. Related Anime: *Fairy Tail.*

> When the young mage, Lucy, runs away from home in order join the Fairy Tail Guild, things don't go exactly as she planned. However, Natsu (the young man who rescues her) just happens to be the Salamander of the Guild. Lucy joins him along with some other friends in order to take on missions for the guild, and she is in for one amazing adventure.

Flame of Recca. Written and Illustrated by Nobuyuki Anzai. VIZ Media, LLC, 2003–2009. 33 Vol. **O** Genre: Action, Adventure, Fantasy, Romantic Comedy. Related Anime: *Flame of Recca.*

> Recca Hanabishi is a young man who claims to be a ninja with the ability to control fire. However, not long after he rescues a young woman with the ability to heal, Recca finds himself approached by a strange woman who tries to get him to kill her. And that's only the beginning of the adventure of a lifetime.

Hoshin Engi. Written and Illustrated by Ryu Fujisaki. VIZ Media, LLC, 2007–2011. 23 Vol. **T** Genre: Fantasy.

> Taikobo has been trained to hunt demons and seal them away forever, and he has every reason to want to given that the demon Dakki is responsible for wiping out his clan. However, he soon finds that there is more to what is going on than he expected, and his adventures are far from being easy,

Hyde & Closer. Written and Illustrated by Haro Aso. VIZ Media, LLC, 2010–. Ongoing Series. 7 Vol. **O** Genre: Action, Comedy, Fantasy.

> Shunpei Closer isn't exactly sure of himself and he's not very talented at much of anything. However, when he is attacked, he finds out that his beloved grandfather just happened to be the King of Sorcerers. Shunpei is his heir, even if he

doesn't know what he's doing yet. Thankfully, the teddy bear, Hyde, which was a gift from said grandfather, can come to life. Hyde will be Shunpei's protector and teacher as he learns how to wield magic and fight his own battles.

InuYasha. Written and Illustrated by Rumiko Takahashi. VIZ Media, LLC, 1998–2011. 56 Vol. 5 VIZ Big Vol. O Genre: Adventure, Fantasy, Romance. Related Anime: *InuYasha, InuYasha: The Final Act, InuYasha the Movie: Affections Across Time, InuYasha the Movie: The Castle Beyond the Looking Glass, InuYasha the Movie: Swords of an Honorable Ruler, InuYasha the Movie: Fire on the Mystic Island.*

> When Kagome falls down a well in her family's shrine, she finds herself transported back in time to the feudal era. Attacked by a demon, Kagome accidentally releases the half-demon Inuyasha from his imprisonment. Soon the two of them set off on a quest to find all the pieces of the Shikon Jewel. But Kagome will find that surviving in the fuedal era, finding the jewel, and juggling high school is a task that is far more difficult than it seems. Winner of the Shogakukun Award.

Kobato. Written and Illustrated by CLAMP. Yen Press, 2010–. Ongoing Series. 5 Vol. T Genre: Adventure, Comedy, Drama, Fantasy, Romance.

> Kobato is on a quest to make her dearest wish come true. However, first she's going to have to heal people's hearts without falling in love. With the help of Ioryogi, a blue plush toy, Kobato is on her way with only her lack of common sense to hinder her.

The Legend of Zelda: Four Swords. Written and Illustrated by Akira Himekawa. VIZ Media, LLC, 2009. 2 Vol. A Genre: Action, Adventure, Fantasy.

> In order to rescue Princess Zelda, Link must master the Four Sword. The sword has split him into four versions of himself, and if he wants to save the princess, Link is going to have to learn to work with himself.

The Legend of Zelda: A Link to the Past. Written and Illustrated by Akira Himekawa. VIZ Media, LLC, 2010. 1 Vol. A Genre: Action, Adventure, Fantasy.

> When a voice in his dream wakes Link one night, he ends up rescuing the Princess Zelda. He is then sent on a quest to find the Master Sword in order to save both Zelda and his homeland.

The Legend of Zelda: Majora's Mask. Written and Illustrated by Akira Himekawa. VIZ Media, LLC, 2009. 1 Vol. A Genre: Action, Adventure, Fantasy.

> When Link's friend Navi goes missing, Link sets off in search of her. Along the way, Skull Kid steals the Ocarina of Time from Link, and Link is in for another great adventure.

The Legend of Zelda: The Minish Cap. Written and Illustrated by Akira Hime-kawa. VIZ Media, LLC, 2009. 1 Vol. **A** Genre: Action, Adventure, Fantasy.

When a strange man named Vaati turns Princess Zelda to stone, Link must find the pieces of the Picori Blade in order to save her.

The Legend of Zelda: Ocarina of Time. Written and Illustrated by Akira Hime-kawa. VIZ Media, LLC, 2008. 2 Vol. **A** Genre: Action, Adventure, Fantasy.

Link is a young boy who has never really fit in with the others in the Kokiri Forest. When the fairy Navi arrives to take Link to the Great Deku Tree, it is the beginning of a great adventure. Link will have to find a way to protect both Princess Zelda and the entire Kingdom of Hyrule from the evil Ganondorf.

The Legend of Zelda: Oracle of Ages. Written and Illustrated by Akira Hime-kawa. VIZ Media, LLC, 2009. 1 Vol. **A** Genre: Action, Adventure, Fantasy.

Link finds himself sent back in time to keep an evil sorceress from killing one of his ancestors and thus changing the future. If Link fails, he may cease to exist completely.

The Legend of Zelda: Oracle of Seasons. Written and Illustrated by Akira Hime-kawa. VIZ Media, LLC, 2009. 1 Vol. **A** Genre: Action, Adventure, Fantasy.

Link was born with the mark of the triforce on one of his hands. This destines him for greatness. So he sets out to take the Knight's Trial without knowing he is only starting on an adventure.

MÄR: Märchen Awakens Romance. Written and Illustrated by Nobuyuki Anzai. VIZ Media, LLC, 2005–2007. 15 Vol. **T** Genre: Action, Adventure, Comedy, Fantasy, Romance. Related Anime: MÄR.

Ginta doesn't exactly have a lot going for him. He is short and near-sighted as well bad at school and at sports. He has had the same dream over a hundred times, but that doesn't count for much. Then he finds himself sent to another world, and everything changes.

O-Parts Hunter. Written and Illustrated by Seishi Kishimoto. VIZ Media, LLC, 2006–2009. 19 Vol. **O** Genre: Action, Adventure, Fantasy.

After her father dies, Ruby takes on his job of treasure hunting for O-Parts, magical artifacts that can grant certain people powers. She also comes across a boy by the name of Jio who wants to take over the world. The two of them become traveling companions as they search for answers about their pasts.

Train + Train. Written by Hideyuki Kurata. Illustrated by Tomomasa Takuma. Go!comi, 2007–2008. 6 Vol. **T** Genre: Action, Adventure, Fantasy.

On the planet Deloca, high school is conducted on trains, which travel the world to provide students with an interesting hands-on experience. There are two choices: the Standard Train or the Special Train. Reiichi was planning on taking the Standard Train. Then he got handcuffed to Arena, a mysterious young warrior. Now he finds himself on the Special Train. High school is not going to be what he expected.

Tsubasa: Reservoir Chronicle. **Written and Illustrated by CLAMP. Del Rey, 2004–2010. 28 Vol. T Genre: Fantasy, Romance. Related Anime:** *Tsubasa Chronicle, Tsubasa Chronicle the Movie: The Princess of the Country of Birdcages, Tsubasa Tokyo Revelations, Tsubasa Shunraiki.*

> Syaoran might be just a humble archeologist, but he has been friends with Princess Sakura of Clow since childhood. When Sakura visits him at his dig site, disaster strikes. The only way to save Sakura now is for Syaoran to travel through dimensions collecting feathers that contain Sakura's memories. So along with an amnesiac Sakura, he sets out. Syaoran is joined by the warrior, Kurogane, and the magician, Fai, both traveling for their own reasons. Together the four to them will attempt to find Sakura's feathers. But there may be more to this mission than any of them knows.

Venus Versus Virus. **Written and Illustrated by Atsushi Suzumi. Seven Seas, 2008–2010. O Genre: Action, Fantasy, Yuri. Related Anime:** *Venus versus Virus.*

> Sumire has always been able to see ghosts, but it isn't until she meets a monster hunter named Lucia that her life takes an interesting turn. Lucia is a member of the Venus Vangard, and she fights monsters called "Viruses" that hunt human souls. Sumire soon finds herself drawn into Lucia's world, and she finds that she might just be able to help in the fight too.

Harem

Love Hina. **Written and Illustrated by Ken Akamatsu. Tokyopop, 2002–2003. 14 Vol. O Genre: Comedy, Harem, Romance. Related Anime:** *Love Hina, Love Hina Christmas Special, Love Hina Spring Special, Love Hina Again.*

> Thanks to a childhood promise, Keitaro is determined to get into Tokyo University. However, he's failed the exams twice. Still, he's not about to give up, which is how he ends up running his family's boardinghouse. The catch is it's now a girls' dorm, and he's the only guy around. Living with five beautiful women will be interesting, if it doesn't kill him first. Winner of the Kodansha Award.

Historical Fiction

Barefoot Gen. **Written and Illustrated by Keiji Nakazawa. Last Gasp, 2004–2010. 10 Vol. T Genre: Drama, Historical Fiction.**

> Gen and his family live in Hiroshima. When the bomb is dropped on their city, Gen struggles to survive and take care of his family. But despite the destruction and chaos around him, Gen also finds reasons to hope. Considered a classic.

Buddha. Written and Illustrated by Osamu Tezuka. Vertical, 2004–2005. 8 Vol. **T** Genre: Drama, Historical Fiction, Humor, Supernatural.

> Siddhartha's life from his birth to his journey toward enlightenment has been retold in manga in ways that are both humorous and enlightening. Considered a classic, it has won the Eisner Award, the Harvey Award, and the Bungeishunju.

Peace Maker. Written and Illustrated by Nanae Chrono. Tokyopop, 2007–2008. 5 Vol. **O** Genre: Action, Adventure, Drama, Historical Fiction.

> When their parents are murdered, Tetsunosuke and Tatsunosuke are left are their own. Tatsu, the older of the two, being a pacifist, takes a job as an accountant. However, Tetsu wants revenge for their family. He decides to join the Shinsengumi, but convincing them to let a 15-year-old who looks 10 join their ranks may not be easy. A prequel to *Peace Maker Kurogane*.

Peace Maker Kurogane. Written and Illustrated by Nanae Chrono. Tokyopop, 2009–. Ongoing Series. 6 Vol. **O** Genre: Action, Adventure, Drama, Historical Fiction. Related Anime: *Peacemaker Kurogane*.

> The Shinsengumi are now Kyoto's official police force, and Tetsu is now officially working for them as the Vice-Commander's page. But the Shinsengumi have their enemies, and soon will find themselves caught up in one of the bloodiest periods of Japan's history. Tetsu must choose his path carefully as he is caught up in it all.

Rurouni Kenshin. Written and Illustrated by Nobuhiro Watsuki. VIZ Media, LLC, 2003–2010. 28 Vol. 9 VIZ Big Vol. **O** Genre: Action, Adventure, Historical Fiction, Romance, Samurai. Related Anime: *Rurouni Kenshin, Samurai X, Samurai X: Trust & Betrayal, Samurai X: Reflection*.

> Kenshin Himura was once the Hitokiri Battousai, one of the most feared assassins of the revolution. But that was nearly 10 years ago. He has since become a wanderer and made a vow not to kill again. When he arrives in Tokyo, Kenshin rescues Kaoru Kamiya, a young kendo instructor, who ends up offering him a home. All Kenshin really wants to do is live in peace, but there are enemies both old and new that he'll have to face before that can happen.

Horror

Cirque Du Freak. Written by Darren Shan. Illustrated by Takahiro Arai. Yen Press, 2009–. 12 Vol. **T** Genre: Adventure, Fantasy, Horror, Supernatural.

> Darren's life changed when he came to the Cirque Du Freak. As he is drawn into the shadowy world of the freak show, he will find his entire world shifting.

Deadman Wonderland. Written by Jinsei Kataoka. Illustrated by Kazuma Kondou. Tokyopop, 2010–. Ongoing Series. 8 Vol. **O** Genre: Action, Horror, Science Fiction.

> Ten years after the Great Tokyo Earthquake destroyed much of the country, middle school student Ganta finds himself framed for the murder of his

classmates and sentenced to the Deadman Wonderland Prison. There he finds himself in a grim game for survival and maybe with a little luck, he might find the answers to his questions about just why this is happening to him.

The Drifting Classroom. **Written and Illustrated by Kazuo Umezu. VIZ Media, LLC, 2006–2008. 11 Vol.** Ⓜ **Genre: Horror.**

> After a strange earthquake, Sho finds his elementary school transported to a wasteland. Back home, there is just a hole in the ground. Sho and his fellow students quickly find themselves in a desperate struggle to survive, and it's clear that not everyone will. Winner of the Shogakukun Award.

Nightmare Inspector: Yumekui Kenbun. **Written and Illustrated by Shin Mashiba. VIZ Media, LLC, 2008–2009. 9 Vol.** Ⓣ **Genre: Fantasy, Horror, Science Fiction.**

> Those people suffering from their nightmares can find help at the Silver Star Teahouse. They provide more than just tea there. There a customer will find Hiruko, a dream eater. And for a price, he can deal with your worst nightmares.

Variante. **Written and Illustrated by Igura Sugimoto. CMX, 2004–2008. 4 Vol.** Ⓜ **Genre: Horror, Mystery.**

> Aiko should be dead. After seeing her family slaughtered by a monster, she does not expect to wake up in some sort of hospital. But the truth of what is going on is still unknown to Aiko, and before long, she will have to decide just what role she is willing to play in it all.

Martial Arts

Dragon Ball. **Written and Illustrated by Akira Toriyama. VIZ Media, LLC, 2000–2009. 16 Vol. 5 VIZ Big Vol.** Ⓣ **Genre: Action, Adventure, Fantasy, Martial Arts, Science Fiction. Related Anime:** *Dragon Ball.*

> Goku is a rather strange kid. With a monkey tail and super strength, he's never left the woods where he lives. However, when a girl named Bulma stumbles across him during her search for the Dragon Balls, Goku ends up teaming up with her and leaving his home. Whoever collects all seven Dragon Balls can summon the dragon and be granted one wish. But Bulma and Goku aren't the only ones who want the Dragon Balls, and their journey isn't going to be an easy one.

Dragon Ball Z. **Written and Illustrated by Akira Toriyama. VIZ Media, LLC, 2000–2010. 26 Vol. 9 VIZBig Vol.** Ⓐ **Genre: Action, Adventure, Fantasy, Martial Arts, Science Fiction. Related Anime:** *Dragon Ball Z, Dragon Ball Z Kai, Dragon Ball GT.*

> A continuation of Dragon Ball, Goku is now all grown up and has a family of his own. But he can't rest on his laurels, for Earth is threatened by Saiyans

who have come to destroy it. Now Goku and his friends will have to defend their planet, and that will only be the start of their next set of adventures.

Knights of the Zodiac: Saint Seiya. Written and Illustrated by Masami Kurumada. VIZ Media, LLC, 2003–2010. 28 Vol. **T** Genre: Fantasy, Martial Arts. Related Anime: *Knights of the Zodiac.*

Seiya is a young man who is training in Greece in order to win a Bronze Cloth and become one of 88 Saints. He finds himself agreeing to participate in a tournament against other Saints in order to get help to find his missing sister. But Seiya may find both friends and enemies at the tournament, and it might just be the start of his adventure.

Real Bout High School. Written by Reiji Saiga. Illustrated by Sora Inoue. Tokyopop, 2002–2004. 6 Vol. **T** Genre: Action, Comedy, Martial Arts. Related Anime: *Real Bout High School.*

At Ryoko's school, the teachers grade the students' fights rather than break them up. Ryoko herself is the top student until Shizuma transfers in. When the principal proposes a tournament, then their rivalry really begins to heat up. After all, only one of them can be the best.

YuYu Hakusho. Written and Illustrated by Yoshihiro Togashi. VIZ Media, LLC, 2003–2009. 19 Vol. **T** Genre: Fantasy, Martial Arts, Supernatural. Related Anime: *YuYu Hakusho, Yu Yu Hakusho the Movie: Poltergeist Report.*

Yusuke Urameshi, a teenage delinquent, changed his life by dying. When he gets hit by a car and dies, saving a little boy in the process, Yusuke is given a second chance at life. Yusuke's second chance comes with some certain strings, but he's never been one to turn down a good fight, and this definitely promises to be one. So now he's the spirit detective, and if that means fighting demons, Yusuke's not going to complain. Winner of the Shogakukun Award.

Mecha

Mobile Fighter G Gundam. Written by Hajime Yadate and Yoshiyuki Tomino. Illustrated by Kouichi Tokita. Tokyopop, 2003. 3 Vol. **Y** Genre: Action, Martial Arts, Mecha, Science Fiction. Related Anime: *Mobile Fighter G Gundam.*

In the future, disputes between countries are solved with Gundam fighters. These giant robotic suits are piloted by humans. The 13th Gundam Tournament is about to start, but this year, there is something wrong. The Dark Gundam seeks to destroy the Earth and brainwashes pilots in order to do so. Perhaps the best hope for the world is Neo-Japan's pilot, Domon Kasshu—if he can survive the tournament, that is.

Mobile Suit Gundam: Ecole Du Ciel. Written and Illustrated by Haruhiko Mikimoto. Tokyopop, 2005–. Ongoing Series. 11 Vol. **T** Genre: Action, Mecha, Military, Science Fiction.

Asuna isn't exactly the best student at Ecole du Ciel, a military school, but when she risks flunking out, she finds that she might just be cut out to be a mobile suit pilot after all. But the school also hides secrets, and she and her classmates maybe facing more than just a war.

Mobile Suit Gundam: Lost War Chronicles. Written by Tomohiro Chiba. Illustrated by Masato Natsumoto. Tokyopop, 2006. 2 Vol. T Genre: Action, Drama, Mecha, Science Fiction.

The One Year War is over, but that does not mean that every thing is now at peace. Two men are working to make sure that there is both peace and a future for everyone, but Ken Bederstadt and Matt Healy are going to have their work cut out for them.

Mobile Suit Gundam Wing. Written and Illustrated by Koichi Tokita. Tokyopop, 2000–2001. 3 Vol. Y Genre: Mecha, Military, Science Fiction. Related Anime: *Mobile Suit Gundam Wing*.

Five teenagers with advanced mobile suits called Gundams are sent to Earth from the space colonies with a mission: to damage the United Earth Sphere Alliance, which has oppressed the colonies for years. However, they will find that things are not so simple as that, and together the five of them will struggle to figure out what peace is and if it can exist for them.

Mobile Suit Gundam Wing: Battlefield of Pacifists. Written and Illustrated by Koichi Tokita. Tokyopop, 2002. 1 Vol. Y Genre: Mecha, Military, Science Fiction.

What happened in between the events of Gundam Wing and Endless Waltz? Battlefield of Pacifists is one possible take on those events as the Gundam pilots find themselves dealing with the remnants of plots from the past even as a fragile peace is threatened.

Mobile Suit Gundam Wing: Endless Waltz. Written and Illustrated by Koichi Tokita. Tokyopop, 2002. 1 Vol. Y Genre: Mecha, Military, Science Fiction. Related Anime. *Mobile Suit Gundam Wing: Endless Waltz*.

Endless Waltz provides a conclusion to the Gundam Wing series. Once more, Earth and the space colonies are near war, and the Gundam Pilots scramble to put a stop to it. Has the world learned the lessons of the previous wars yet or is it doomed to keep repeating the same wars over and over again?

Mobile Suit Gundam Wing: Ground Zero. Written and Illustrated by Reku Fuyunagi. VIZ Media, LLC, 2001. 1 Vol. Y Genre: Mecha, Military, Science Fiction.

What happened in between the events of Gundam Wing and Endless Waltz? Ground Zero is one possible take on those events as the Gundam pilots find themselves at loose ends now that the fighting is over.

Neon Genesis Evangelion: The Shinji Ikari Raising Project. Written and Illustrated by Osamu Takehashi. Dark Horse: 2009–. Ongoing Series. 10 Vol. **T** Genre: Comedy, Drama, Mecha, Romance, Science Fiction.

> In an alternate universe from the original *Neon Genesis Evangelion*, life is a little brighter. Shinji Ikari is a fairly ordinary high school student. His best friend since childhood is Asuka. When Rei, a new student, arrives, however, his life starts to get rather interesting.

Mystery

Case Closed. Written and Illustrated by Gosho Aoyama. VIZ Media, LLC, 2004–. Ongoing Series. 71 Vol. **O** Genre: Comedy, Drama, Detective, Mystery. Related Anime: *Case Closed, Case Closed: The Time-Bombed Skyscraper, Case Closed: The Fourteenth Target, Case Closed: The Last Wizard of the Century, Case Closed: Captured in Her Eyes, Case Closed: Countdown to Heaven, Case Closed: The Phantom of Baker Street.*

> High school student Jimmy Kudo is the guy the police call when they can't solve a mystery. However, when he sticks his nose where he shouldn't, Jimmy finds himself in a world of trouble. Force-fed poison that ends up shrinking him instead of killing him, Jimmy is now an elementary school student. Taking the name Conan Edogawa, Jimmy is determined to unravel the mystery behind those who shrank him and get back to his normal life. But this may be the toughest mystery he's ever faced, and being a kid again is going to make things more difficult than he expects. Winner of the Shogakun Award.

Future Diary. Written and Illustrated by Sakae Esuno. Tokyopop, 2009–. 11 Vol. **O** Genre: Horror, Mystery, Supernatural, Suspense.

> Yukiteru's main hobby is keeping a diary on his cell phone. However, his cell phone is rather special. It can predict the future. But as it turns out, he's not the only one with a special cell phone, and soon Yukiteru finds himself in a deadly game pitted against the others with Future Diaries.

Pandora Hearts. Written and Illustrated by Jun Mochizuki. Yen Press, 2009–. Ongoing Series. 12 Vol. **O** Genre: Action, Comedy, Fantasy, Mystery, Psychological Thriller, Romance. Related Anime: *Pandora Hearts.*

> Oz Vessalius finds his coming-of-age ceremony memorable, mostly because he ends up thrown in the Abyss, an eternal prison. He finds himself saved by a girl named Alice. Now he just has to figure out the mysteries of the Abyss, Alice, and an organization called Pandora.

Parody

Excel Saga. Written and Illustrated by Rikdo Koshi. VIZ Media, LLC, 2003–. Ongoing Series. 25 Vol. **T** Genre: Action, Parody, Science Fiction. Related Anime: *Excel Saga.*

> Excel and Hyatt might currently have minimum-wage jobs, but that's not all they do. The two girls are also members of ACROSS, a secret organization run by

Il Palazzo. Their mission: to take over the world. They haven't even managed to take over the city they live in yet. Still, that's not going to stop them.

Hayate the Combat Butler. Written and Illustrated by Kenjiro Hata. VIZ Media, LLC, 2006–. Ongoing Series. 25 Vol. O Genre: Parody, Romantic Comedy. Related Anime: *Hayate the Combat Butler.*

Hayate has had to work part-time jobs since childhood to pay off his parents' gambling debts. When they sell his organs to the Yakuza to pay off a debt, Hayate attempts a kidnapping in order to pay the money back. However, things don't go quite as planned, and he ends up rescuing the girl he meant to kidnap. She promptly hires him as her new butler, and Hayate's life may never be the same.

Romance

Densha Otoko: The Story of the Train Man Who Fell in Love with a Girl. Written and Illustrated by Wataru Watanabe. CMX, 2005–2007. 3 Vol. T Genre: Romance.

When an ordinary geek on the train stands up to a guy hassling a pretty girl, he finds that his life changes. She wants to thank him. He has no problem with that, but he's not used to dating at all, especially dating pretty girls. What is a geek to do except post online asking for help? With a cadre of online friends giving advice, does he have a chance with what could be the girl of his dreams?

Pita-Ten. Written and Illustrated by Koge-Donbo. Tokyopop, 2004–2005. 8 Vol. T Genre: Drama, Fantasy, Romance.

Kotaro's life has been pretty lonely and sad lately, but all that changes when a strange girl moves in next door. Misha claims that she is an angel, and it's her mission to make sure that Kotaro's life is happy and safe. Unfortunately, she doesn't know much about living on Earth, which may cause more than a few problems. At least Kotaru's life won't be boring now.

Strawberry 100%. Written and Illustrated by Mizuki Kawashita. VIZ Media, LLC, 2007–. 19 Vol. O Genre: Comedy, Harem, Romance.

Junpei, an aspiring movie director and a high school student, gets inspiration through a chance encounter. The only problem is that he doesn't know the name or the face of his new muse. So he embarks upon a quest that may lead him to dreams, romance, and inspiration.

Tuxedo Gin. Written and Illustrated by Tokihiko Matsuura. VIZ Media, LLC, 2003–2005. 15 Vol. O Genre: Action, Comedy, Romance.

Ginji Kusanagi had everything going for him. He was just about to make his debut as a pro boxer, and he had a date with the girl of his dreams, Minako. Then he gets killed in a motorcycle accident. But fate gives him a second chance. The only catch is he has to get reincarnated as a penguin and live through its lifetime. Then he can be reincarnated as himself. Gin's determined to go through with it, but life as a penguin is going to be a challenge.

Romantic Comedy

Cheeky Angel. Written and Illustrated by Hiroyuki Nishimori. VIZ Media, LLC, 2004–2008. 20 Vol. **O** Genre: Action, Romantic Comedy.

> Megumi is probably the prettiest girl in school, even if she acts like a guy. There is a reason for that. Until six years ago, Megumi was a boy. Then a genie misheard his wish and suddenly he's a girl. Megumi is searching for a book that might reverse the wish, but along the way she's got plenty on her plate, especially when the local delinquent starts falling for her. Winner of the Shogakukun Award.

Inukami!. Written by Mamizu Arisawa. Illustrated by Mari Matsuzawa. Seven Seas, 2008–2011. 5 Vol. **O** Genre: Fantasy, Harem, Romantic Comedy.

> Inukami are mystical dog-like beings, and Keita Kawahira comes from a family known for taming them. However, he seems to lack that particular talent, and so has been abandoned by his family. When he meets Yoko, a beautiful Inukami, it seems like he might have a chance after all, but he also might be getting in over his head. Also available in a two-volume omnibus.

Kashimashi: Girl Meets Girl. Written by Satoru Akahori. Illustrated by Yumimaru Katsura. Seven Seas, 2006–2008. 5 Vol. **O** Genre: Romantic Comedy, Science Fiction, Yuri. Related Anime: *Kashimashi: Girl Meets Girl, Kashimashi: Girl Meets Girl (OVA)*.

> Hazumu tried to escape into the outdoors after the girl he liked rejected him. Unfortunately for him, an alien crash-lands their space ship on him. The alien does bring Hazuma back to life, only now he's a girl. Then Hazumu lands herself in the middle of a love triangle, and things really get complicated.

Pretty Face. Written and Illustrated by Yasuhiro Kano. VIZ Media, LLC, 2007–2008. 6 Vol. **O** Genre: Romantic Comedy.

> Masashi Rando is a high school student and a karate champion until the day he's in a bus accident. His face is burned beyond recognition, but the plastic surgeon reconstructs it from the picture in his wallet. The catch, however, is that the picture was of Masashi's crush, Rina. So now he looks like a girl, and his crush thinks that he just might be her long-lost twin sister. What's a guy to do?

Ranma ½. Written and Illustrated by Rumiko Takehashi. VIZ Media, LLC, 2003–2006. 36 Vol. **O** Genre: Martial Arts, Romantic Comedy. Related Anime: *Ranma ½, Ranma ½ (O.V.A.), Ranma ½: Big Trouble in Nekonron, China, Ranma ½: Nihao My Concubine*.

> Ranma Saotome has spent the last 10 years on a training journey with his father. However, when they reach a training ground in China, an accident occurs. Both Ranma and his father fall into cursed springs. Now when splashed with cold

water, Ranma's father turns into a panda. Ranma turns into a girl. Hot water turns them both back into their normal forms. Things get even more complicated when Ranma's father drags him back to Japan in order to fulfill an old promise. Ranma will marry Akane Tendou and keep both families' martial arts traditions alive. Of course, neither Ranma nor Akane have agreed to this, but according to their families they don't have a choice.

Rizelmine. Written and Illustrated by Yukiru Sugusaki. Tokyopop, 2005. 1 Vol. T Genre: Romantic Comedy, Science Fiction.

Rizel is a genetically engineered girl whose tears can cause explosions. She was created by the government. Her loneliness is beginning to cause far too much damage, so the government decides to marry her off. Enter Tomonori, a 15-year-old who just found out that he's married and that his life is about to get very interesting.

Toradora. Written by Yuyuko Takemiya. Illustrated by Zekkyo. Seven Seas, 2011–. Ongoing Series. 4 Vol. O Genre: Drama, Romantic Comedy. Related Anime: _Toradora_.

Ryūji's looks cause everyone to assume that he's a delinquent despite the fact that he's really gentle and gets good grades. This doesn't help him get any closer to his crush, Minori. To make matters worse, he crosses paths with Taiga, the most feared girl in the school. But while they don't get off to the best start, they might be able to help one another. After all, Taiga is Minori's best friend, and she also just happens to have a crush on Ryūji's best friend. Perhaps they could help one another with their crushes, if they don't kill each other first.

Video Girl Ai. Written and Illustrated by Masakazu Katsura. VIZ Media, LLC, 2004–2006. 15 Vol. O Genre: Romantic Comedy, Science Fiction. Related Anime: _Video Girl Ai_.

Yota's nickname is actually Dateless. He's fallen for a classmate of his, but she's in love with his best friend. After renting a video in order to cheer himself up, though, Yota never expected a girl to pop out of his TV screen. She says her name is Ai, and she is there to help him with his love life.

Samurai

Samurai Champloo. Written and Illustrated by Masaru Gotsubo. Tokyopop, 2008. 1 Vol. T Genre: Action, Comedy, Drama, Samurai. Related Anime: Samurai Champloo.

A series of coincidences bring together Mugen and Jin, both wandering swordsmen of rather different temperaments, with Fuu, a young woman searching for her father. Fuu ends up saving the men, and they agree to help her as well as not fight one another until they've found him. The three of them set off on their search and find plenty of adventure along the way.

Samurai Deeper Kyo. Written and Illustrated by Akimine Kamijyo. Tokyopop, 2003–2009. 34 of 38. Vol. Del Rey, 2009–2010. 2 Omnibus Vol. **O** Genre: Samurai, Supernatural. Related Anime: *Samurai Deeper Kyo.*

> Kyoshiro Mibu and Demon Eyes Kyo are currently sharing a body. Kyo is a legendary samurai, and Kyoshiro was once his rival. Now as the two of them share a body, Kyo hunts for a way to regain his own form. Tokyopop released 34 volumes of the series before discontinuing it. Del Rey published the remaining volumes as two omnibus volumes.

Science Fiction

A.I. Love You. Written and Illustrated by Ken Akamatsu. Tokyopop, 2004–2005. 8 Vol. **O** Genre: Science Fiction, Romance.

> Hiroshi's a computer geek with bad luck and a knack for programming artificial intelligences. However, when a freak accident occurs, one of his A.I.s is turned into a girl. Now there's suddenly a girl in his life that he can relate to, but does that mean he has a chance with her?

Angelic Layer. Written and Illustrated by CLAMP. Tokyopop, 2002–2003. 5 Vol. **A** Genre: Action, Comedy, Drama, Fantasy, Science Fiction. Related Anime: *Angelic Layer.*

> Misaki has just moved to Tokyo to live with her aunt and go to school. She quickly gets caught up in the game Angelic Layer, where people battle using dolls called Angels. Misaki names her angel Hikaru, and while the two of them might be new to Angelic Layer, they definitely are making a splash.

Apollo's Song. Written and Illustrated by Osamu Tezuka. Vertical, 2010. 2 Vol. **O** Genre: Drama, Romance, Science Fiction.

> *Apollo's Song* follows the young boy Shogo as he explores the ideas and concepts of love between a man and a woman.

Aqua. Written and Illustrated by Kozue Amano. Tokyopop, 2007–2008. 2 Vol. **T** Genre: Adventure, Drama, Science Fiction, Slice of Life.

> Akari has just arrived on the planet Aqua. It used to be known as Mars until it was terraformed during the past 150 years. Now the planet is 90 percent covered in water, and Akari is there to learn how to be a gondolier and guide.

Aria. Written and Illustrated by Kozue Amano. Tokyopop, 2008–. 12 Vol. **O** Genre: Adventure, Drama, Science Fiction, Slice of Life. Related Anime: *Aria the Animation, Aria the Natural, Aria the Origination, Aria the OVA: Arietta.*

> Akari is an Undine, a guide and gondolier on the canal streets of Neo-Venezia. She left Earth in order to come here to train as an Undine. As Akari explores the city, she will make friends and explore the new world she now lives on.

Astro Boy. Written and Illustrated by Osamu Tezuka. Dark Horse, 2002–2004. 23 Vol. **T** Genre: Action, Adventure, Science Fiction. Related Anime: *Astro Boy* (1963), *Astro Boy* (1982), *Astro Boy* (2003).

> Astro Boy was built by Dr. Temna in order to replace his son Tobio, who died as a child. However, when he realizes that Astro can never truly replace Tobio, he abandons the robot and sells him to the circus. Astro soon finds himself adopted by a Dr. Ochanomizu, who treats him as his son, and the young robot soon becomes a hero and ambassador with many adventures. This series is considered a classic.

MegaMan: NT Warrior. Written and Illustrated by Ryo Takamisaki. VIZ Media, LLC, 2004–2008. 13 Vol. **A** Genre: Adventure, Science Fiction. Related Anime: *MegaMan: NT Warrior*.

> In a future where most problems have been solved, World Three is out to destroy the peace. That's where Lan comes in. The fifth grader and his Netnavi (a navigation program), MegaMan, make for a pretty unstoppable team. When the two of them stumble upon World Three's plot, they begin to fight back.

The Melancholy of Haruhi Suzumiya. Written by Nagaru Tanigawa. Illustrated by Gaku Tsugano. Yen Press, 2008–. Ongoing Series. 4 Vol. **O** Genre: Comedy, Science Fiction. Related Anime: *The Melancholy of Haruhi Suzumiya*.

> Kyon's first day of high school is hijacked by his classmate, Haruhi Suzumiya. The next thing he knows he's been drafted into her SOS Brigade. It also becomes clear to him that of the five members of the brigade he quite possibly is the only normal human among them. Haruhi can't stand boredom, and the brigade gets involved with whatever crazy stunts she comes up with. Kyon had thought he was going to be a typical apathetic high school student. Somehow, he doesn't think that is going to happen now.

Metropolis. Written and Illustrated by Osamu Tezuka. Dark Horse, 2003. 1 Vol. **T** Genre: Science Fiction.

> Considered a classic by many, *Metropolis* is the story of Michi, an artificial life form that has no idea she's not human. It explores the nature of humanity, especially in a technological society.

Phoenix. Written and Illustrated by Osamu Tezuka. VIZ Media, LLC, 2003–2008. 12 Vol. **O** Genre: Science Fiction, Spiritual.

> Phoenix is a tale of reincarnation and the search for eternal life. It moves forward and backward in time, and it is considered one of Tezuka's most important works.

Saber Marionette J. Written by Satoru Akahori. Illustrated by Yumisuke Kotoyoshi. Tokyopop, 2003–2004. 5 Vol. **O** Genre: Adventure, Comedy, Romance, Science Fiction. Related Anime: *Saber Marionette J*.

> There are no women on Terra II. There are, however, female androids called Marionettes. Of course, it is also taboo to fall in love with them. So what's

Otaru to do when he falls for a rather special Marionette by the name of Lime? She just happens to have emotions and a personality. And she also may hold the key to a new future for all of the planet.

Scryed. Written by Yosuke Kuroda. Illustrated by Yasunori Toda. Tokyopop, 2003. 5 Vol. O Genre: Adventure, Science Fiction. Related Anime: *S-cry-ed*.

After the Great Uprising, things have certainly changed. There are now those with special powers called Alter Users, who can alter matter into what they will, and most of them use those powers to their own advantage. There is also Holy, a special police force that fights Alters. However, at times, neither of them are what is the best for the public in general. Enter Kazuma, an Alter who is definitely going to change things.

Silent Möbius. Written and Illustrated by Kia Asamiya. VIZ Media, LLC, 1992–2003. 12 Vol. O Genre: Action, Science Fiction, Supernatural. Related Anime: *Silent Mobius*.

When the Entities came to Earth, Earth needed someone to protect it. That's where the A.M.P. comes in. It consists of six young women with a variety of special abilities. Led by Rally Cheyenne, they may be the only thing that stands between Earth and disaster.

To Terra. Written and Illustrated by Keiko Takemiya. Vertical, 2007. 3 Vol. O Genre: Psychological, Science Fiction, Supernatural. Related Anime: *Toward the Terra, Toward the Terra* (TV Series).

In a future where computers control almost everything, a race called the Mu, who have psychic powers, has emerged. Humans have decided that the Mu are a threat and must be destroyed. Most children with the potential to be Mu are killed before they reach adulthood, though the adult Mu try to save as many as they can. When Jomy takes his Maturity Check, he finds himself pulled into a whole new world where he just might be the best hope for the Mu. Winner of the Shogakukun Award and the Seiun Award.

Wāqwāq. Written and Illustrated by Ryu Fujisaki. VIZ Media, LLC, 2009–2010. 4 Vol. T Genre: Science Fiction.

Humanity lives in fear of the machines that roam the world. They are protected by the Guardians. Shio is a young guardian who ends up entrusted with a girl named Matsuda. She is believed to be a Kami because she has red blood, and people hope that she can bring peace to the land. But first the two of them will have to survive.

Slice of Life

Azumanga Daioh. Written and Illustrated by Kiyohiko Azuma. ADV, 2003–2004. 4 Vol. Yen Press, 2009. 1 Vol. T Genre: Comedy, School, Slice of Life. Related Anime: *Azumanga Daioh: The Animation*.

Ordinary life can be surprisingly amusing. Follow the lives of six high school students and two of their teachers. Everyone has quirks, but life would be boring without them.

Bakuman. Written by Tsugumi Ohba. Illustrated by Takeshi Obata. VIZ Media, LLC, 2010–. Ongoing Series. 11 Vol. **T** Genre: Comedy, Drama, Romance, Slice of Life.

> Moritaka enjoys drawing. When his classmate, Akita, who happens to be an aspiring writer, discovers this, he convinces Moritaka to team up with him in order to create manga. Moritaka's a little skeptical though. Becoming a mangaka isn't easy, but with a little encouragement, he might give the dream a chance.

Yotsuba&!. Written and Illustrated by Kiyohiko Azuma. Yen Press, 2009–. Ongoing Series. 10 Vol. **A** Genre: Comedy, Slice of Life.

> Yotsuba is a five-year-old who doesn't know much about the world. But that doesn't stop her from being endlessly curious. Moving to a new town definitely gives her plenty of things to explore.

Sports

Air Gear. Written and Illustrated by Oh!great. Del Rey, 2006–2010. Kodansha, 2011–. Ongoing Series. 39 Vol. **O** Genre: Action, Comedy, Sports. Related Anime: *Air Gear.*

> Ikki lives with the Noyamano sisters and is probably the toughest guy in the area. He also happens to be fascinated with flying. When he gets beaten by the Skull Saders, a gang of Storm Riders (people who use Air Treks, a type of high-powered inline skates), Ikki thinks he's lost it all. However, the Noyamano sisters have something up their sleeves. They just happen to be Storm Riders themselves, and they think Ikki has what it takes to join them. And Ikki's not going to give up until he's proven himself. Volumes 15, 16, and 17 were released in an omnibus format. Winner of the Kodansha Award.

Cross Game. Written and Illustrated by Mitsuru Adachi. VIZ Media, LLC, 2010–. 8 Omnibus Vol. **T** Genre: Romantic Comedy, Sports. Related Anime: *Cross Game.*

> Ko is the son of the owner of a sports store. While he doesn't seem to be that interested in sports, secretly he's been training to be as good a pitcher as the girl next door, Aoba. As they grow older, both of them will struggle to attain their dreams in the field of baseball, and along the way they may learn some things about themselves as well. Winner of the Shogakukun Award.

Eyeshield 21. Written by Riichiro Inagaki. Illustrated by Yusuke Murata. VIZ Media, LLC, 2005–. 37 Vol. **O** Genre: Comedy, Drama, Sports. Related Anime: *Eyeshield 21.*

> Sena is fast. He has to be if he wants to get away from bullies. However, he's just started high school and is determined not to get picked on anymore. But the captain of the football team (who rather looks like a demon) has his eye on Sena, and it may turn out to a very interesting year.

Prince of Tennis. Written and Illustrated by Takeshi Konomi. VIZ Media, LLC, 2004–2011. 42 Vol. **A** Genre: Comedy, Drama, School, Sports. Related Anime: *Prince of Tennis*.

> Ryoma Echizen is a teenage tennis ace. After transferring to a private school known for its tennis team, he gets things off to a quick start by defeating most of the upperclassmen and earning a spot on the school tennis team. As the team gears up for the National Championships, they work on improving their skills, and Ryoma begins to discover just what the game means to him.

Slam Dunk. Written and Illustrated by Takehiko Inoue. VIZ Media, LLC, 2008–. 31 Vol. **T** Genre: Comedy, Drama, Sports.

> Hanamachi Sakuragi has been rejected by 50 girls in a row. It's not exactly encouraging. However, when he meets Haruko, his life changes both because she could be the girl of his dreams and because she introduces him to basketball. Hanamachi might have started playing the game in order to impress her, but this might just be the game for him, and he's determined for his team to succeed. Winner of the Shogakukun Award.

Whistle!. Written and Illustrated by Daisuke Higuchi. VIZ Media, LLC, 2004–2010. 24 Vol. **A** Genre: Sports.

> When Sho transferred to a new school in order to play soccer, things don't exactly go well. At his older school, the soccer team had never let him play, claiming he was too short. When his new teacher accidentally introduces him as a star player from his old school, it doesn't take long for things to fall apart. But Sho is determined to be the best soccer player he can be, and he'll practice day and night to prove it.

Supernatural

Black Butler. Written and Illustrated by Yana Toboso. Yen Press, 2010–. Ongoing Series. 11 Vol. **O** Genre: Action, Comedy, Mystery, Supernatural. Related Anime: *Black Butler*.

> The Earl Phantomhive, a loyal servant of Queen Victoria and a giant in the area of commerce, happens to be a 12-year-old boy named Ciel. But his young age is not a problem for Ciel—not when he has his butler Sebastian to carry out his orders and wishes, and Sebastian does so with a skill that isn't quite human.

Bleach. Written and Illustrated by Tite Kubo. VIZ Media, LLC, 2004–. Ongoing Series. 47 Vol. **T** Genre: Action, Adventure, Horror, Supernatural. Related Anime: *Bleach, Bleach: Memories of Nobody, Bleach: Diamond Dust Rebellion*.

> Ichigo Kurosaki was a normal high school student who had the ability to see the dead. It was that ability that got him turned into a shinigami or Soul Reaper: those who send wandering spirits to Soul Society and fight spirits who have turned evil. But Soul Society isn't the paradise it seems. Nothing about dealing

with death is simple, and Ichigo is caught right in the middle. Winner of the Shogakukun Award.

Blood+. Written and Illustrated by Asuka Katsura. Dark Horse, 2008–2009. 5 Vol. **O** Genre: Adventure, Supernatural. Related Anime: *Blood+.*

Saya's life is fairly normal for an amnesiac, though she does keep having horrible nightmares. However, those nightmares prove to be connected to her past, and as Chriopterans, shape shifters that crave human blood, threaten humanity, it may be up to Saya to save everyone.

Blue Exorcist. Written and Illustrated by Kazue Kato. VIZ Media, LLC, 2011–. Ongoing Series. 5 Vol. **O** Genre: Action, Fantasy, Supernatural.

The human world and the demon world exist like mirror images. Demons can only come into the human world by possessing things in it. However, Satan, the god of demons, has a problem. There hasn't been a vessel strong enough for him to possess. So he created Rin, his son by a human world. Now Satan plans on possessing Rin, but his son may not go along with his plans. At least, not without a fight.

Buso Renkkin. Written and Illustrated by Nobuhiro Watsuki. VIZ Media, LLC, 2006–2008. 10 Vol. **O** Genre: Action, Supernatural. Related Anime: *Buso Renkin.*

When Kazuki Muto wakes up one morning, he thinks his dream of rescuing a girl from a monster and getting killed was just a dream. However, when he and his sister are attacked by another monster, the girl from his dream shows up. Tokiko tells them that the monster is a homunculus, and the only thing that can kill them is a weapon called a Buso Renkin. So Kazuki's finding that life just got much more interesting as he joins Tokiko in her fight.

Chibi Vampire. Written and Illustrated by Yuna Kagesaki. Tokyopop, 2006–2009. 14 Vol. **O** Genre: Horror, Romantic Comedy, Supernatural. Related Anime: *Karin.*

Karin might look like a cute school girl, but she has a secret: she's a vampire. In fact, that's part of her problem. Unlike the rest of her family, Karin produces blood instead of drinking it, and she must bite people to expel the excess blood. To make things worse, not only does the new transfer student, Kenta, think there's something strange about her, but he might just hold some of the answers to her problems.

Chikyu Misaki. Written and Illustrated by Yuji Iwahara. CMX, 2005–2006. 3 Vol. **T** Genre: Mystery, Supernatural.

When Misaki inherits her great-grandfather's home, she moves to Hohoro, a little town by a lake. She soon finds that one of her new friends is in fact a legendary creature. Misaki will have her work cut out for her in making a new home and protecting her friends, but it could be that inheriting the house was the best thing to happen to her.

Dororo. Written and Illustrated by Osamu Tezuka. Vertical, 2008. 3 Vol. 🆃 Genre: Action, Historical Fiction, Supernatural.

> An orphaned thief, Dororo runs across Hyakkimaru, a man who hunts demons in order to reclaim his life. Dororo soon joins Hyakkimaru in his journey, and the two of them travel together through the war-torn countryside. Winner of the Eisner Award.

Genju no Seiza. Written and Illustrated by Matsuri Akino. Tokyopop, 2006–. Ongoing Series. 14 Vol. 🅾 Genre: Comedy, Fantasy, Supernatural.

> Fuuto might not have had exactly a normal life, but it gets a whole lot stranger when he finds out that he just happens to be the reincarnated spiritual leader of a little country named Dhalashar. Now he's also having visions and seeing ghosts, and he's about to embark on a journey that may change his life.

Hikaru No Go. Written by Yumi Hotta. Illustrated by Takeshi Obata. VIZ Media, LLC, 2006–2011. 23 Vol. 🅰 Genre: Games, Psychological, School, Supernatural. Related Anime: *Hikaru No Go.*

> Hikaru's a pretty typical kid, though when he finds a bloodstained Go board in his attic, things start to get interesting. That Go board just happens to be haunted by an ancient Go master, and when he ends up taking up residence in Hikaru's mind, Hikaru finds a new interest in the game of Go and a number of adventures. Winner of the Shogakukun Award.

Kekkaishi. Written and Illustrated by Yellow Tanabe. VIZ Media, LLC, 2005–. Ongoing Series. 32 Vol. 🆃 Genre: Action, Comedy, Drama, Romance, Supernatural. Related Anime: *Kekkaishi.*

> Yoshimori and Tokine are both demon exterminators, kekkaishi, as well as next-door neighbors. Despite the fact that their families don't get along, the two of them have been friends for awhile and work together well. This is a good thing since they definitely have their work cut out for them. Winner of the Kodansha Award.

Kurozakuro. Written and Illustrated by Yoshinori Natsume. VIZ Media, LLC, 2010–. 7 Vol. 🅾 Genre: Adventure, Supernatural.

> Mikito is sick of being bullied, but he's not exactly able to stand up for himself. Then he meets a strange kid named Zakuro. Zakuro claims that he can help Mikito. But there is a catch: Mikito may no longer be entirely human now.

Mail. Written and Illustrated by Housui Yamazaki. Dark Horse, 2006–2007. 3 Vol. 🅾 Genre: Horror, Supernatural.

> Reiji Akiba has an interesting job. He's a private eye, but he specializes in cases that deal with ghosts. Armed with a sanctified gun, Reiji's one detective with the most unusual cases.

Nora: The Last Chronicle of Devildom. Written and Illustrated by Kazunari Kakei. VIZ Media, LLC, 2008–2010. 9 Vol. **O** Genre: Action, Comedy, Supernatural.

> Nora happens to be a rather disobedient demon. As a punishment, he's sent into the human world in order to hunt down renegade demons. The catch is Nora's powers are now controlled by Kazuma, a human high school student. The two of them are supposed to work together, but they can't even seem to get along.

Nura: Rise of the Yokai Clan. Written and Illustrated by Hiroshi Shiibashi. VIZ Media, LLC, 2011–. Ongoing Series. 14 Vol. **T** Genre: Action, Supernatural.

> Rikuo Nura is stuck in the middle. He's part human and part yokai, not to mention the fact that his grand father is a powerful yokai leader. Rikuo's always lived with yokai, so he doesn't mind him, but he finds his classmates aren't exactly of the same mind. Plus, there's the fact that he's his grandfather's heir, and there are quite a few yokai who aren't pleased about that either. Rikuo will have to figure out just where his place in the world is, and what he wants to do with his life.

Psycho Busters. Written by Yuya Aoki. Illustrated by Akinari Nao. Del Rey, 2006–2010. 6 Vol. **O** Genre: Fantasy, Supernatural.

> Kakeru wanted something interesting to happen in his life, and he got it when he met three psychics on the run from a government organization. Getting roped into helping them wasn't exactly what he had in mind when he wanted something to happen, but at this point, Kakeru's in too deep to get out. Besides, he seems to have extraordinary luck when it comes to surviving, or is it a psychic ability of his own? Volumes 6 and 7 of this series are published in an omnibus volume.

The Record of a Fallen Vampire. Written by Kyo Shirodaira. Illustrated by Yuri Kimura. VIZ Media, LLC, 2008–2010. 9 Vol. **T** Genre: Fantasy, Mystery, Supernatural.

> A thousand years ago, the Vampire King Strauss lost his queen and his kingdom. Now he wanders the world searching for his lost queen, who has been hidden from him. However, he is pursued by dhampire that want to kill him as well as the Black Swan, an entity that actually has the power to destroy both him and his queen, should he ever find her. Still, there is another threat looming, and Strauss may find himself out of his depth.

Rin-Ne. Written and Illustrated by Rumiko Takehashi. VIZ Media, LLC, 2009–. Ongoing Series. 5 Vol. **O** Genre: Romantic Comedy, Supernatural.

> Sakura has been able to see ghosts ever since she was spirited away for a week when she was a child. By the time she's in high school, she'd like to stop seeing them. However, one day Sakura seems to be the only one who

can see her ever-absent classmate, Rinne Rokudo. It's only later that she learns Rinne's job is to guide souls that are bound to earth by regrets, and it seems like Sakura may end up helping him out.

Rosario + Vampire. Written and Illustrated by Akihisa Ikeda. VIZ Media, LLC, 2008–2009. 10 Vol. O Genre: Action, Harem, Romance, Supernatural. Related Anime: *Rosario + Vampire.*

Tsukune can't seem to get into any high school except for one: Yokai Academy. However, on his first day there it soon becomes clear that this is not a normal high school. In fact, the school is actually for supernatural creatures and only for supernatural creatures. If that weren't problem enough, Tsukune quickly makes friends with Moka, a vampire attracted to the sweet taste of his blood, and it doesn't take long for her to discover that he's just a human. One thing is for sure, Tsukune won't forget his first year of high school.

Rosario + Vampire: Season II. Written and Illustrated by Akihisa Ikeda. VIZ Media, LLC, 2010–. Ongoing Series. 8 Vol. O Genre: Action, Harem, Romance, Supernatural. Related Anime: *Rosario + Vampire Capu2.*

Sequel to Rosario + Vampire. Tsukune is now in his second year at Yokai Academy. He still has to keep the fact that he's human a secret, and he still has more girls than he needs interested in him. A new year at the school brings new adventures, challenges, and friends.

Shaman King. Written and Illustrated by Hiroyuki Takei. VIZ Media, LLC, 2003–2010. 32 Vol. T Genre: Action, Adventure, Comedy, Fantasy, Supernatural. Related Anime: *Shaman King.*

Yoh Asakura just happens to be a shaman as well as a middle school student. Some of his best friends are ghosts. But it's not all fun and games. Yoh is a link between worlds, helping ghosts move on to the afterlife—and not all spirits are friendly ones.

Soul Eater. Written and Illustrated by Atsushi Ohkubo. Yen Press, 2009–. Ongoing Series. 19 Vol. O Genre: Action, Adventure, Comedy, Supernatural. Related Anime: *Soul Eater.*

Maka Albran, a weapon meister, and her weapon, the scythe Soul Eater Evans, make for a formidable team, even if they don't always get along. The two of them are working toward turning Soul into a death scythe, the ultimate weapon used by Death himself. They just might manage that, too, if they can stop fighting with one another long enough to fight their enemies.

Togari. Written and Illustrated by Yoshinori Natsume. VIZ Media, LLC, 2007–2008. 8 Vol. O Genre: Action, Supernatural.*

Tobei was once a ruthless criminal until he was beheaded at age 16. After spending 300 years in hell, he is given a second chance. He has to kill 108 spirits in 108 days. There are a few conditions though, and if he doesn't manage this task, his fate might be even worse than before.

<u>Zombie-Loan</u>. **Written and Illustrated by Peach-Pit. Yen Press, 2007–. Ongoing Series. 13 Vol. O Genre: Action, Comedy, Romance, Supernatural.**

> Michiru has Shinigami Eyes, the power to tell how close someone is to death by reading the rings around the person's throat. However, when she tries to help a pair of classmates, she finds that they've already made a deal. In return for their lives, they now hunt zombies for an office called Zombie Loan, and now that Michiru knows this, her life is about to get a lot more complicated.

Thriller

<u>Death Note</u>. **Written by Tsugumi Ohba. Illustrated by Takeshi Obata. VIZ Media, LLC, 2005–2007. 12 Vol. O Genre: Mystery, Psychological, Supernatural, Thriller. Related Anime:** *Death Note.*

> Light Yamagi's life begins to change when he stumbles across the Death Note. He can kill anyone by writing their name in the book and even specify how they should die. Light has unimaginable power now, and he plans on using it. With the Death Note, he will be able to reshape the world into a better place. But when criminals start to die, Light finds himself known to the world at large as Kira, a dangerous serial killer. Kira is attracting all sorts of attention, and whether he is a hero or a criminal is up for debate.

Western

<u>Gun Blaze West</u>. **Written and Illustrated by Nobuhiro Watsuki. VIZ Media, LLC, 2008. 3 Vol. O Genre: Adventure, Western.**

> Viu Bannes is determined to be the best gunfighter in the west. After winning a gun belt in a arm wrestling contest and meeting a mysterious stranger, Viu's adventure is about to take off.

<u>Zombiepowder</u>. **Written and Illustrated by Tite Kubo. VIZ Media, LLC, 2006–2007. 4 Vol. Traing: O Genre: Action, Comedy, Science Fiction, Western.**

> A chance encounter takes Elwood Shepard from a life of petty crime to a life of traveling with the infamous criminals Gamma Akutabi and C. T. Smith, searching for zombie powder. But they're not the only ones who want the powder, and it's a rough world out there.

Shonen Anime

Action

<u>Get Backers</u>. **ADV, 2008. 49 25 Min. Episodes. 10 Discs. T Genre: Action, Adventure, Comedy, Drama, Supernatural.**

> If you lose something, Ginji and Ban can get it back, for a fee of course. In fact, they offer a 100 percent success rate when they take a job. This duo will do just about anything to get the job done, and that can prove to make some jobs very interesting.

Jing: King of Bandits. ADV, 2003. 13 25-Min. Episodes. 3 Discs. **T** Genre: Action, Adventure, Comedy, Fantasy.

> Jing may be young, but his reputation as the bandit king has spread far and wide. Of course, some people don't believe that he's the bandit king when they first meet, but they often change their minds once they see him in action. Jing's earned his reputation for a reason, and when he's involved, adventure isn't far behind.

The Law of Ueki. Geneon, 2005. 51 25-Min. Episodes. 13 Discs. **T** Genre: Comedy, Action.

> There is a contest to determine who will get to be the next Celestial King. Each candidate gives a power to a junior high school student, and then the students battle it out. Kosuke Ueki is one such student. He has the power to turn to trash into trees, and the battle is about to start.

Adventure

Elemental Gelade. Geneon, 2005. 26 25-Min. Episodes. 6 Discs. **T** Genre: Action, Adventure, Fantasy, Romance.

> In Guardia, humans coexist with Edel Raids. The Edel Raids can fuse with a human to become a living weapon. When sky pirate Coud Van Giruet captures an Edel Raid named Ren on a raid, he finds himself drawn into an adventure he never expected. As they journey to find a legendary land of gold, they'll have to defeat enemies and maybe find something besides gold.

Fullmetal Alchemist: Brotherhood. Funimation, 2010–2011. 64 25-Min. Episodes. 10 Discs in 5 Sets. **T** Genre: Adventure, Fantasy, Science Fiction.

> Alchemy gives its users the ability to change the world around them, but it comes with a price. When Edward and Alphonse Elric attempt to resurrect their dead mother using it, Edward loses an arm and a leg, and Alphonse's soul and personality are trapped in a metal suit of armor. In order to reclaim what they have lost, Edward sets out to become a State Alchemist and find the Philosopher's Stone. But the brothers have a long journey ahead of them, and it won't be easy.

Naruto. VIZ Media, LLC, 2009–2010. 220 25-Min. Episodes. 48 Discs in 8 Sets. **T** Genre: Action, Adventure, Fantasy.

> Naruto Uzumaki is determined to succeed as a ninja and become the next Hokage of his village. Not even the fact that he's dead last at the ninja academy is going to stop him. But there are more than just missions and adventures in Naruto's future. Secrets of the past and dangerous enemies also lurk there, but no matter what happens, Naruto isn't one to give up on his dream.

Naruto Shippuden. VIZ Media, LLC, 2010–. Ongoing Series. 206 25-Min. Episodes. 24 Discs in 6 Sets. **T** Genre: Action, Adventure, Fantasy.

> It's been two and a half years since Naruto left his teammates in order to train. Now he has returned and is still determined to bring Sasuke back to Konoha. However, a criminal organization begins to rear its head and they are targeting

Naruto. Personal missions may have to take a backseat to the safety of Konoha and its people, and Naruto will find himself tested as he never has been before.

One Piece. Funimation, 2008–. Ongoing Series. 489 25-Min. Episodes. 34 Discs in 17 Sets. T Genre: Action, Adventure, Comedy, Drama.

Monkey D. Luffy has been determined to find the legendary One Piece treasure and become the Pirate King since childhood. Now that he has the power to stretch like rubber (acquired when he accidentally ate the fruit of the Gum Gum), Luffy is off to find the treasure. Along the way he'll acquire a crew and a ship, and together they'll make a name for themselves as pirates.

Pokemon: Indigo. VIZ Media, LLC, 2006–2008. 80 25-Min. Episodes. 9 Discs in 3 Sets. Y Genre: Action, Adventure, Comedy, Drama, Fantasy, Science Fiction.

Ash is now 10 years old and ready to set out on his Pokemon journey. However, Pikachu, his very first Pokemon, doesn't quite get along with him. The two of them will have to learn to work together as they face other Pokemon trainers, Gym Leaders, and Team Rocket. And if Ash wants to truly become a Pokemon Master, he has a lot of work ahead of him.

Comedy

Cromartie High School. ADV, 2003. 26 12.5-Min. Episodes. 4 Discs. T Genre: Comedy, Parody.

Cromartie High School is known for its delinquents. When Takashi transfers in, everyone assumes he has to be a tough guy. After all, who else would come to Cromartie? Takashi isn't exactly a delinquent himself, but he'll do what he has to in order to fit in at his new school, even if it is strange, weird, and confusing.

Hetalia. Funimation, 2008–2009. 52 5-Min. Episodes. 2 Discs. O Genre: Comedy, Historical.

World history has never been so interesting as it is in *Hetalia*, an allegorical tale where the countries of the world are now the main characters. Join Germany, Italy, and Japan as they begin to form a partnership and set events in motion that will lead to some of the most famous periods of history.

Harem

Tenchi Universe. Geneon, 1997. 26 25-Min. Episodes. 8 Discs. T Genre: Adventure, Comedy, Fantasy, Harem.

Tenchi Masaki thought he was an ordinary high school student with normal concerns. That was before he had six alien women decide to move into his family home. With two princesses, a space pirate, a mad scientist, and a pair of Galaxy Police officers along with his own father and grandfather in the house, chaos is the natural order of things. And that's before a galaxy-wide plot interferes with their lives. One thing is for sure, Tenchi's life is no longer normal or boring.

Historical Fiction

Rurouni Kenshin. Anime Works, 1997–2006. 95 25-Min. Episodes. 22 Discs. **T** Genre: Action, Adventure, Historical Fiction, Romance, Samurai.

Kenshin Himura was once the Hitokiri Battousai, one of the most feared assassins of the revolution. But that was nearly 10 years ago. He has since become a wanderer and made a vow not to kill again. When he arrives in Tokyo, Kenshin rescues Kaoru Kamiya, a young kendo instructor, who ends up offering him a home. All Kenshin really wants to do is live in peace, but there are enemies both old and new that he'll have to face before that can happen, and creating a life in a time of peace may be his biggest challenge yet.

Fantasy

InuYasha. VIZ Media, LLC, 2004–2009. 167 25-Min. Episodes. 55 Discs in 7 Sets. **T** Genre: Adventure, Fantasy, Romance.

When Kagome falls down a well in her family's shrine, she finds herself transported back in time to the feudal era. Attacked by a demon, Kagome accidentally releases the half-demon Inuyasha from his imprisonment. Soon the two of them set off on a quest to find all the pieces of the Shikon Jewel. But Kagome will find that surviving in the feudal era, finding the jewel, and juggling high school is a task that is far more difficult than it seems. And she might just find herself torn between the two times for more than one reason.

Tsubasa: Reservoir Chronicle. Funimation, 2005. 52 25-Min. Episodes. 8 Discs in 2 Sets. 9 Discs in Collected Memories Ed. **T** Genre: Fantasy, Romance.

Syaoran might be just a humble archeologist, but he has been friends with Princess Sakura of Clow since childhood. When Sakura visits him at his dig site, disaster strikes. The only way to save Sakura now is for Syaoran to travel through dimensions collecting feathers that contain Sakura's memories. Along with an amnesiac Sakura, he sets out. Joined by the warrior, Kurogane, and the magician, Fai, both traveling for their own reasons, they set off. Together the four to them will attempt to find Sakura's feathers. But there may be more to this mission than any of them knows.

Martial Arts

Dragon Ball. Funimation, 2009–2010. 153 25-Min. Episodes. 25 Discs in 5 Sets. **T** Genre: Action, Fantasy, Martial Arts, Science Fiction.

Goku is a rather strange kid. With a monkey tail and super strength, he's never left the woods where he lives. However, when a girl named Bulma stumbles across him during her search for the Dragon Balls, Goku ends up teaming up with her and leaving his home. Whoever collects all seven Dragons Balls can summon the dragon and be granted one wish. But Bulma and Goku aren't the only ones who want the Dragon Balls, and their journey isn't going to be an easy one.

Dragon Ball Z. Funimation, 1996–2009. 291 25-Min. Episodes. 54 Discs in 9 Sets. **T** Genre: Action, Fantasy, Martial Arts, Science Fiction.

A continuation of Dragon Ball, Goku is now all grown up and has a family of his own. But he can't rest on his laurels, for Earth is threatened by Saiyans who have come to destroy it. Now Goku and his friends will have to defend their planet, and that will only be the start of their next set of adventures.

YuYu Hakusho. Funimation, 2008. 112 21-Min. Episodes. 16 Discs in 4 Sets. **T** Genre: Martial Arts, Supernatural.

Yusuke Urameshi, a teenage delinquent, changed his life by dying. When he gets hit by a car and dies saving a little boy in the process, Yusuke is given a second chance at life. Yusuke's second chance comes with some certain strings, but he's never been one to turn down a good fight, and this definitely promises to be one.

Mecha

Mobile Suit Gundam. Bandai, 2004. 43 25-Min. Episodes. 10 Discs. **T** Genre: Mecha, Military, Science Fiction.

In the year 0079 UC, the Earth Federation is at war with the Principality of Zeon. The two sides are currently stalemated, but the Earth Federation is developing a secret weapon called Gundam. When a surprise attack leaves the new Federation warship White Base crewed by inexperienced officers and civilians, a young man named Amuro ends up piloting Gundam, and now he may hold the fate of the war in his hands.

Mobile Suit Gundam Wing. Bandai, 1995. 49 25-Min. Episodes. 10 Discs in 2 Sets. **T** Genre: Mecha, Military.

Five teenagers with advanced mobile suits called Gundams are sent to Earth from the space colonies with a mission: to damage the United Earth Sphere Alliance, which has oppressed the colonies for years. However, they will find that things are not so simple as that, and together the five of them will struggle to figure out what peace is and if it can exist for them.

Mobile Suit Gundam Wing: Endless Waltz. Bandai, 2000. 180 Min. 1 Disc. **T** Genre: Mecha, Military.

A sequel to the series *Gundam Wing*. A fragile peace between Earth and the space colonies has been established, and the Gundam pilots prepare to destroy their Gundams once and for all. However, a young woman shatters the peace, planning on taking control of both Earth and the space colonies. Once again the Gundam pilots find themselves fighting to make a peaceful future reality.

Military

Pumpkin Scissors. Funimation, 2006. 24 25-Min. Episodes. 6 Discs. 4 Discs in Complete Series Ed. **T** Genre: Military, War.

> The war between the empire and its enemy is over, but the country remains ravaged by the effects of that war. That is where Military Sate Section Three comes in. The unit, called Pumpkin Scissors, is supposed to provide war relief. However, its members soon find out that not everyone is as interested in rebuilding the country as they are. But the team led by Alice Malvin isn't about to give up either, and they have a number of surprises up their sleeves.

Romance

Boys Be. . . . The Right Stuf, 2006. 13 25-Min. Episodes. 4 Discs. **T** Genre: Comedy, Romance, School.

> Three high school boys have one thing on their minds: girls. However, all three of them have their own problems when it comes to love. Kyoichi has fallen for a long-time friend and doesn't know whether to risk that friendship for something more. Makoto trusts in the *Dr. Mitsuboshi Love Manual*, but he may have met a girl that it doesn't work on. And Yoshihiko has no idea how to deal with a girl when he finally meets one he's interested in. One thing is for sure though, high school romance is always complicated.

Romantic Comedy

Ranma ½. VIZ Media, LLC, 2007–2008. 161 25-Min. Episodes. 34 Discs in 7 Sets. **T** Genre: Martial Arts, Romantic Comedy.

> Ranma Saotome has spent the last 10 years on a training journey with his father. However, when they reach a training ground in China, an accident occurs. Both Ranma and his father fall into cursed springs. Now, when splashed with cold water, Ranma's father turns into a panda. Ranma turns into a girl. Hot water turns them both back into their normal forms. Things get even more complicated when Ranma's father drags him back to Japan in order to fulfill an old promise. Ranma will marry Akane Tendou and keep both families' martial arts traditions alive. Of course, neither Ranma nor Akane have agreed to this, but according to their families they don't have a choice.

Samurai

Samurai Champloo. Geneon, 2004. 26 25-Min. Episodes. 7 Discs. **O** Genre: Comedy, Drama, Samurai.

> A series of coincidences bring together Mugen and Jin, both wandering swordsmen of rather different temperaments, with Fuu, a young woman searching for her father. Fuu ends up saving the men, and they agree to help her as well as not fight one another until they've found him. The three of them set off on their search and find plenty of adventure along the way.

Sword of the Stranger. Bandai, 2007. 102 Min. **T** Genre: Action, Samurai.

> Kotaro is a young boy traveling on his own with only his dog, Tobimaru, for a companion. They are pursued by strange warriors from the Ming Dynasty in China. When a warrior with no name takes Kotaro under his wing, it will change both of their lives.

Science Fiction

Angelic Layer. ADV, 2005. 26 25-Min. Episodes. 5 Discs. **Y** Genre: Action, Comedy, Drama, Science Fiction.

> Misaki has just moved to Tokyo to live with her aunt and go to school. She quickly gets caught up in the game *Angelic Layer,* where people battle using dolls called Angels. Misaki names her angel Hikaru, and while the two of them might be new to *Angelic Layer,* they definitely are making a splash.

.hack//Sign: Bandai, 2002. 26 25-Min. Episodes. 6 Discs. **T** Genre: Adventure, Fantasy, Mystery, Science Fiction.

> Tsukasa awakes to find himself in *The World,* an online game. He is missing parts of his memory, and he's not really sure what is going on. However, he can't log out of the game like the rest of the characters. Whatever is going on, Tsukasa soon finds himself swept up in an adventure as he and his friends try to unravel the mysteries surrounding him.

.hack//Sign: Legend of the Twilight. Bandai, 2003. 12 25-Min. Episodes. 3 Discs. **T** Genre: Adventure, Fantasy, Mystery, Science Fiction.

> When his twin sister, Rena, wins a contest, Shugo finds himself drawn into *The World,* an online game. Though they no longer live together, *The World* gives them a chance to hang out. When a mysterious woman heals Shugo and gives him a strange bracelet, Shugo finds that *The World* is far more dangerous than he expected. As he and Rena try to find some answers, it may be up to Shugo to save *The World* before it is destroyed completely.

The Irresponsible Captain Tylor. The Right Stuf, 2009. 26 25-Min. Episodes. 5 Discs. **T** Genre: Adventure, Comedy, Military, Science Fiction.

> Justy Ueki Tylor has a plan in order to be set for life. He will join United Planets Space Force, get a cushy desk job, and be taken care of for the rest of his life. However, propelled both by his own ineptitude and his extreme luck, Tylor ends up the captain of a ship and is sent off to patrol the border. While Tylor might not know what he is doing, his results seem to work. Even the enemy can't decide whether the man is a military genius or a complete idiot. And he and his crew may be the United Planets Space Force's best hope in winning the war.

The Melancholy of Haruhi Suzumiya. Bandai, 2010. 28 25-Min. Episodes. 8 Discs in 2 Sets. **T** Genre: Comedy, Science Fiction.

> Kyon's high school life is almost immediately hijacked by his classmate, Haruhi Suzumiya, before it starts. The next thing he knows, he's been drafted

into her SOS Brigade. It also becomes clear to him that of the five members of the brigade, he quite possibly is the only normal human. Haruhi can't stand boredom, and the brigade gets involved with whatever crazy stunts she comes up with. Kyon had thought he was going to be a typical apathetic high school student. Somehow, he doesn't think that is going to happen now.

s-Cry-ed. Bandai, 2003. 26 25-Min. Episodes. 6 Discs. T Genre: Adventure, Science Fiction.

After the Great Uprising, things have certainly changed. There are now those with special powers called Alter Users who can alter matter into what they will, and most of them use those powers to their own advantage. There is also Holy, a special police force that fights Alters. However, at times, neither of them are what is the best for the public in general. Enter Kazuma, an Alter who is definitely going to change things.

Steamboy. Sony Pictures, 2005. 130 Min. 1 Disc. PG-13 Genre: Steampunk, Science Fiction.

When Ray's grandfather sends him a mysterious package, Ray finds himself being pulled into intrigue and danger. Ray will have to make his own decisions about how to use technology and his own skills as an inventor, and making the wrong decisions could led to more deaths than just his own.

Slice of Life

BECK: Mongolian Chop Squad. Funimation, 2004. 26 25-Min. Episodes. 6 Discs. O Genre: Music, Romance, Slice of Life.

Koyuki is pretty much your average junior high school student. However, when he rescues a dog from some kids, he meets Ryusuke, an aspiring musician. Koyuki finds himself being drawn into a band. But getting a band off the ground isn't easy. Then again, the four members of BECK aren't about to give up either.

Sports

Prince of Tennis. VIZ Media, LLC, 2001. 52 23-Min. Episodes. 12 Discs in 4 Sets. Y Genre: Comedy, Drama, School, Sports.

Ryoma is a teenage tennis ace. He starts at his new high school by defeating most of the upperclassmen and earning a spot on the school tennis team. As the team gears up for the National Championships, they work on improving their skills, and Ryoma begins to discover just what the game means to him.

Supernatural

Bleach. VIZ Media, LLC, 2008–. Ongoing Series. 311 25-Min. Episodes. 35 Discs in 9 Sets. T Genre: Action, Adventure, Horror, Supernatural.

Ichigo Kurosaki was a normal high school student who had the ability to see the dead. It was that ability that got him turned into a shinigami or Soul Reaper:

those who send wandering spirits to Soul Society and fight spirits who have turned evil. But Soul Society isn't the paradise it seems. Nothing about dealing with death is simple, and Ichigo is caught right in the middle.

Blood+. Sony Pictures, 2008–2009. 50 25-Min. Episodes. 10 Discs in 2 Sets. Rating **O** Genre: Adventure, Supernatural.

Saya's life is fairly normal for an amnesiac, though she does keep having horrible nightmares. However, those nightmares prove to be connected to her past, and as Chriopterans, shape shifters that crave human blood, threaten humanity, it may be up to Saya to save everyone.

Soul Eater. Funimation, 2008–2009. 51 23-Min. Episodes. 8 Discs in 4 Sets. **T** Genre: Action, Adventure, Comedy, Supernatural.

Maka Albran, a weapon meister, and her weapon, the scythe Soul Eater Evans, make for a formidable team, even if they don't always get along. The two of them are working toward turning Soul into a death scythe, the ultimate weapon used by Death himself. They just might manage that too, if they can stop fighting with one another long enough to fight their enemies. And as students at Death Weapon Meister Academy, there are plenty of fights ahead.

Thriller

Death Note. VIZ Media, LLC, 2008–2009. 37 25-Min. Episodes. 10 Discs in 2 Sets. **O** Genre: Mystery, Psychological, Supernatural, Thriller.

A rather bored if very talented high school student, Light Yamagi's life begins to change when he stumbles across the Death Note. He can kill anyone by writing the person's name in the book and even specify how the person should die. Light has unimaginable power now, and he plans on using it. With the Death Note, he will be able to reshape the world into a better place. But when criminals start to die, Light finds himself known to the world at large as Kira, a dangerous serial killer. Kira is attracting all sorts of attention, and whether he is a hero or a criminal is up for debate.

Chapter 2

Shojo Manga and Anime

Originally, Shojo manga was marketed toward girls ages 10 to 18, but like Shonen manga, it often appeals to other audiences as well. Shojo titles have a range of genre and age levels that they cover, though they often focus on relationships and romance even if romance isn't the main genre of a title.

Shojo manga is the second largest of the groups of manga published in North America and have a great range of subjects and titles. While they may have had a targeted audience, they often appeal to both adults and young men as well as teenage girls. The titles in this section are organized by their main genre, though all of the genres that a title fits into are included with each entry.

Shojo Manga

- From Japan

- Marketed toward girls ages 10 to 18

- Read right to left

- Often focus on romance and friendship

Shojo Manga

Action

<u>Blank Slate</u>. **Written and Illustrated by Aya Kanno. VIZ Media, LLC, 2008. 2 Vol. O Genre: Action, Adventure, Drama, Mystery.**
Zen has no memory whatsoever, but he does have a bounty hunter for a partner and a definite skill for crime. However, as secrets from his past begin to surface, things take a far more sinister turn, and Zen's past may hold things worse than his present.

Cowboy Bebop: Shooting Star. Written and Illustrated by Cain Kuga. Tokyopop, 2003. 2 Vol. **T** Genre: Action, Adventure, Comedy, Crime, Drama. Romance, Science Fiction. Related Anime: *Cowboy Bebop*.

> If you need a bounty hunter, the crew of the Bebop are the best. Spike, Jet, Faye, and Ed all have their own pasts and histories, but you can't argue with their results. Of course, since they have more morals than most bounty hunters, they often go hungry. But when trouble comes calling, these four make for a formidable team.

Library Wars: Love & War. Written and Illustrated by Kiiro Yumi. VIZ Media, LLC, 2010–. Ongoing Series. 6 Vol. **O** Genre: Action, Comedy, Romance, Science Fiction.

> When censorship laws are passed in Japan, the libraries band together and create the Library Defense Force. Iku Kasahara has dreamed of joining the LDF because one of their agents rescued her favorite book back when she was in school. She's wanted to be like that agent ever since. But now that she's started her training, she might find that working for the LDF is much harder than she imagined.

Punch!. Written and Illustrated by Rie Takada. VIZ Media, LLC, 2006–2007. 3 Vol. **O** Genre: Action, Comedy, Romance.

> Despite the fact that everyone else in her family has been involved in martial arts like boxing and wrestling, Elle has no interest in it. She just wants an ordinary life. However, her grandfather just happens to have engaged her to a boxer at his gym. When Elle meets Kazuki, a street fighter, she has an idea about how to get her life back on track to what she wants. What she didn't plan on was falling in love.

Saiyuki Reload. Written and Illustrated by Kazuya Minekura. Tokyopop, 2005–. 10 Vol. **O** Genre: Action, Adventure, Fantasy. Related Anime: *Saiyuki Reload, Saiyuki Reload: Burial*.

> A sequel to *Saiyuki, Saiyuki Reload* continues Sanzo, Goku, Gojyo, and Hakkai's journey west. The four companions continue on even as they encounter more challenges and trials along the way, and there are still enemies out to stop them.

Adventure

Dream Saga. Written and Illustrated by Megumi Tachikawa. Tokyopop, 2004–2005. 5 Vol. **Y** Genre: Adventure, Fantasy, Romance.

> When Yuuki finds a magical red stone, she ends up transported to a dream world called Takamagahara. There she finds it her responsibility to help save the Sun God from danger, but balancing her life between her own world and Takamagahara may hinder her in her efforts.

Magic Knight Rayearth. Written and Illustrated by CLAMP. Tokyopop, 2002–2003. 3 Vol. Dark Horse, 2011. 1 Vol. **Y** Genre: Action, Adventure, Magical Girl, Mecha. Related Anime: *Magic Knight Rayearth, Rayearth*.

> On a routine trip to Tokyo Tower, Hikaru, Umi, and Fuu suddenly find themselves transported to a strange world called Cephiro. Told that they are Magic Knights, the three girls are sent on a quest to rescue Princess Emeraude, who has

been kidnapped by a man named Zagato. As the girls set off on their journey, they must learn to work together and truly become the Magic Knights everyone says they are. Recently republished as an omnibus by Dark Horse.

Magic Knight Rayearth II. **Written and Illustrated by CLAMP. Tokyopop, 2003–2004. 3 Vol. Dark Horse, 2011. 1 Vol. Y Genre: Action, Adventure, Magical Girl, Mecha. Related Anime:** *Magic Knight Rayearth II.*

A sequel to *Magic Knight Rayearth.* Called back to Cephiro, Hikaru, Umi, and Fuu find themselves once again needed by the friends they left behind. Without a Pillar, Cephiro is in danger from three invading countries as well as internal strife. The Magic Knights once again are called to defend Cephiro, and hopefully find a solution for the people of Cephiro to live in peace. Recently republished as an omnibus by Dark Horse.

Vampire Doll. **Written and Illustrated by Erika Kari. Tokyopop, 2006–2009. 6 Vol. T Genre: Adventure, Comedy, Fantasy.**

Guilt-na-Zan was a vampire aristocrat who had been sealed away for a hundred years. Now, thanks to the exorcist Kyoji, he's been released and resurrected as a female doll who can only return to his true form when he sucks Kyoji's sister's blood. Together the three of them will end up fighting evil, if they can get along long enough to do so.

Comedy

Cactus's Secret. **Written and Illustrated by Nana Haruta. VIZ Media, LLC, 2010. 4 Vol. T Genre: Comedy, Drama, Romance, School.**

When Miku tries to confess to her crush, Kyohei, he thinks it's just a joke. She cannot seem to convince the guy that she's in love with him, and now he's started calling her Cactus since she's so prickly with him. Miku is torn. Should she give up on him or keep trying to make him see that she really likes him?

Café Kichijouji De. **Written by Yuki Miyamoto. Illustrated by Kyoko Negishi. DMP, 2005–2006. 3 Vol. T Genre: Comedy, Supernatural.**

Things at Café Kichijouji are never boring. Even the smallest problem can turn into complete chaos. But the staff there is friendly, and something is always going on.

From Eroica with Love. **Written and Illustrated by Yasuko Aoike. CMX, 2004–2010. Ongoing Series. 15 of 36 Vol. T Genre: Comedy.**

Eccentric aristocrat by day, art thief by night, Dorian Red Gloria leads an interesting life. When an art professor decides to stop the art thief known only as Eroica, he has no idea what sort of adventures he has just let himself in for.

Gals!. **Written and Illustrated by Mihona Fujii. CMX, 2005–2007. 10 Vol. T Genre: Comedy, Drama, Romance. Related Anime:** *Super Gals! Kotobuki Ran.*

Ran enjoys hanging out in Shibuya with her friends and having fun. Of course, Shibuya is never boring, and while Ran enjoys her lifestyle, she comes from a family of police officers and knows a thing or two about dealing with trouble. Fashion, friends, and fun are what's important to Ran, and she's not about to miss a moment of it.

Gravitation. Written and Illustrated by Maki Murakami. Tokyopop, 2003–2005. 12 Vol. **O** Genre: Comedy, Romance, Yaoi. Related Anime: *Gravitation, Gravitation: Lyrics of Love.*

> Shuichi is determined to be a rock star. He's got a band, Bad Luck, but he can't write lyrics. When a stranger named Eiri Yuki criticizes his attempts to write lyrics, Shuichi finds himself fascinated by the man. As Shuichi attempts to make himself a part of the Eiri's life, they may find that some things can't be fought.

Here Is Greenwood. Written and Illustrated by Yukie Nasu. VIZ Media, LLC, 2004–2006. 9 Vol. **O** Genre: Comedy, Drama, Romance. Related Anime: *Here Is Greenwood.*

> After his older brother married Kazuya's first love, he moves into the Greenwood dorm at school. However, since he transferred into the dorm so late, there's only one room left: Shun Kisagiri's. And Shun just happens to be a girl. What a girl is doing at a boys' school is definitely one question, and Kazuya's going to have plenty to distract him from his broken heart.

Kamikaze Girls. Written by Novala Takemoto. Illustrated by Yukio Kanesada. VIZ Media, LLC, 2006. 1 Vol. **O** Genre: Comedy.

> Momoko is stranded in the rural countryside away from Tokyo and its shops. Ichigo is a member of an all-girls biker gang. An unlikely pair, together they set out on a journey to Tokyo in order to make their dreams come true.

Kyo Kara MAOH!. Written by Tomo Takabayashi. Illustrated by Temari Matsumoto. Tokyopop, 2008–. Ongoing Series. 8 Vol. **T** Genre: Adventure, Comedy, Drama, Fantasy, Romance. Related Anime: *Kyo Kara Maoh, Kyo Kara Maoh R.*

> Yuri Shibiya is having a bad day. First he gets his head stuck in a toilet by bullies at school. Then he gets transported to a parallel universe. There he quickly gets made king of the Mazoku, a new race, and now they want him to lead them against humanity in a war. And did he mention his new fiancée is a guy?

Love Master A. Written and Illustrated by Kyoko Hashimoto. Go!Comi, 2007–2008. 2 Vol. **T** Genre: Comedy, Romance, School.

> Aria just transferred to a new school. She was looking for a normal high school experience. Unfortunately, her reputation of having bad luck with romance has preceded her. Hence her nickname, the Love Master. What is a girl to do except start working to fix up couples instead? But will Aria ever find love for herself?

Me & My Brothers. Written and Illustrated by Hari Tokeino. Tokyopop, 2007–2010. 11 Vol. **T** Genre: Comedy, Drama, Romance.

Sakura's parents died when she was three and she has been raised by her grandmother ever since. However, when her grandmother dies, she suddenly finds out that she has four step-brothers from her mother's previous marriage. Sakura's brothers move in with her, and Sakura finds she has a lot to learn about family.

My Heavenly Hockey Club. Written and Illustrated by Ai Morigana. Del Rey, 2005–2009. Kodansha Comics, 2011–. 14 Vol. **T** Genre: Comedy, Romance.

When Hana is invited to join the school hockey club, she needs come convincing. But once she's told that the hockey club gets to travel and eat out a lot, and given that food is one of Hana's weaknesses, she agrees to join. But being the only girl on an all-male team and playing a game she doesn't know much about isn't going to be easy.

Pick of the Litter. Written and Illustrated by Yuriko Suda. Tokyopop, 2007–2010. 5 Vol. **T** Genre: Comedy, Supernatural.

Riku turned up in Tokyo five years ago with no memory. His life is pretty normal now, but he still wonders about his past. Then he runs into a group of strange people claiming to be his family. As it turns out, he's from another world, where his family runs a shop—and Riku's just agreed to work there part time. The fifth volume is an omnibus containing what originally had been volumes five and six.

Portrait of M & N. Written and Illustrated by Tachibana Higuchi. Tokyopop, 2010–. 6 Vol. **T** Genre: Comedy, Romance.

Mitsuru and Natsuhiko both have their secrets, and they'd like to keep them secret. Mitsuru is a masochist while Natsuhiko is a narcissist. Both of them would like to manage a school life free of too much trouble, but will that really be possible?

The Recipe for Gertrude. Written and Illustrated by Nari Kusakawa. CMX, 2006–2007. 5 Vol. **A** Genre: Comedy.

Sahara's life is turned around when she meets a demon named Gertrude. He was created with a recipe from a spell book, and Gertrude is now searching for it in order to destroy it. He enlists Sahara's help, and the two of them are in for an adventure of a lifetime.

Ultra Cute. Written and Illustrated by Nami Akimoto. Tokyopop, 2006–2007. 9 Vol. **Y** Genre: Comedy, Romance.

For years Ami and Noa had always fallen for the same guy and ended up scaring him off with their competitiveness over him. However, they've finally fallen for different guys. There's one catch, though: Ami suspects their new objects of affection might just be players. She is determined to protect Noa's feelings as well as maybe get the upper hand with these guys.

Detective

Clamp School Detectives. Written and Illustrated by CLAMP. Tokyopop, 2003. 3 Vol. **A** Genre: Comedy, Detective. Related Anime: *Clamp School Detectives*.

> Nokoru, Suoh, and Akira are the Clamp School Detectives. The three of them are students at the Clamp School and provide a detective service to those classmates who need it as well as others. Whether it is finding lost items or accepting a challenge from another classmate, these are the people to call.

Drama

After School Nightmare. Written and Illustrated by Setona Mizushiro. Go!comi, 2006–2008. 10 Vol. **O** Genre: Drama, Psychological.

> Mashiro gets a surprise when he finds out that the only way he can graduate is to participate in an after-school class where he must enter a nightmare and fight other students for a mysterious key. To make matters worse, his darkest secret might be exposed. Mashiro is neither male nor female. As he struggles to find the key and with it his identity, Mashiro will find that being able to graduate may be the largest challenge he ever faces.

Banana Fish. Written and Illustrated by Akimi Yoshida. VIZ Media, LLC, 1998–2009. 19 Vol. **O** Genre: Drama, Adventure.

> A rash of mysterious suicides strikes New York City just as Ash, a young gang leader, is given a sample of something by a dying man. As Ash begins to look into the connections between the deaths, he will find that people will stop at nothing to keep the truth hidden.

Confidential Confessions. Written and Illustrated by Reiko Momochi. Tokyopop, 2003–2005. 6 Vol. **O** Genre: Drama.

> Confidential Confessions is a collection of short stories dealing with serious issues that teens may face. From suicide to sexual harassment to running away from home, the teens in this manga have faced all sorts of problems, and they've found that sometimes though there are no happy endings, there may be new beginnings to be found.

Dear Myself. Written and Illustrated by Eiki Eiki. DMP, 2006. 1 Vol. **O** Genre: Drama, Romance, Yaoi.

> Hirofumi wakes up one morning to find that he's missing two years of his memories. Among other things he has forgotten, Hirofumi seems to have forgotten his relationship with Daigo. Can the two of them work things out or will this be the end of them?

Doubt!!. Written and Illustrated by Kaneyoshi Izumi. VIZ Media, LLC, 2005–2006. 6 Vol. **O** Genre: Drama, Romance.

> Ai's always been something of an ugly duckling, but when a classmate completely humiliates her, she decides to change things. Transferring to a new high school, Ai reinvents herself and hopes to make a new start. However, being

popular isn't entirely as she expected, and while she may look good on the outside, her self-confidence isn't entirely there. Still, she's determined to see her plan through, and falling in love along the way won't hurt either.

Hot Gimmick. Written and Illustrated by Miki Aihara. VIZ Media, LLC, 2003–2006. 12 Vol. 4 VIZBIG Vol. **O** Genre: Comedy, Drama, Romance.

Hatsumi's life is currently a mess. Caught in the act of buying a pregnancy test for her sister, she finds herself being blackmailed by her neighbor into being his slave. Then there's the fact that her childhood crush seems to be taking an interest in her, but the blackmail is interfering with her being able to do much. Relationships are never easy, and Hatsumi's going to have a tough time sorting hers out.

Imadoki! Nowadays. Written and Illustrated by Yuu Watase. VIZ Media, LLC, 2004–2005. 5 Vol. **O** Genre: Drama, Comedy, Romance.

Tanpopo has moved from Hokkaido to Tokyo to attend Meio Academy, but she feels more than a little out of her depth, especially with the way she keeps getting bullied. In order to make some real friends and get to know the young man she met on her first day, Tanpopo starts a planting committee to plant real flowers around the school to replace the fake ones around the grounds. But her determination may get her in more thankless trouble.

Kodocha: Sana's Stage. Written and Illustrated by Miho Obana. Tokyopop, 2002–2003. 10 Vol. **T** Genre: Drama, Romantic Comedy. Related Anime: *Kodocha.*

Sana just happens to be a child star with the urge to fix things for the people around her. It doesn't always work, but she means well. However, when a new boy in her class at school starts causing trouble, Sana may find more than just a problem to fix. Winner of the Kodansha Award.

Peach Girl. Written and Illustrated by Miwa Ueda. Tokyopop, 2000–2004. 18 Vol. **T** Genre: Comedy, Drama, Romance. Related Anime: *Peach Girl.*

High school is a little rough for Momo. A former swim team member, she had bleached hair and a tan, making most of the school think she's an airheaded beach bunny. Throw in a malicious best friend and a love triangle and Momo may be in over her head. She's not sure what her heart wants, but she's going to have to figure it out, and the sooner, the better. The second half of the series was published as *Peach Girl: Change of Heart,* volumes 1 through 10. Winner of the Kodansha Award.

Peach Girl: Sae's Story. Written and Illustrated by Miwa Ueda. Tokyopop, 2006–2007. 3 Vol. **O** Genre: Drama, Comedy, Romance.

In a spin-off of *Peach Girl,* Momo's friend Sae faces repeating a year of high school. While most of her friends have moved on, Sae is stuck in the same place, and she will be faced with some hard realizations about her life and her heart. But maybe she can manage to find a future that she wants for herself.

Princess Princess. Written and Illustrated by Mikiyo Tsuda. DMP, 2006–2007. 5 Vol. **O** Genre: Drama, Comedy, Yaoi. Related Anime: *Princess Princess*.

Toru has just transferred to an elite all-boys school, and he has to admit he's gotten a warm welcome. Of course, his classmates seem to want him to dress up as a girl and make him a "Princess," and the other two Princesses in the school don't mind the idea either. Toru is going to find his new school to be an experience, but what kind he doesn't know yet.

Princess Princess Plus. Written and Illustrated by Mikiyo Tsuda. DMP, 2009. 1 Vol. **O** Genre: Drama, Comedy, Yaoi.

In this sequel to *Princess Princess*, the new Princesses have been chosen, but they don't seem to get along very well. It is up to the former Princesses and the student council to get the two of them to get along and keep the Princess system intact.

Revolutionary Girl Utena. Written and Illustrated by Chiho Saito. VIZ Media, LLC, 2003–2004. 5 Vol. **O** Genre: Drama, Fantasy, Psychological, Surreal, Yuri. Related Anime: *Revolutionary Girl Utena, The Adolescence of Utena*.

Utena's goal in life is to become a prince. She was inspired by the young man who rescued and comforted her after her parents died. Now a high school student at Ohtori Academy, she finds herself drawn into a world of duels and intrigue as she tries to protect the Rose Bride, a young woman named Anthy.

Sand Chronicles. Written and Illustrated by Hinako Ashihara. VIZ Media, LLC, 2008–2011. 10 Vol. **O** Genre: Drama.

When Ann moves from Tokyo to a little town in the countryside, she finds that her whole life has changed. She is not used to living where everyone knows everyone, but when tragedy strikes, Ann may find that this is the best community for her. Winner of the Shogakukun Award.

Fantasy

Angel Sanctuary. Written and Illustrated by Kaori Yuki. VIZ Media, LLC, 2004–2007. 20 Vol. **O** Genre: Fantasy, Romance. Related Anime: *Angel Sanctuary*.

The reincarnation of an angel that betrayed Heaven, Setsuna is doomed to a miserable life. He finds himself torn in more than one way. Caught in a war between Heaven and Hell, he must figure out what role he will play in all this.

Baron: The Cat Returns. Written and Illustrated by Aoi Hiiragi. VIZ Media, LLC, 2005. 1 Vol. **A** Genre: Fantasy. Related Anime: *The Cat Returns*.

When Haru rescues a cat from getting run over, she sets in motion a series of events that will change her life forever. Desperate for help, Haru turns to Baron and his friends for assistance. Together with Baron, Haru hopes to be able to escape the fate that she accidentally incurred.

Basara. Written and Illustrated by Yumi Tamura. VIZ Media, LLC, 2003–2007. 27 Vol. **O** Genre: Fantasy, Science Fiction, Romance.

In a postapocalyptic Japan, hope is not entirely lost. A child of destiny will be born to lead a revolution against the people's oppressors. However, that child of destiny is Sarasa's twin brother, Tatara, and he is dead. Vowing revenge, Sarasa takes on the mantle of leader and masquerades as a boy, with plans to change the world. Winner of the Shogakukun Award.

Dazzle. Written and illustrated by Minari Endoh. Tokyopop, 2006–. Ongoing Series. 12 Vol. **T** Genre: Fantasy, Action, Drama.

At age 14, Rahzel finds herself sent off by her father to see the world. It isn't long before she runs across Alzeid, a young man bent on revenge. Once Rahzel convinces Alzeid to let her be his traveling companion, their adventure together begins, and neither of them may be ready for the result.

Demon Sacred. Written and Illustrated by Natsumi Itsuki. Tokyopop, 2010–. 11 Vol. **T** Genre: Fantasy.

A strange occurrence during Rena's honeymoon leaves her twin daughters in dire straights. Rina has contracted Return Syndrome, and while both she and her sister Mona are 14, Rina only looks 9 years old. Furthermore, the disease may kill her. Mona will do just about anything to save her twin, including dealing with demons.

Fairy Cube. Written and Illustrated by Kaoru Yuki. VIZ Media, LLC, 2008. 3 Vol. **O** Genre: Fantasy, Horror, Romance.

Ian can see fairies. That doesn't help him much, because while he can see fairies and spirits, he can't protect himself or the girl he likes from a spirit called Tokage. Under Tokage's influence, Ian's father stabs him, and Tokage possesses Ian's body. Ian is left as a spirit himself, and if he ever wants reclaim his own life, Ian will have figure out how he can save the fairies' world and maybe even his own.

From Far Away. Written and Illustrated by Kyoko Hikawa. VIZ Media, LCC, 2004–2007. 14 Vol. **T** Genre: Adventure, Fantasy, Romance.

When Noriko finds herself transported to another world, her only ally is the mysterious Izark who seems to have taken her under his wing. As they travel together, their fates seemed to be far more entwined than either expects, and neither of them knows how their journey will end. Winner of the Seiun Award.

Fushigi Yûgi: Genbu Kaiden. Written and Illustrated by Yuu Watase. VIZ Media, LLC, 2005–. Ongoing Series. 9 Vol. **O** Genre: Adventure, Fantasy, Historical, Romance.

A prequel to *Fushigi Yûgi*, *Fushigi Yûgi: Genbu Kaiden* follows the adventures of Takiko. When she tries to destroy her father's translation of *The*

Universe of the Four Gods, she finds herself sucked into the story instead. Now as Priestess of Genbu, she must gather her seven celestial warriors, but in a world completely different from her own, Takiko is going to have her work cut out for her.

Fushigi Yûgi: The Mysterious Play. **Written and Illustrated by Yuu Watase. VIZ Media, LLC, 2003–2006. 18 Vol. O Genre: Fantasy, Romance. Related Anime:** *Fushigi Yûgi, Fushigi Yûgi OVA, Fushigi Yûgi OVA 2, Fushigi Yûgi Eikoden.*

When Miaka and her friend Yui get sucked into a world contained inside the book *The Universe of the Four Gods*, she finds herself named the Priestess of Suzaku. Miaka will have to face friends who have become enemies and find new allies if she wishes to return home, and even so, she may not be able to leave before losing her heart to the enigmatic martial artist, Tamahome.

Haruka: Beyond the Stream of Time. **Written and Illustrated by Tohko Mizuno. VIZ Media, LLC, 2008–. Ongoing Series. 14 Vol. O Genre: Fantasy, Romance.**

Akane's first day of school takes an interesting turn when she and two friends get transported to what appears to be the Heian period of Japan. Then Akane learns that she is supposed to be the Priestess of the Dragon God. However, there are those that are her enemies as well, and Akane will find that her very life may be in danger.

Heaven's Will. **Written and Illustrated by Satoru Takamiya. VIZ Media, LLC, 2009. 1 Vol. T Genre: Fantasy.**

Sudou can see ghosts, which turns out to be a problem for her. However, when she meets Seto, an exorcist in need of some practice, it seems like a stroke of luck. The two of them decided to team up in order to help one another, and end up forming a partnership that just might help them both.

The Key to the Kingdom. **Written and Illustrated by Kyoko Shitou. 2007–2008. 6 Vol. O Genre: Adventure, Drama, Fantasy.**

When both the king and the crown prince of Landor are killed in battle, Asta is left to inherit the thrown. However, the young prince first must prove himself by finding the key to the kingdom. But Asta is not the only one searching for the key, and there is a real chance that he could die on his quest. Whoever finds the key will be the next ruler of Landor, and Asta has both allies and enemies waiting for him.

La Corda d'Oro. **Written and Illustrated by Yuki Kure. VIZ Media, LCC, 2006–. Ongoing Series. 14 Vol. T Genre: Fantasy, Music, Romance. Related Anime:** *La Corda d'Oro: Primo Passo.*

When Kahoko sees a fairy at school, she finds herself owner of a magical violin as well as a contestant in a school competition. Kaho isn't a musician, however, and she finds the whole affair confusing and frustrating. The music competition might bring her love and fame or it could bring her down with its rivalries and bitterness.

Mamotte! Lollipop. Written and Illustrated by Michiyo Kikuta. Del Rey, 2007–2008. 8 Vol. **T** Genre: Fantasy, Romantic Comedy. Related Anime: *Save Me! Lollipop.*
> When Nina accidentally swallows the Crystal Pearl (she thought it was a piece of candy), she finds herself the target of a sorcery exam with a number of student wizards coming after her. Thankfully, two of the wizards have agreed to protect her until they can make a magic potion to recover the Crystal Pearl. However, the potion will take six months to make, so Nina's life is going to be interesting for awhile.

MeruPuri: Mächen Prince. Written and Illustrated by Matsuri Hino. VIZ Media, LLC, 2005–2006. 4 Vol. **T** Genre: Comedy, Fantasy, Romance.
> Airi just wants to end up living in a nice home with a loving husband, and her school has a legend that the longer your streak of being on time to class, the better boyfriend you will end up with. However, one morning in her rush to get to school, she drops a star-shaped mirror that is an heirloom of her family's. When she goes back to find it, Airi finds a little boy. Aram claims to have come through the mirror, and his presence in her life will change everything.

Mugen Spiral. Written and Illustrated by Mizuho Kusanagi. Tokyopop, 2007. 2 Vol. **T** Genre: Fantasy, Romance.
> Yayoi is a young mystic from a long line of mystics. When Ura, the son of the demon king, tries to steal her powers, she seals him in the body of a black cat. However, Yayoi ends up bringing him home with her, and before long, the two find that they just might not be enemies after all.

Red River. Written and Illustrated by Chie Shinohara. VIZ Media, LLC, 2004–2010. 28 Vol. **O** Genre: Drama, Fantasy, Historical, Romance.
> Yuri's life is going pretty well. At 15, she's just had her first kiss and she's gotten into the high school she wanted. Then she finds herself pulled into the ancient Middle East by an evil queen. Yuri escapes being sacrificed, but she finds herself caught up in a whirlwind of power, politics, and war. Yuri will have a part to play in all this if she wants to go home, and if she wants to survive. Winner of the Shogakukun Award.

RG Veda. Written and Illustrated by CLAMP. Tokyopop, 2005–2007. 10 Vol. **T** Genre: Adventure, Fantasy, Romance.
> Three hundred years ago after the Heavenly Emperor was killed by his wife and the God of Thunder, a prophecy was made. Now the child of that prophecy, Ashura, along with the Six Stars, begins a journey that just might fulfill that prophecy.

R.I.P.: Requiem in Phonybrian. Written and Illustrated by Mitsukazu Mihara. Tokyopop, 2006. 1 Vol. **O** Genre: Fantasy, Romance.
> When a bored angel witnesses a young undertaker's attempt to take his own life, she gives him one of her wings. However, now the both of them are trapped between heaven and hell as well as stuck with one another.

Silver Diamond. Written and Illustrated by Shiho Sugiura. Tokyopop, 2008–. Ongoing Series. 23 Vol. **T** Genre: Adventure, Fantasy, Romance, Supernatural, Yaoi.

> Rakan is an ordinary teen with an interest in plants. An orphan, his entire life changes when he finds a mysterious man named Chigusa in his garden. Rakan is soon pulled into another world where his powers with plants mark him as a Sanome and make him the best hope of saving Chigusa's world.

Soul Rescue. Written and Illustrated by Aya Kanno. Tokyopop, 2006–2007. 2 Vol. **T** Genre: Action, Fantasy.

> Renji's an angel who has been banished to Earth until he can save 10,000 souls. Unfortunately for him, he's never been good at much except fighting, so he might just be stuck on Earth forever.

Tsubasa: Those with Wings. Written and Illustrated by Natsuki Takaya. Tokyopop, 2009. 3 Vol. **O** Genre: Adventure, Fantasy.

> Kotoboki is a thief who is trying to make a new start at a legal way of life. However, she gets drawn into the search for Tsubasa, a legendary item that supposedly grants wishes. Along with a military officer named Raimon, Kotobiki joins the race to find Tsubasa, all the while entertaining the hopes of one day having a normal life. But Tsubasa may not be what people think, and Kotobuki may find that happiness doesn't come from a wish.

Vampire Game. Written and Illustrated by Judal. Tokyopop, 2003–2006. 15 Vol. Rated: **T** Genre: Comedy, Fantasy, Romance.

> A hundred years ago the Vampire King Duzell was defeated by King Phelios in a great battle. As they both lay dying, Duzell swore revenge on his enemy's reincarnation. What he didn't expect was to be reincarnated as a cat. Adopted by the Princess Ishtar, Duzell will have his work cut out for him finding Phelios, especially since the 15-year-old princess can be more of a hindrance than a help at times.

Wish. Written and Illustrated by CLAMP. Tokyopop, 2002–2003. 4 Vol. **T** Genre: Fantasy.

> When the young doctor, Shuichiro, rescues an angel named Kohaku, the angel offers him a wish in return. But there is nothing that Shuichiro wants, as he's perfectly happy with his life. Since Kohaku is honor-bound to grant his wish, she moves in with him. Both of them may find that this situation is far more complicated than either of them expects.

X/1999. Written and Illustrated by CLAMP. VIZ Media, LLC, 2003–. Ongoing Series. 18 Vol. **O** Genre: Fantasy. Related Anime: *X/1999* (film), *X/1999* (OVA), *X/1999* (TV Series).

> Kamui returns home to Tokyo in a troubled state after his mother's death. He is determined to protect his friends Fuma and Kotori even if he's not exactly sure how to do that yet. Chaos and darkness swirl around Kamui, and he will have to

make a choice about where he stands as the end of the world approaches. This series is on hiatus in Japan.

Historical Fiction

<u>Kaze Hikaru</u>. **Written and Illustrated by Taeko Watanabe. VIZ Media, LLC, 2005–. Ongoing Series. 28 Vol. O Genre: Action, Historical Fiction.**
> Seizaburo Kamiya has just joined the Mibu-Roshi, a group of warriors loyal to the Shogunate. He might not have much experience, but he does have a lot of passion for their cause. And he's managed to get the great Soji Okita to mentor him. He also has a secret. Seizaburo is really Sei, a young woman who is determined to get revenge for her murdered father and brother. To do so, her real identity will have to stay a secret. Winner of the Shogakukun Award.

<u>Le Chevalier d'Eon</u>. **Written by Tou Ubukata. Illustrated by Kiriko Yumeji. Del Rey, 2007–2010. 8 Vol. O Genre: Historical Fiction, Horror, Mystery. Related Anime:** *Chevalier: Le Chevalier D'Eon.*
> When his older sister, Lia, shows up dead and floating in the river Seine, d'Eon decides that someone needs to get to the bottom of her murder. He joins the French secret police, and soon d'Eon finds that he has only scratched the tip of the iceberg.

<u>Tail of the Moon</u>. **Written and Illustrated by Rinko Ueda. VIZ Media, LCC, 2006–2009. 15 Vol. O Genre: Adventure, Comedy, Historical Fiction, Romance.**
> While Usagi is the great-granddaughter of the leader of a ninja clan, she is an utter failure as a ninja, so instead, she is sent to secure a marriage with Hanzo Hattori, a local nobleman. Unfortunately, Hanzo seems to have no intention of marrying anyone—not to mention that she has competition for his hand in marriage. Usagi is determined to see her first mission through, and love is never easy in dangerous times.

<u>Tail of the Moon Prequel: The Other Hanzo(u)</u>. **Written and Illustrated by Rinko Ueda. VIZ Media, LLC, 2009. 1 Vol. O Genre: Adventure, Comedy, Historical Fiction, Romance.**
> A prequel to *Tail of the Moon, The Other Hanzo(u)* gives the back story of Princess Sara and her relationship with both men named Hanzo before the series Tail of the Moon starts.

<u>Wanted</u>. **Written and Illustrated by Matsuri Hino. VIZ Media, LLC, 2008. 1 Vol. O Genre: Action, Historical Fiction, Romance.**
> When Ameria's crush Luce is captured by pirates, she is determined to rescue him. She disguises herself as a boy and takes a job on Captain Skulls' ship. But things are not quite as they seem abroad Skulls' ship, and Ameria's not the only one with a secret.

Horror

<u>Pet Shop of Horrors</u>. **Written and Illustrated by Matsuri Akino. Tokyopop, 2003– 2005. Ongoing Series. 6 Vol. O Genre: Horror, Mystery.**

> At Count D's shop, one can find the most perfect pet ever imagined. However, a strict contract comes with each pet, and if it is broken, the consequences can be dire. Even as a police detective tries to figure out the mysteries behind Count D, people continue to purchase pets, and each has his or her own story. The series tends to be episodic and tied together with a few recurring characters.

<u>Pet Shop of Horrors: Tokyo</u>. **Written and Illustrated by Matsuri Akino. Tokyopop, 2008–. Ongoing Series. 6 Vol. O Genre: Horror, Mystery.**

> A sequel to the series *Pet Shop of Horrors, Pet Shop of Horrors: Tokyo* provides further stories of Count D's pet shop, this time in a new location. Like the previous series, the stories are episodic in nature and are tied together with a few reoccurring characters.

<u>Sengoku Nights</u>. **Written and Illustrated by Kei Kusonoki and Kaoru Ohashi. Tokyopop, 2006. 2 Vol. T Genre: Action, Horror.**

> Masayoshi Kurozuka just happens to be the reincarnation of a woman named Oni-hime. Unfortunately for him, that means he has a number of bloodthirsty ghosts pursuing him who would like very much to harm him. If Masayoshi wants to find his destiny, he's going to have to survive.

Magical Girl

<u>Alice 19th</u>. **Written and Illustrated by Yuu Watase. VIZ Media, LLC, 2003–2004. 7 Vol. O Genre: Adventure, Fantasy, Magical Girl, Romance.**

> Alice Seno lives in the shadow of her older sister Mayura. However, one day when she rescues a rabbit, she is given the ability to use the Lotis Words. But this power ends up costing Alice her sister, and now she'll do what she has to in order to get Mayura back.

<u>Cardcaptor Sakura</u>. **Written and illustrated by CLAMP. Tokyopop, 2003. 12 Vol. Dark Horse, 2010–. 4 Vol. A Genre: Fantasy, Magical Girl, Romance. Related Anime:** *Cardcaptor Sakura, Cardcaptor Sakura: The Movie, Cardcaptor Sakura Movie 2: The Sealed Card.*

> When Sakura Kinomoto accidentally releases a set of magic cards from a book in her father's library, she finds her life changed. The cards are the Clow Cards, and it is now Sakura's task to collect them all before they cause too much trouble. Each card has its own powers, and as Sakura collects them she gains access to those powers. But she's not the only one interested in the cards, and capturing them all may be a challenge. The second half of the series was released by Tokyopop as *Master of the Clow* volumes 1 through 6. Dark Horse Comics is currently reissuing the series as four omnibus volumes. Winner of the Seiun Award.

I.O.N. Written and Illustrated by Arina Tanemura. VIZ Media, LCC, 2008. 1 Vol. **T** Genre: Magical Girl, Romance.

> Ion Tsubaburagi uses the letters of her first name as a good luck mantra. However, when she gets involved with the school's Psychic Research Club, an accident occurs that gives Ion telekinetic powers. Having psychic powers isn't easy and the fact that Ion's falling for one of the other club members doesn't help either.

Kamichama Karin. Written and Illustrated by Koge-Donbo. Tokyopop, 2005–2007. 7 Vol. **Y** Genre: Comedy, Drama, Magical Girl, Romance.

> Karin is your average girl on a good day. On a bad day, well, she's rather below average. Quite frankly, she's been rather miserable lately. However, when she finds out that her mother's ring allows her to borrow the power of a god, things start to change in her favor. However, she's not the only one with powers, and not all of the others may be friendly.

Kamichama Karin Chu. Written and Illustrated by Koge-Donbo. Del Rey, 2008–2010. 7 Vol. **T** Genre: Comedy, Drama, Magical Girl, Romance.

> A sequel to *Kamichama Karin, Kamichama Karin Chu* follows the continuing adventures of Karin and her friends. This time Karin ends up traveling through time in order to keep her future from changing and to protect her friends.

Kamikaze Kaito Jeanne. Written and Illustrated by Arina Tanemura. CMX, 2005–2007. 7 Vol. **E** Genre: Magical Girl, Romance.

> Maron isn't exactly a normal teenager. With the assistance of Finn Fish, she transforms into the thief Kamikaze Kaito Jeanne. She tracks down and steals demon-possessed paintings in order to exorcise them. But she has some competition when it comes to getting hold of those paintings, not to mention the fact that she also has to attend high school.

Magical x Miracle. Written and Illustrated by Yuzu Mizutani. Tokyopop, 2006–2007. 6 Vol. **T** Genre: Drama, Fantasy, Magical Girl.

> Merleawe has come to Viegald in order to study to be a wizard. However, Viegald's Master Wizard Sylthfarn has just gone missing, and Merleawe looks almost exactly like him. She agrees to pretend to be Sylthfarn in order to help keep the peace of the country, but Merleawa isn't entirely sure she can pull this off. Meanwhile, what does this mean for her own dreams?

Mink. Written and Illustrated by Megumi Tachikawa. Tokyopop, 2004–2005. 6 Vol. **Y** Genre: Magical Girl, Romance.

> When Mink accidentally buys a strange software disc instead of the latest music album she intended to buy, she finds that the program is from the future and lets her be what she wants. Mink soon creates Cyber Idol Mink. She quickly becomes the hottest sensation around. However, there is one catch. It's

illegal for her to use future software in the present, and if someone finds out, Mink herself might disappear.

Mistress Fortune. Written and Illustrated by Arina Tanemura. VIZ Media, LLC, 2011. 1 Vol. 🅃 Genre: Magical Girl, Romance.

Kisaki just happens to work for the PSI as well as being a junior high school student. She also happens to be in love with her partner, Ginior. Unfortunately, that happens to be against the rules, and she doesn't know if he feels the same way. To make things worse, it sounds like she's going to be transferred, and she really doesn't know what to do about it all.

Pichi Pichi Pitch: Mermaid Melody. Written and Illustrated by Pink Hanamori. Del Rey, 2006–2007. 7 Vol. 🅃 Genre: Magical Girl.

Lucia has a secret. She is actually a mermaid. She's posing as a human while she looks for the boy she entrusted her magical pearl too, and it looks like she's finally found him. The only problem is he doesn't recognize her, and she can't tell him who she really is or she'll turn into sea foam. Meanwhile, some water demons are causing trouble, and Lucia really needs that pearl. She's got to get her pearl back and maybe even manage a romance too.

Sailor Moon. Written and Illustrated by Naoko Takeuchi. Tokyopop, 1998–2001. 18 Vol. 🅃 Genre: Adventure, Comedy, Drama, Fantasy, Magical Girl, Romance. Related Anime: _Sailor Moon._

Bunny is a rather clumsy schoolgirl. When she rescues a cat one day, she finds herself caught up in a war against evil. With a brooch that allows her to transform into Sailor Moon, a soldier for love and justice, and with her cat, Luna to guide her, Bunny will have to do her best to save the world and hopefully get to school on time too. The series was released as _Sailor Moon_ for the first 11 volumes, followed by _Sailor Moon SuperS_, which had 4 volumes, and _Sailor Moon Stars_, which had 3 volumes. The series will be released by Kodansha Comics in 2011. Winner of the Kodansha Award.

Shugo Chara!. Written and Illustrated by Peach-Pit. Del Rey, 2006–2010. Kodansha Comics, 2011–. 12 Vol. 🅃 Genre: Magical Girl.

Amu is a shy elementary school student. When she wishes for the confidence to be herself, she ends up with eggs containing guardian characters. With their help, Amu will discover her true self and make some new friends along the way. Winner of the Kodansha Award.

St. ♥ Dragon Girl. Written and Illustrated by Natsumi Matsumoto. VIZ Media, LLC, 2008–2010. 8 Vol. 🅃 Genre: Fantasy, Magical Girl, Martial Arts, Romantic Comedy.

Momoka and Ryuga are childhood friends. Momoka is a martial artist while Ryuga is a master of ancient Chinese magic. When Ryuga summons the dragon spirit that is the guardian of his family, it accidentally possesses Momoka instead.

Now the two of them have teamed up to fight demons and perhaps discover that their friendship might be something more.

Sugar Sugar Rune. Written and Illustrated by Moyoco Anno. Del Rey, 2005–2008. 8 Vol. **Y** Genre: Comedy, Fantasy, Magical Girl, Romance, Supernatural.

Chocolat and Vanilla are best friends. The girls also happen to be witches and in the running to become Queen of the Magic World. However, to earn the title, they must go to the Human World and earn the hearts of human boys in order to win the right to become Queen. It may be harder than it sounds, and their rivalry may end up ruining their friendship as well. Winner of the Kodansha Award.

Time Stranger Kyoko. Written and Illustrated by Arina Tanemura. VIZ Media, LLC, 2008–2009. 3 Vol. **O** Genre: Comedy, Magical Girl, Romance.

In the 30th century, Kyoko is the Princess of Earth, despite the fact that she doesn't want to be. When her father gives her the chance at freedom, she jumps at it. The catch is Kyoko must find 12 holy stones and 12 telepaths in order to awaken her twin sister, who has been in a coma since birth.

Tokyo Mew Mew. Written and Illustrated by Mia Ikumi and Reiko Yoshida. Tokyopop, 2003–2006. 7 Vol. **Y** Genre: Drama, Magical Girl. Related Anime: *Tokyo Mew Mew*.

Ichigo was a normal 11-year-old until her DNA was combined with the DNA of an almost extinct cat. And she's not the only one. Four other girls have also been combined with other almost extinct animals, and together the five of them will become a part of the Mew Project. Their mission: to protect the world from aliens.

Ultra Maniac. Written and Illustrated by Wataru Yoshizumi. VIZ Media, LLC, 2005–2006. 5 Vol. **A** Genre: Magical Girl, Romantic Comedy. Related Anime: *Ultra Maniac*.

Ayu didn't expect to make friends with a witch, but that's exactly what happens when she meets Nina. Unfortunately, Nina isn't exactly a talented witch, and many of her spells backfire on Ayu. It is hard, after all, to impress the boy you like when strange things keep happening around them. But Ayu is going to keep trying, and maybe Nina will be able to help after all.

Wedding Peach. Written and Illustrated by Nao Yazawa. VIZ Media, LLC, 2003–2004. 7 Vol. **T** Genre: Magical Girl, Romance. Related Anime: *Wedding Peach, Wedding Peach DX*.

Momoko Hanasaki is half angel on her mother's side. This is why she can transform into Wedding Peach. She is the only thing standing in between the innocent humans and the demons who want to destroy all the love and happiness on the planet. With her friends, Angel Lily and Angel Daisy, Wedding Peach will fight to protect love and maybe find a true love of her own.

Mystery

The Cain Saga. Written and Illustrated by Kaori Yuki. VIZ Media, LLC, 2006–2007. 5 Vol. M Genre: Historical Fiction, Horror, Mystery.

Earl Cain Hargreaves has a knack for solving mysteries. But he has yet to solve the mysteries of his own past. As he searches for his own answers, he also solves mysteries for others, exposing the darker side of Victorian England.

Godchild. Written and Illustrated by Kaori Yuki. VIZ Media, LLC, 2006–2008. 8 Vol. O Genre: Historical Fiction, Horror, Mystery.

A sequel to *The Cain Saga*, Godchild follows the adventures of Lord Cain, his sister Mary Weather, and his valet, Riff, as they investigate crimes in Victorian London. However, never far away in the shadows is Cain's half brother, who is part of a secret society with nefarious purposes.

Kamen Tantei. Written and Illustrated by Matsuri Akino. Tokyopop, 2006–2007. 4 Vol. T Genre: Detective, Mystery.

Masato and Haruka are a pair of aspiring young mystery writers who publish under the name Taro Suzuki. The two of them willingly take on any mysteries that come their way. However, when they hit a dead end, the mysterious Kamen Tantei or Masked Detective shows up to lend a hand. But just who is the Masked Detective and what is he up to?

Legal Drug. Written and Illustrated by CLAMP. Tokyopop, 2004–. Ongoing Series. 3 Vol. O Genre: Action, Comedy, Mystery, Supernatural, Yaoi.

Kazahaya Kudo has the ability to see visions when he touches a person or an object. What he doesn't have is a job until he gets hired at Green Drug Pharmacy. He's not the only one at Green Drug with supernatural powers, and he finds himself along with his coworker Rikuo Himura being sent on some special assignments that make use of those powers. This series is on haitus in Japan.

Loveless. Written and Illustrated by Yun Kouga. Tokyopop, 2006–. Ongoing Series. 9 Vol. O Genre: Drama, Fantasy, Mystery, Romance, Yaoi. Related Anime: *Loveless*.

When Ritsuka starts at a new school after the death of his brother, Seimei, he meets Soubi who claims to have known his brother. Soon the two of them are looking into Seimei's death and fighting battles side by side. But when your true name is Loveless, what does the future hold for you?

Suki. Written and Illustrated by CLAMP. Tokypop, 2004. 3 Vol. T Genre: Mystery, Romance.

Hinata lives alone in her house with a collection of teddy bears. When her new next-door neighbor turns out to be her substitute teacher at school, Hinata ends up developing a crush on him. But there is more going on than simply teenager romance, and both Hinata and Shiro may learn a few things.

<u>Zodiac P.I</u> **Written and Illustrated by Natsumi Ando. Tokyopop, 2003. 4 Vol.**
Y Genre: Action, Fantasy, Mystery.

> Lili has a talent she uses to track down criminals and solve crimes. The teenager uses the help of her Star Ring in order to transform into the Detective Spica as well as read horoscopes in order to solve the mysteries. Whatever the mystery, Lili is ready to find out what the truth is.

Romance

<u>Backstage Prince</u>. **Written and Illustrated by Kanako Sakurakoji. VIZ Media, LLC, 2007. 2 Vol. T Genre: Romance, School.**

> When Akari accidentally injures one of her classmates, she ends up acting as his assistant. As it turns out, Ryusei is a kabuki actor. He is hampered in part by the fact that no one has been able to stand him long enough to be his assistant. But Akari finds that there is a softer side to him, and she may turn out to be more than just Ryusei's assistant.

<u>Beast Master</u>. **Written and Illustrated by Kyousuke Motomi. VIZ Media, LLC, 2009–2010. 2 Vol. O Genre: Comedy, Romance.**

> Yuiko loves animals, but they don't seem to share her feelings. However, when a new transfer student arrives at school who has a knack with animals, Yuiko manages to be the only one to befriend him. Despite having lived in the wild most of his life, Leo is a nice enough guy save for one thing: when he sees blood, he flies into a berserk rage. Still, Yuiko refuses to give up on him, and maybe she can help tame his inner beast.

<u>B.O.D.Y.</u> **Written and Illustrated by Ao Mimori. VIZ Media, LLC, 2008–. 14 Vol O Genre: Romance.**

> Ryoko has a crush on her classmate Ryunosuke despite the fact that her friends can't see why she likes him. When she finds out that he works part time at a host club where she could pay to date him, it almost seems too good to be true. But Ryoko wants to win his heart as well, and that could take a little more work.

<u>Captive Hearts</u>. **Written and Illustrated by Matsuri Hino. VIZ Media, LLC, 2008–2009. 5 Vol. T Genre: Comedy, Romance, Supernatural.**

> Megumi is pretty happy with his life right up until Suzuka comes back into his life. Then he finds himself bowing and scraping to her and generally acting like a servant. As it turns out, his family is cursed to serve hers. Unfortunately, for the two of them, this makes having a relationship rather difficult unless they can find some way to break the curse.

<u>Cherry Juice</u>. **Written and Illustrated by Haruka Fukushima. Tokyopop, 2007–2008. 4 Vol. T Genre: Comedy, Drama, Romance.**

> Minami and Otome are step-siblings who are finally getting along. It only took five years after their parents got married. However, when Otome starts dating Minami's best friend, Minami finds that he might have more than

just a crush on his stepsister after all. But can a romantic relationship between a pair of step-siblings really work?

Dengeki Daisy. Written and Illustrated by Kyousuke Motomi. VIZ Media, LLC, 2010–. Ongoing Series. 8 Vol. **O** Genre: Comedy, Drama, Romance.

Before Teru's older brother passes away, he gives her a phone so she can contact DAISY. Teru has never met DAISY, but he seems to know when she needs him and sends her texts. Also, Teru is finding that her school janitor Tasuku Kurosaki always seems to be there when she needs someone in person. But Kurosaki has a few secrets of his own, and Teru's life may be getting more complicated than she knows.

The Devil Does Exist. Written and Illustrated by Mitsuba Takanashi. CMX, 2005–2007. 11 Vol. **T** Genre: Romance.

Kayano's life has been miserable ever since the school bully, Takeru, got hold of the letter she wrote confessing her crush on another classmate. Then things get even worse when her mother announces that she is going to marry Kayano's school principal, who just happens to be Takeru's father. Kayano's pretty sure she's doomed, but maybe there's some hope in this situation after all.

Fruits Basket. Written and Illustrated by Natsuki Takaya. Tokyopop, 2004–2007. 23 Vol. Rated: **T** Genre: Comedy, Drama, Fantasy, Romance. Related Anime: *Fruits Basket.*

Tohru Honda has been orphaned and lives in a tent until her neighbors stumble across her and offer her a home with them, the Sohma family. However, the Sohmas have their own secrets, and Tohru will find herself fighting for her new friends and maybe falling in love along the way. Winner of the Kodansha Award.

Full Moon o Sagashite. Written and Illustrated by Arina Tanemura. VIZ Media, LLC, 2005–2006. 7 Vol. **T** Genre: Magical Girl, Romance, Supernatural. Related Anime: *Full Moon o Sagashite.*

Mitsuki is a 12-year-old with the dream of becoming a singer. However, there is a tumor in her throat, which makes her dreams unlikely. When two death spirits show up to tell her she only has a year left to live, Mitsuki strikes a deal with one of them. He'll help her with her dreams if she'll come quietly when her time arrives. So with a little supernatural help, Mitsuki's career in music is getting off to a running start.

Gentlemen's Alliance Cross. Written and Illustrated by Arina Tanemura. VIZ Media, LLC, 2007–2010. 11 Vol. **O** Genre: Drama, Romance.

Haine's in love with Shizumasa Togu, the emperor-apparent of her school. Not only did he write her favorite book as a child, but he gave her some advice during a hard time in her life. Of course, he doesn't seem to remember her when they meet again in high school, but Haine won't be deterred. However, when she gets appointed to be Shizumasa's bodyguard, Haine will find that there are more secrets hidden in the school than she knows and that winning Shizumasa's love may be much harder than she knows.

Honey Hunt. Written and Illustrated by Miki Aihara. VIZ Media, LLC, 2009–. Ongoing Series. 6 Vol. **O** Genre: Drama, Romance.

> A fairly average teenager, Yura Onozuka tends to be lost in the shadow of her famous parents. When her parents divorce, Yura strikes out on her own, determined to make it as herself rather than as her parents' child. However, the world of show business is not an easy one, and Yura is still figuring out who she is and what she loves.

Kare: First Love. Written and Illustrated by Kaho Miyasaka. VIZ Media, LLC, 2004–2006. 10 Vol. **T** Genre: Drama, Romance.

> Karin has always been something of a plain Jane, and most people don't bother to look beyond her glasses. However, when Kiriya, a student at the local all-boys school, starts taking an interest in her, Karin finds herself being torn between friend Yuka who wants Kiriya for herself and a romance with Kiriya. First loves are never easy, and Karin is not sure what to do.

Kitchen Princess. Written by Miyuki Kobaysahi. Illustrated by Natsumi Ando. Del Rey, 2007–2009. 10 Vol. **T** Genre: Romance.

> Najika loves cooking, and she certainly has the talent for it. However, she keeps searching for the boy she refers to as the Flan Prince. He rescued her once and gave her a dish of flan to cheer her up. This quest brings Najika to Seika Academy. But she may find this school harder than she expected, and it seems that she has found two guys, both of which might be her prince. Winner of the Kodansha Award.

Loveholic. Written and Illustrated by Toko Kawai. DMP, 2007–2008. 2 Vol. **O** Genre: Drama, Romance, Yaoi.

> Nishioka and Matsukawa cannot seem to get along. This is odd since Matsukawa gets along with just about everyone. But even if they don't get along, when they do work together everything seems to go well for the company. So are they really enemies or is there something more there?

The Magic Touch: Oyayubi Kara Romance. Written and Illustrated by Izumi Tsubaki. VIZ Media, LLC, 2009–2010. 9 Vol. **O** Genre: Romance.

> Chiaki's a member of her school's Massage Research Society, and she definitely has a talent for it. However, there is one person at her school that Chiaki would love to get her hands on. Yosuke has to be the tensest person that she's met. But Chiaki may find that Yosuke had more to draw her to him than just the need for a good massage.

Mars. Written and Illustrated by Fuyumi Soryo. Tokyopop, 2002–2003. 15 Vol. **T** Genre: Romance.

> Kira and Rei are almost complete opposites, but fate seems to keep drawing them together. Shy artist Kira is rather surprised when playboy Rei agrees to be her model, and neither of them can help but be drawn to the other. However, there are secrets on both sides that threaten what could possibly be love.

Mars: Horse With No Name. Written and Illustrated by Fuyumi Soryo. Tokyopop, 2000. 1 Vol. **T** Genre: Romance.

A prequel to *Mars, Mars: Horse With No Name* tells the story of Rei and Kira's first meeting, and the struggles at the beginning of their romance.

Mixed Vegetables. Written and Illustrated by Ayumi Komura. VIZ Media, LLC, 2008–2010. 8 Vol. **T** Genre: Comedy, Romance.

Hanayu is the daughter of a pastry chef who wants to be a sushi chef. Hayato is the son of a sushi chef who wants to be pastry chef. Hanayu thinks that maybe marrying into a family that runs a sushi shop might let her follow her dreams without hurting her family's feelings, but neither love or cooking is as easy as it looks.

Monkey High!. Written and Illustrated by Shouko Akira. VIZ Media, LLC, 2008–2009. 8 Vol. **T** Genre: Romance.

Haruna isn't exactly impressed with school. She compares it to living on a monkey mountain. After her father's scandal, she's transferred to a new school, and Haruna doubts it will be any different here. However, her classmate Macharu has been nothing but warm and welcoming, and just maybe this will be a good new start.

The One I Love. Written and Illustrated by CLAMP. Tokyopop, 2004. 1 Vol. **T** Genre: Romance, Slice of Life.

The One I Love is a collection of 12 short stories from all the members CLAMP dealing with love and all that comes with it.

Othello. Written and Illustrated by Satomi Ikezawa. Del Rey, 2004. 7 Vol. **O** Genre: Romance.

Yaya is a rather shy and naïve student whose friends really don't treat her well. Nana is her alter ego, and she's pretty much Yaya's complete opposite. And there's the fact that Yaya doesn't even know that Nana exists. But it may take Nana's help for Yaya to learn to be confident in herself.

Oyayubihime Infinity. Written and Illustrated by Toru Fujieda. CMX, 2006–2007. 6 Vol. **T** Genre: Comedy, Romance, Supernatural.

Tsubame is searching for his reincarnated true love: a girl with a butterfly birthmark on her thumb. Kanoko has the birthmark, but she doesn't really believe his story. Besides, her older sister has the same birthmark. But that might not stop her from falling for Tsubame anyway.

Platinum Garden. Written and Illustrated by Maki Fujita. Tokyopop, 2006–. 15 Vol. **T** Genre: Comedy, Romance.

Kazura isn't exactly pleased to find that she's been given to Mitsuki Magahara in her grandfather's will. But as she starts living with Mitsuki, Kazura will find that there is more going on with her new home than she knows, and that maybe the situation won't be as bad as she thinks.

Sensual Phrase. Written and Illustrated by Mayu Shinjo. VIZ Media, LLC, 2004–2007. 18 Vol. **M** Genre: Romance.

> An almost accident turns out to be a stroke of good luck for Aine, who is trying to break into the music business as a lyricist. The young man who nearly ran her over is Sakuya, the leader of the band Lucifer. He thinks that her lyrics have potential. But neither show business nor romance is easy, and mixing the two of them is definitely going to be a challenge.

Shinobi Life. Written and Illustrated by Shoko Conami. Tokyopop, 2008–. Ongoing Series. 8 Vol. **T** Genre: Comedy, Romance.

> When the ninja Kagetora ends up in the future, he runs across a young woman who appears to be the princess he is sworn to protect. Beni Fujisawa is not only a descendant of Kagetora's Beni-hime, but she is a pretty unhappy one as well. When Kagetora swears to protect her, they both find themselves struggling to make love work even when their situations are against them.

Short-Tempered Melancholic and Other Stories. Written and Illustrated by Arina Tanemura. VIZ Media, LLC, 2008. 1 Vol. **T** Genre: Romance.

> A collection of short romantic stories.

Skyblue Shore. Written and Illustrated by Nanpei Yamada. Tokyopop, 2010–. 6 Vol. **O** Genre: Comedy, Romance.

> Tomo has always loved the beach. However, when her parents divorce, her trips there become infrequent. Then one day on her way to school, she's rescued by a young man whose keychain has the same stone as one given to her by a childhood friend long ago. The beach brought them together once. Now has fate brought them together again?

Stepping On Roses. Written and Illustrated by Rinko Ueda. VIZ Media, LLC, 2010–. Ongoing Series. 6 Vol. **O** Genre: Drama, Historical, Romance.

> Sumi has her hands full taking care of all the orphans her brother brings home. It doesn't help that they are constantly in debt, and that her brother gambles away more money than they can afford to lose. Sumi's little family is constantly teetering on the brink, but just when she is the most desperate, one Soichiro Ashida makes a bargain with her. He will pay for anything she or her family needs. In return, she will marry him and not fall in love with him. Sumi agrees, but the real question is whether both of them will be able to keep their feelings out of their marriage.

The Story of Saiunkoku. Written by Sai Yukino. Illustrated by Kairi Yura. VIZ Media, LLC, 2010–. Ongoing Series. 6 Vol. **T** Genre: Comedy, Fantasy, Romance. Related Anime: *The Story of Saiunkoku.*

> Shurei has always dreamed about working as a civil servant for the Imperial Court, but women aren't allowed to hold such positions. Her family might be nobility, but they are rather poor, and Shurei works hard to make ends meet.

However, the Grand Advisor of the Imperial Court makes her an offer she can't refuse. Apparently, the young Emperor Ryuki refuses to take any responsibility. Shurei is to become his consort for six months and help him learn to become a good ruler. If she can manage it, the reward will be great, but can Shurei really manage it?

Tenshi Ja Nai!!. Written and Illustrated by Takako Shigematsu. Go!Comi, 2005– 2007. 8 Vol. O Genre: Romance.

What Hikaru wants is a nice, ordinary life. She doesn't seem likely to get that. She's been bullied for years, and just when it seems like she'll get a new start at a new school, life throws her another curve. Hikaru's roommate is none other than the celebrity Izumi Kido. But Izumi has some secrets of her own, and Hikaru's life, while not ordinary, will definitely be interesting.

Tokyo Boys and Girls. Written and Illustrated by Miki Aihara. VIZ Media, LLC, 2005–2006. 5 Vol. O Genre: Romance.

Mimori Kosaka has just started high school at Meidai Attached High School and is looking forward to a great freshman year. However, after making new friends and reuniting with old acquaintances, Mimori is finding high school life far more complicated than she expected.

V.B. Rose. Written and Illustrated by Banri Hidaka. Tokyopop, 2008–. 14 Vol. T Genre: Romance.

Ageha not exactly thrilled that her older sister is getting married, but once she visits the Velvet Blue Rose bridal shop, she throws herself into helping make her sister's wedding dress. However, one of the designers is injured. Ageha will have to see if she can step in to save her sister's wedding, and she might just discover some things about herself along the way.

We Were There. Written and Illustrated by Yuki Obata. VIZ Media, LLC, 2008–. Ongoing Series. 14 Vol. O Genre: Comedy, Drama, Romance.

Nanami's high school years get off to an interesting start when she falls for Yano, one of the popular boys in her class. However, Yano has secrets of his own that may make things far more complicated than Nanami expects. Love is never easy, and it definitely may not be a smooth road for Nanami.

Wild @ Heart. Written and Illustrated by Natsumi Ando. Del Rey, 2009. 1 Vol. Y Genre: Comedy, Romance.

Chino just wants to fall in love. However, when she finally does, it's really not what she expects at all. Her father has just brought home a boy who was raised in the jungle. His name is Hyo, and Chino can't help falling for him. But he's also completely uncivilized. So is he really the right guy for Chino fall and does she have a choice in the matter?

Wild Ones. Written and Illustrated by Kiyo Fujiwara. VIZ Media, LLC, 2007– 2010. 10 Vol. T Genre: Adventure, Comedy, Romance.

When her grandfather took her in after her mother dies, Sachie didn't know he was the head of the local yakuza. Now she's trying keep her life normal, but her crush at school has turned out to be both a member of her grandfather's gang and her new bodyguard. Sachie doesn't know where she fits in with her new life, but she wants to make things work out so she has a new family and a chance at love. Volume 7 is titled *Young Love* and is a collection of short stories about the characters of Wedding Peach.

Romantic Comedy

<u>Beauty is the Beast</u>. **Written and Illustrated by Tomo Matsumoto. VIZ Media, 2005–2006. 5 Vol. T Genre: Romantic Comedy.**
> When Eimi moves into the girls' dorm at school, she finds herself falling into an interesting situation. Her dorm mates aren't exactly what she expected, and it seems like most of them have their own little quirks. And one of the first things they want Eimi to do is sneak into the boys' dorm and pull off a secret mission. Little does Eimi know what other surprises are waiting for her.

<u>Boys Over Flowers</u>. **Written and Illustrated by Yoko Kamio. VIZ Media, LLC, 2003–2009. 37 Vol. T Genre: Romantic Comedy.**
> Makino Tsukusa is a working-class girl attending a school for the ultra-rich. She doesn't feel like she fits in, and it doesn't help that she makes enemies of the F4, the four richest boys at the school. But the fact that Makino won't back down impresses Domyoji Tsukasa, the leader of the F4, and enemies might just turn into friends. The final volume of this series is not numbered and is titled *Boys Over Flowers: Jewelry Box*. Winner of the Shogakukun Award.

<u>D.N.Angel</u>. **Written and Illustrated by Yukiru Sugisaki. Tokyopop, 2004–. Ongoing Series. 14 Vol. T Genre: Fantasy, Romantic Comedy. Related Anime: *D.N.Angel*.**
> Daisuke had a problem. Whenever he starts thinking of the girl he loves, his alter ego, a legendary thief, takes control. There is a cure for this condition, however: she must return his love. But when you can't romance a girl without pulling a heist, it might be harder than it sounds.

<u>Fall in Love Like a Comic!</u>. **Written and Illustrated by Chitose Yagami. VIZ Media, LLC, 2007–2008. 2 Vol. T Genre: Romantic Comedy.**
> Rena has a secret. She might be a high school student, but she's also a professional mangaka. However, she's never been on a date or had a romance of her own. When Tomoyo, the most popular boy in school, accidentally finds out her secret, Rena asks him out. She's hoping that real romance will help her writing, but real love doesn't quite work the same way it does in comic books.

<u>Guru Guru Pon-Chan</u>. **Written and Illustrated by Satomi Ikezawa. Del Rey, 2005–2007. 9 Vol. T Genre: Romantic Comedy.**
> Ponta is the Koizumi family dog. When she eats an invention of Grandpa Koizumi, she transforms into a human girl, though the effect wears off after

awhile. However, when Ponta falls in love with a human boy, she is determined to learn how to be a proper human and win his love. Winner of the Kodansha Award.

Hana-Kimi. Written and Illustrated by Hisaya Nakajo. VIZ Media, LLC, 2004–2008. 23 Vol. **O** Genre: Romantic Comedy.

Mizuki has transferred to a new school in order to be closer to her idol Izumi. However, there is a catch. Izumi attends an all-boys school, so Mizuki will have to keep the fact that she's a girl under wraps. And when she ends up being Izumi's roommate, she may just find her work cut out for her.

High School Debut. Written and Illustrated by Kazune Kawahara. VIZ Media, LLC, 2008–2010. 13 Vol. **T** Genre: Drama, Romantic Comedy.

In middle school, Haruna spent all her free time on softball, but now in high school she'd like to give romance a try. Unfortunately, she seems to be an utter failure at it. So she asks upperclassman Yoh to coach her. His one stipulation is that she can't fall for him. Haruna could use a friend like him, but it might be harder to keep her end of the bargain than she thinks.

Kare Kano: His and Hers Circumstances. Written and Illustrated by Masami Tsuda. Tokyopop, 2003–2007. **T** Genre: Romantic Comedy. Related Anime: *His and Hers Circumstances.*

Yukino seems like she has it all to her classmates. With perfect grades and good looks, she seems like she's at the top. Then the new student, Soichiro, knocks her out of her position as top student. Yukino is determined to get her place on top back, but she didn't count on falling in love as well.

Kimi Ni Todoke: From Me to You. Written and Illustrated by Karuho Shiina. VIZ Media, LLC, 2009–. Ongoing Series. 12 Vol. **T** Genre: Romantic Comedy.

Sawako never asked to look like a character from a horror movie, and she's too shy to really change her classmates' opinions. When one of the popular boys takes an interest in her, Sawako finds that maybe making friends isn't so hard after all. But she may make some enemies as well. Winner of the Kodansha Award.

Maid Sama!. Written and Illustrated by Hiro Fujiwara. Tokyopop, 2009–. Ongoing Series. 11 Vol. **T** Genre: Romantic Comedy, Slice of Life. Related Anime: *Maid Sama!*

Misaki Ayuzawa is known as the demon president of Seika High School. This mostly has to do with the fact that she's the student council president of a school that was until recently just for boys. Even now boys outnumber girls four to one. However, Misaki has a secret. Her part-time job is at a Maid Café, and she's afraid it will undermine her respect at school. When Takumi Usui discovers this by accident, Misaki finds herself with a friend she never expected and maybe even a love interest.

Marmalade Boy. Written and Illustrated by Wataru Yoshizumi. Tokyopop, 2002–2003. 8 Vol. **T** Genre: Romantic Comedy. Related Anime: *Marmalade Boy.*

Miki finds it hard enough to be a teenager, and when her parents drop a bombshell on her, her life just gets more difficult. Her parents are divorcing one another, so they each can marry a member of another couple that's divorcing. Oh, and they're all going to share a house. To make matters worse, Miki learns that her new crush is now her stepbrother. Somehow, she needs to figure out her relationships, but they just seem to get more and more confusing.

Metamo Kiss. Written and Illustrated by Sora Omote. Tokyopop, 2007. 3 Vol. **T** Genre: Romantic Comedy.

Kohamaru's family has a rather odd quirk. They call can switch bodies with their soul mate, and he's just found his. However, there's one problem. She happens to have a crush on his twin brother.

Missile Happy!. Written and Illustrated by Miki Kiritani. Tokyopop, 2007–2009. 5 Vol. **T** Genre: Romantic Comedy.

Mikako isn't about to let her older sister marry just anyone, even if their uncle wants her to. So in order to investigate one of the potential candidates, Mikako winds up living with him. But what she didn't expect was that Rou would be a 17-year-old high school student or that she might just be falling for him herself.

My Girlfriend's a Geek. Written by Pentabu. Illustrated by Rize Shinba. Yen Press, 2010–2011. 5 Vol. **O** Genre: Romantic Comedy.

Taiga is a broke college student. All he really wants at this point is a good job and a girlfriend. He manages to land a part-time job and to ask out a pretty girl named Yuiko. She even says yes. However, Yuiko happens to be a rather specific sort of geek, and Taiga has no idea what he's just gotten himself into.

Orange Planet. Written and Illustrated by Haruka Fukushima. Del Rey, 2009–2010. 3 Vol. **T** Genre: Romantic Comedy.

Rui had boy problems, but they are not the typical sort. Her main problem is that there are two boys in love with her. And figuring out which one actually holds her heart may be a job and a half.

Otomen. Written and Illustrated by Aya Kanno. VIZ Media, LLC, 2009–. Ongoing Series. 11 Vol. **T** Genre: Romantic Comedy.

Asuka might be the coolest guy in the school, but he has a secret. He absolutely loves sewing, cooking, and romances. However, he's expected to act manly, and so he tries to hide his hobbies. Then he meets Ryo. She can't cook or sew, and says she only likes tough guys. Asuka doesn't know if he has a chance with her or not, but maybe he's found a girl who might accept him as he is.

Ouran High School Host Club. Written and Illustrated by Bisco Hatori. VIZ Media, LLC, 2005–. 17 Vol. **T** Genre: Drama, Romantic Comedy. Related Anime: *Ouran High School Host Club*.

Haruhi just happens to be the only scholarship student at Ouran High School, which is known for its exclusive and wealthy students. She is just looking for a quiet place to study when she stumbles upon the Host Club. When Haruhi accidentally breaks an expensive vase, the boys of the Host Club decide she must join the club in order to pay for it. However, there's one little problem: they seem to think that she is a he.

Penguin Revolution. Written and Illustrated by Sakura Tsukuba. CMX, 2006– 2009. 7 Vol. T Genre: Romantic Comedy.

Yukari has the ability to spot a potential star from the vision of wings she can see on their back. This comes in handy when she gets hired as Ryoko Katsuragi's manager. There's just two small catches. Yukari must convince everyone that she's a boy for the job, and Ryoko just happens to be a he rather than a she. However, both of them are determined to succeed in the world of show business, and together they just might.

S • A: Special A. Written and Illustrated by Maki Minami. VIZ Media, LLC, 2007–2010. 17 Vol. T Genre: Romantic Comedy. Related Anime: *S • A: Special A*.

Hikari is determined to beat her rival, Kei. No matter what he seems to do, Kei is always number one. She's been trying to best him since they were both six years old. Now in an elite high school, Hikari is determined to beat him if it's the last thing she does. But while she sees Kei as her rival, he just happens to be in love with her. Now the real question is, will Hikari ever notice or will she continue to be blinded by her competitiveness?

Skip-Beat!. Written and Illustrated by Yoshiki Nakamura. VIZ Media, LLC, 2006–. Ongoing Series. 27 Vol. T Genre: Romantic Comedy.

Kyoko followed Sho to Tokyo because she loved him. However, he's no longer interested in her now that he is famous. Kyoko knows that she deserves better than just being tossed aside, so now she's determined to become a star herself. She joins a talent agency where Sho's rival, Ren, works. It is going to take hard work to surpass Sho, but Kyoko might just find something other than fame as well.

Train Man. Written and Illustrated by Machiko Ocha. Del Rey, 2006. 1 Vol. T Genre: Romantic Comedy.

When geeky Ikumi rescues a pretty girl from a drunk on the train, it seems like a dream come true. She wants to get together sometime, but Ikumi doesn't know anything about romance. So he posts to an online message board asking for help. But can advice from the Internet help Ikumi win the heart of the girl of his dreams?

The Wallflower. Written and Illustrated by Tomoko Hayakawa. Del Rey, 2004– 2010. Kodansha Comics, 2011–. Ongoing Series. 27 Vol. O Genre: Drama, Romantic Comedy. Related Anime: *The Wallflower*.

It seemed like a perfect set up to the four 15-year-old boys. A whole mansion to live in and none of them had to pay rent. There is one catch, however. During the three years they live there they must turn Sunako into a lady worthy of such a mansion. Sunako loves horror movies, is completely antisocial, and shuns anything that has to do with beauty. But there might be a friendship in the cards for these five teenagers—if they survive living with one another. Volumes 22, 23, and 24 were released in an omnibus volume.

Science Fiction

Absolute Boyfriend. Written and Illustrated by Yuu Watase. VIZ Media, LLC, 2006–2008. 6 Vol. **O** Genre: Romantic Comedy, Science Fiction.

Riiko has been rejected by every single guy she's ever asked out. When an act of kindness leads her to a rather strange company, Riiko ends up ordering something called a Nightly Lover Figure. What she ends up with is a young man programmed to be the perfect boyfriend. Has Riiko's luck with romance finally changed?

Chicago. Written and Illustrated by Yumi Tamura. VIZ Media, LLC, 2002–2003. 2 Vol. **T** Genre: Science Fiction.

Rei and her partner, Uozumi, accidentally stumble upon a plot during a search-and-rescue mission. With their lives in danger, the two of them join Rescue Inc., run out of the bar Chicago. So Rei will save other people's lives while she searches for the answers she needs.

Clover. Written and Illustrated by CLAMP. Dark Horse, 2009. 1 Vol. **T** Genre: Cyberpunk, Fantasy, Science Fiction.

Sue has spent her entire life in isolation. As a Clover, she is a classified as top secret by the military. Now Kazuhiko has been assigned to escort her to visit the Fairy Park. But the two share a connection even if Kazuhiko doesn't know it yet.

Jyu-Oh-Sei. Written and Illustrated by Natsumi Itsuki. Tokyopop, 2008–2009. 3 Vol. **T** Genre: Drama, Romance, Science Fiction. Related Anime: *Jyu-Oh-Sei*.

Life was pretty normal for twins Rai and Thor on the space colony Juno until the day they come home to find their parents murdered. Shipped off to a secret prison planet, the twins will have to fight to survive and try to unravel the mysteries that now surround them.

Moon Child. Written and Illustrated by Reiko Shimizu. CMX, 2006–2009. 13 Vol. **T** Genre: Fantasy, Science Fiction.

A young amnesiac may hold the key to saving Earth's future, even if he doesn't know it. But there is more than just one mystery surrounding Jimmy, and the fact that he doesn't know who he is might jeopardize things. With the fate of the world hanging in the balance, some people are willing to risk everything.

Neon Genesis Evangelion: Angelic Days. Written and Illustrated by Fumino Hayashi. ADV, 2006–2007. 6 Vol. **T** Genre: Romantic Comedy, Science Fiction.

Shinji Ikari is pretty typical for a high school student. His best friend, Asuka, tends to give him a hard time, and high school is high school. But things start to change when the new student, Rei, transfers to his class, and Shinji finds that he might be involved in a struggle that is more than just surviving high school.

Neon Genesis Evangelion: Campus Apocalypse. Written and Illustrated by Mingming. Dark Horse, 2010–. 4 Vol. ☐T Genre: Action, Drama, Romance, Science Fiction.

Though a student at NERV Academy, Shinji Ikari has never been privy to its secrets—until now, that is. But some of his fellow students spend their nights fighting to protect the world from what they call Angels, and Shinji is going to join them.

Please Save My Earth. Written and Illustrated by Saki Hiwatari. VIZ Media, LLC, 2003–2007. 21 Vol. ☐O Genre: Science Fiction.

Alice hasn't had an easy time fitting in and making new friends since moving to Tokyo. However, a strange turn of events soon brings her into contact with some other teenagers who share a secret. They all have been dreaming of their past lives, lives that were connected. But their shared past holds some dark secrets, and these may spill over into the teens' present life as well.

Tower of the Future. Written and Illustrated by Saki Hiwatari. CMX, 2003–2008. 11 Vol. ☐T Genre: Romantic Comedy, Science Fiction.

Takeru finds his life changing as his high school exams approach. Between family secrets, mysterious strangers, and tragedy, Takeru will find his entire life altering and more than one mystery unfolding.

Slice of Life

Ashiteruze Baby. Written and Illustrated by Yoko Maki. VIZ Media, LLC, 2006–2007. 7 Vol. ☐T Genre: Drama, Romance, Slice of Life.

Kippei is handsome, popular, and your regular high school playboy. Then his aunt abandons her five-year-old daughter, Yuzuyu, on his family's doorstep and somehow, Kippei ends up being the one responsible for keeping an eye on her. Kippei doesn't know anything about raising a little girl, but he's not about to abandon Yuzuyu, and he just might get some help from the one girl who has never given him the time of day before.

Baby & Me. Written and Illustrated by Marimo Ragawa. VIZ Media, LLC, 2006–2010. 18 Vol. ☐T Genre: Slice of Life.

Takuya is stuck taking care of his little brother all the time. Their mother has passed away, and their father works long hours, leaving Takuya left to pick up the slack. It eats up all his time, and it's enough to drive a kid crazy. But when it comes down to it, Takuya does care about his little brother, and maybe there is a way to make his family work. Winner of the Shogakukun Award.

Flower of Life. Written and Illustrated by Fumi Yoshinaga. DMP, 2007–2009. 4 Vol. ☐O Genre: Comedy, Slice of Life.

Harutaro Hanazono transfers to a new school a month after the start of the year. He finds himself making new friends and maybe a few enemies as high school begins, and Harutaro knows that at least high school is one place he won't forget.

Happy Happy Clover. Written and Illustrated by Sayuri Tatsuyama. VIZ Media, LLC, 2009–2010. 5 Vol. **A** Genre: Comedy, Fantasy, Slice of Life.

Clover, a bunny rabbit, lives in the Crescent Forest with her friends. She's always up for another adventure whether it is making new friends or making mischief.

Happy Hustle High. Written and Illustrated by Rie Takada. VIZ Media, LLC, 2005–2006. 5 Vol. **O** Genre: Romance, Slice of Life.

Hanabi's a tomboy who's been protecting her less assertive friends for years at their all-girls school. However, when their school merges with an all-boys school, Hanabi meets Yasuki, the student council vice president, and quickly falls for him. The only problem is Yasuki claims he has no interest in girls or dating. But Hanabi's willing to take on the job of student council representative in order to change his mind.

Itazura Na Kiss. Written and Illustrated by Kaoru Tada. DMP, 2010–. 12 Omnibus Vol. **T** Genre: Romantic Comedy, Slice of Life.

Kotoko finally confesses to her longtime crush, Naoki, who is popular, smart, and athletic. However, he just rejects her out of hand. Then to make matters worse, her family's home is destroyed by an earthquake. So Kotoko and her father move in with a good friend of her father's and his family. Oh, and his son just happens to be Naoki. Kotoko doesn't know if fate is rubbing her nose in failure or giving her a second chance at love.

Karakuri Odette. Written and Illustrated by Julietta Suzuki. Tokyopop, 2009–2011. 6 Vol. **T** Genre: Comedy, Science Fiction, Slice of Life.

When Odette, an android who looks a like a teenage girl, sees some girls on TV, she asks her creator to let her go to school. She wants to learn what the difference is between herself and real girls. He agrees, and Odette sets off to learn what real life is like.

Love ♥ Com. Written and Illustrated by Aya Nakahara. VIZ Media, LLC, 2007–2010. 17 Vol. **T** Genre: Romantic Comedy, Slice of Life.

Risa is the tallest girl in her class, and Atsushi is the shortest guy. Their classmates think that pairing them up together all the time is hilarious. But the two of them have entered a pact in order to help each other get the real objects of their affection. That pact may help Risa and Atsushi become friends, but it also might help them become something more as well. Winner of the Kodansha Award.

W Juliet. Written and Illustrated by Emura. VIZ Media, LLC, 2004–2007. 14 Vol. **T** Genre: Comedy, Romance, Slice of Life.

Tomboy Ito and ladylike Makoto have seemingly nothing in common save for a love of acting. Both members of the high school drama club, they make for an unlikely pair of best friends. However, they share a secret. Makoto is a very good actor because she is in fact a he. In order to win the freedom to pursue his own choice of career, Makoto made a deal with his father: he would transfer to a new school and spend the rest of his time in high school pretending to be a girl. If no one finds out the truth, Makoto can choose his own career. Otherwise, he has to take over the family business. When Ito finds out by mistake, she promises help Makoto, but they have two more years of high school, and that's a long time to keep a secret.

Sports

Crimson Hero. Written and Illustrated by Mitsuba Takanashi. VIZ Media, LCC, 2005–. Ongoing Series. 18 Vol. T Genre: Sports.
Nobara Sumiyoshi is determined to make it in the world of volleyball, even if her family wants her to work as a hostess at their traditional restaurant instead. When her own mother stoops to dirty tricks to deter Nobara from her dreams, Nobara decides that it's time to stop playing defense and go on the offense.

Dragon Girl. Written and Illustrated by Toru Fujieda. Yen Press, 2010–2011. 2 Vol. T Genre: Sports, Romance.
Rinna plans on following in her father's footsteps and becoming the captain of the Shoryu Senior High cheering squad. There's one little problem, though. It's an all-boys school. However, Rinna isn't about to let that stop her. And the school's just announced that it will now be coed. While that might take her one step closer to her dreams, she still has a ways to go, and it won't be easy. Rinna's not about to give up.

Forbidden Dance. Written and Illustrated by Hinako Ashihara. Tokyopop, 2003–2004. 4 Vol. T Genre: Drama, Sports.
After an accident during a competition, Aya loses confidence in herself and her dancing abilities. After watching the group COOL perform, Aya is determined to dance again. However, returning to the world of dance will be harder than Aya expects, and she will be pushed to her limits in order to achieve her full potential.

Girl Got Game. Written and Illustrated by Shizuru Seino. Tokyopop, 2004–2005. 10 Vol. T Genre: Comedy, Romance, Sports.
Kyo is a great basketball player, and she loves the game. However, her father is determined that she be on the team Seisyu. The boys' team, that is. So Kyo is posing as a guy in order to play basketball with some of the best. Now she just has to keep the fact that that she's a girl a secret and try not to fall too hard for her new roommate.

Sugar Princess. Written and Illustrated by Hisaya Nakajo. VIZ Media, LLC, 2008. 2 Vol. A Genre: Romance, Sports.
During Maya's first time ice skating, she accidentally lands a double axel. One of the coaches at the rink sees her and convinces her to take skating lessons. Shun,

her new teacher, doesn't seem too pleased to be coaching her. But when the ice rink is threatened with closing, Maya and Shun will team up to keep their ice rink open.

Swan. Written and Illustrated by Kyoko Ariyoshi. CMX, 2005–2010. 15 of 21 Vol. **A** Genre: Drama, Sports.

Masumi Hijiri is a young ballet dancer at a school in a remote part of the country. When she is given the opportunity to compete for a spot in an exclusive ballet, Masumi finds it to be an opportunity of a lifetime and a challenge she never expected. Only time will tell if she can make it in the competitive world of ballet. This series has been discontinued at the present time with 15 of the 21 volumes published in English. Considered a classic.

Supernatural

Black Bird. Written and Illustrated by Kanoko Sakurakoji. VIZ Media, LLC, 2009–. Ongoing Series. 11 Vol. **O** Genre: Romantic Comedy, Supernatural.

Misao has always been able to see things other people couldn't. She's done her best to ignore them and have a normal life, but when she turns 16, the things she sees start trying to kill her. Also, her childhood friend, Kyo, has returned to her life. As it happens, Kyo is a demon and is determined to protect her. What Misao can't figure out is if that's a good thing. Winner of the Shogakukun Award.

Bloody Kiss. Written and Illustrated by Kazuko Furumiya. Tokyopop, 2009. 2 Vol. **T** Genre: Fantasy, Romance, Supernatural.

When Kiyo inherits her grandmother's mansion, she also inherits the two vampires, Kuroboshi and his servant Alshu, living there. Things get even more complicated when Kuroboshi decides that he wants to make Kiyo his bride, the human female that provides a vampire with his only source of blood. Now Kiyo has to settle into her new home and community and try to figure out just what to do with one very handsome vampire who seems fixated on her.

Broken Angels. Written and Illustrated by Setsuri Tsuzuku. Tokyopop, 2006–2007. 5 Vol. **O** Genre: Fantasy, Romance, Supernatural.

Sunao Fujiwara typically dresses like a boy and has the power to control water. Interestingly enough, she's not the strangest person at her high school. While Sunao acts as a sort of counselor for her schoolmates and others she meets, secrets from her own dark past threaten her life.

Ceres, Celestial Legend. Written and Illustrated by Yuu Watase. VIZ Media, LLC, 2003–2006. 14 Vol. **O** Genre: Action, Fantasy, Romance, Supernatural. Related Anime: *Ceres Celestial Legend*.

Aya's 16th birthday has not exactly been fun. The party at her grandfather's is presented with a mummified hand. Her twin brother Aki gets injuries all over his body, and her family tries to kill her. Aya is rescued, but her life is still in danger. She will have to get to the bottom the mystery of the Heavenly Maidens if she ever wants to have a normal life again. Winner of the Shogakukun Award.

The Demon Ororon. Written and Illustrated by Hakase Mizuki. Tokyopop, 2004. 4 Vol. T Genre: Romance, Supernatural.

Chiaki takes care of a strange injured man named Ororon who claims to be a demon. He offers to grant her a wish in return for her help, and she wishes for him to stay with her forever. Ororon moves in, and secrets of Chiaki's past begin to be revealed as well as dangers hunting Ororon. Neither of them knows what the future may hold now.

The Devil Within. Written and Illustrated by Ryo Takagi. Go!Comi, 2007. 2 Vol. O Genre: Comedy, Supernatural.

Rion doesn't trust men at all. She's convinced that they're all devils. However, just when she meets a guy she thinks she could like, Rion's father presents her with three men to choose a fiancé from. Her life just got far more complicated, and there are still more secrets to come.

Eerie Queerie!. Written and Illustrated by Shuri Shiozu. Tokyopop, 2004. 4 Vol. O Genre: Comedy, Drama, Romance, Supernatural, Yaoi.

Mitsuo is a high school student with a special ability. He can see ghosts. However, this can be rather problematic. Especially when possessed by a girl, he can end up in some very awkward situations.

Gaba Kawa. Written and Illustrated by Rie Takada. VIZ Media, LLC, 2006. 1 Vol. T Genre: Fantasy, Romance, Supernatural.

Rara is a demon who has come to the mortal world following her crush, the demon Akusawa. However, when she mistakes the human for her crush, Rawa finds herself starting to fall for a mortal. Retsu Aku has the sixth sense when it comes to the supernatural, and he finds Rawa just as irresistible as she does him. But it is forbidden for a demon to fall in love with a human, so Rawa may have to choose between her heart and her life.

Gakuen Alice. Written and Illustrated by Tachibana Higuchi. Tokyopop, 2007–. Ongoing Series. 23 Vol. T Genre: Comedy, Romance, Supernatural. Related Anime: *Gakuen Alice*.

When her best friend, Hotaru, moves away to attend a new school, Mikan misses her so much that she runs away to join her friend. Alice Academy is reserved for students with special abilities called Alices, but Mikan is accepted anyway, even though she doesn't know what her Alice is. Fitting into a new school is never easy even when it's a normal one, and Alice Academy is anything but normal.

Heaven!!. Written and Illustrated by Shizuru Seino. Tokyopop, 2007–2008. 3 Vol. T Genre: Comedy, Romance, Supernatural.

Rinne can see ghosts, and she has the ability to exorcise them using her trusty paper fan. However, when Uzaki, the school bad boy, saves her from becoming a ghost herself, Rinne finds that she is in an interesting situation. Uzaki's spirit is now residing in a pink toy monkey while a ghost named Keiju is possessing Uzaki's body. Rinne definitely has her work cut out for her if she is going to sort out this mess.

Hell Girl. Written and Illustrated by Miyuki Eto. Del Rey, 2008–2010. 9 Vol. **O** Genre: Horror, Mystery, Supernatural. Related Anime: *Hell Girl, Hell Girl: Two Mirrors, Hell Girl: Three Vessels.*

The Hell Girl will get your revenge for you, but there is a price to her services: your soul. Ai Enma is not your ordinary schoolgirl at all. To contact her, you must go to the Hell Correspondence website and type in the name of the one on whom you wish revenge. But remember, revenge always comes with a price. Volumes 7, 8, and 9 were released together in an omnibus volume.

Her Majesty's Dog. Written and Illustrated by Mick Takeuchi. Go!Comi, 2005–2008. 11 Vol. **O** Genre: Romance, Supernatural.

Amane's not like most girls at her new Tokyo school. She's lived in a sheltered village most of her life, and she also just happens to be a powerful medium. Her fellow transfer student, Hyoue, is her demon guardian. Together the two of them will have their work cut out for them: surviving high school and dealing with dangerous spirits.

Kamisama Kiss. Written and Illustrated by Julietta Suzuki. VIZ Media, LLC, 2010–. Ongoing Series. 8 Vol. **T** Genre: Comedy, Supernatural.

Nanami's father has skipped town in order to avoid his gambling debts, leaving his daughter homeless. When an act of kindness results in an offer of a home, Nanami accepts having nowhere else to go. However, she finds that her new home is a shrine, and she is now a local deity. With duties that she doesn't under stand and a rather grumpy, if cute, ex-familiar on her hands, Nanami has more than just a roof over her head to worry about now.

Land of the Blindfolded. Written and Illustrated by Sakura Tsukuba. CMX, 2004–2006. 9 Vol. **A** Genre: Romance, Supernatural.

Sometimes Kanade can see bits and pieces of the future, but she's never sure if she could try and change it. Her classmate Arou can see into the past, and he's certain that one should never meddle. Neither of them is sure what to do about their powers, but at least they are a common bond that leads to a friendship, if not something more.

Mad Love Chase. Written and Illustrated by Kazusa Takashima. Tokyopop, 2009–2011. 5 Vol. **O** Genre: Action, Comedy, School, Supernatural.

Kujou Yamato isn't a normal teenager, though he wishes he were. In fact, he's actually Kaito, the Prince of the Demon World. He and his cat have run away from an arranged marriage. Posing as humans, Kaito is now a high school student while his cat, Levun, has taken a job as the school nurse. However, Kaito's father has sent a trio of demons to find his son and return him, so both Kaito and Levun are going to have their work cut out for them if they don't want to go back.

Millennium Snow. Written and Illustrated by Bisco Hatori. VIZ Media, LLC, 2007. 2 Vol. **T** **Genre: Romance, Supernatural.**

Seventeen-year-old Chiyuki is not expected to survive to the next snow because he has heart problems. Toya is a young vampire who so far has refused to partner with a human. When he partners with a human, he will drink the person's blood, and it will enable them both to live for a thousand years. But Toya does not like blood or humans that much. Can Chiyuki change his mind about humans before her own life ends?

Natsume's Book of Friends. Written and Illustrated by Yuki Midorikawa. VIZ Media, LLC, 2010–. Ongoing Series. 10 Vol. **T** **Genre: Drama, Supernatural.**

The fact that Takashi Natsume has always been able to see spirits and demons has set him apart from his peers. However, when his grandmother, who also had this power, passes away, Takashi inherits her Book of Friends, where she bound the names of many demons and spirits. And now they want to be free. Takashi must learn to return the names to their owners, and try to survive the spirits and demons who now want to kill him.

NG Life. Written and Illustrated by Mizuho Kusanagi. Tokyopop, 2009–2011. 9 Vol. **T** **Genre: Romantic Comedy, Supernatural.**

Keidai might be a fairly ordinary high school student, but he also just happens to remember his past life as a Roman in Pompeii. This causes him some problems when he runs into some familiar faces from his past. His Roman wife has been reincarnated as a male while his best male friend is now a girl. Keidai tries to make sense of his relationships both past and future even as he deals with falling in love once again.

Phantom Dream. Written and Illustrated by Natsuki Takaya. Tokyopop, 2008–2010. 5 Vol. **O** **Genre: Mystery, Romance, Supernatural.**

Tamaki, the last in a long line of priests that fight the evil forces that threaten humans, has to balance normal school life along with fighting the supernatural forces out there. However, there is both danger and more than one faction involved in his work. When his beloved friend Asahi gets caught up in some supernatural trouble, Tamaki will find that he has to fight for not only his own life but for that of the girl he loves as well.

Rasetsu. Written and Illustrated by Chika Shiomi. VIZ Media, LLC, 2009–2011. 8 Vol. **O** **Genre: Mystery, Supernatural.**

When Yako from *Yurara* comes looking for some help with a possessed book, he doesn't expect to find Rasetsu. Not only does she have a remarkable resemblance to the ghost Yako fell in love with, but she also has problems of her own with evil spirits. If Rasetsu does not find her true love by the time she is 20, an evil spirit will claim her as his own. Rasetsu and Yako make for good partners when it comes to dealing with spirits, but will they remain just partners or might they become something more?

<u>Shirahime Syo</u>. Written and Illustrated by CLAMP. Tokyopop, 2003. 1 Vol. **T** Genre: Supernatural.

> A collection of short stories about the Yuki-Onna or Snow Woman, a character from Japanese folklore.

<u>Tokyo Babylon</u>. Written and Illustrated by CLAMP. Tokyopop, 2004–2005. 7 Vol. **T** Genre: Detective, Supernatural, Yaoi.

> Suburu is the 13th head of the Sumeragi clan. A powerful magician, his job is to deal with restless spirits and give peace to the dead. However, it is not always easy work, nor is it always safe.

<u>Trinity Blood</u>. Written by Sunao Yoshida. Illustrated by Kiyo Kyujo. Tokyopop, 2006–. Ongoing Series. 12 Vol. **O** Genre: Action, Supernatural. Related Anime: *Trinity Blood.*

> After Armageddon, two powers have risen in the world: the vampires and the humans. They seem to be constantly in a stalemated war with one another. Abel Nightroad is a traveling priest from the Vatican who works to protect humans from dangerous vampires and hopes for a path of peace between the two races. But while the forces of evil might be against him, Abel has a secret of his own up his sleeve.

<u>Vampire Knight</u>. Written and Illustrated by Matsuri Hino. VIZ Media, LLC, 2007–. Ongoing Series. 13 Vol. **O** Genre: Romance, Supernatural. Related Anime: *Vampire Knight, Vampire Knight Guilty.*

> Yuki Cross has no memory prior to 10 years ago when Kaname Kuran saved her from a vampire. She now lives at Cross Academy, the adopted daughter of the headmaster. There are two groups of students at Cross Academy: the Day Class and the mysterious Night Class, who just happen to be a group of young vampires. Yuki believes that vampires and human can live together in peace, but the secrets of her past may cause more problems than Yuki knows.

<u>Yurara</u>. Written and Illustrated by Chika Shiomi. VIZ Media, LLC, 2007–2008. 5 Vol. **O** Genre: Mystery, Supernatural.

> Yurara has been able to see spirits and ghosts for years but tries to hide the fact. On her first day of high school, Yurara finds a ghost in her assigned seat. However, her new classmates Mai and Yako chased it off for her. But they can't banish the ghost completely, and Yurara's mysterious guardian makes an appearance.

Shojo Anime

Comedy

<u>Gravitation</u>. The Right Stuf, 2004. 13 25-Min. Episodes. 4 Discs. **T** Genre: Comedy, Romance, Yaoi.

> Shuichi is determined to be a rock star. He's got a band, Bad Luck, but he can't write lyrics for his songs that well. When a stranger named Eiri Yuki

criticizes his attempts to write lyrics, Shuichi finds himself by fascinated and inspired by the man. As Shuichi attempts to make himself a part of the Eiri's life, they may find that some things can't be fought.

Gravitation: Lyrics of Love. **The Right Stuf, 1999. 60 Min. 1 Disc. T Genre: Comedy, Romance, Yaoi.**

Shuichi and his band are in trouble. If he can't come up with new lyrics and songs for his band, it may be the end for them. However, Shuichi is heartbroken over the loss of Yuki and is having more than a little trouble pulling himself together. Can the band get him to snap out of it in time to save them? And will Yuki ever return to Shuichi or is he destined to be heartbroken forever?

Here Is Greenwood. **Media Blasters, 2004. 6 30-Min. Episodes. 2 Discs. T Genre: Comedy, Drama, Romance.**

After his older brother marries Kazuya's first love, he moves into the Greenwood dorm at school. However, since he transferred into the dorm so late, there's only one room left: Shun Kisagiri's. And Shun just happens to be a girl. What a girl is doing at a boys' school is definitely one question, and Kazuya's going to have plenty to distract him from his broken heart since he's been assigned to the one dorm at the school known for its weirdos.

Drama

Peach Girl. **Funimation, 2005. 25 20-Min. Episodes. 6 Discs. T Genre: Comedy, Drama, Romance.**

High school is a little rough for Momo. A former swim team member, she had bleached hair and a tan, making most of the school think she's an airheaded beach bunny. Throw in a malicious best friend and a love triangle and Momo may be in over her head.

Revolutionary Girl Utena: The Movie. **Software Sculptors, 2001. 80 Min. 1 Disc. 13 & Up Genre: Drama, Fantasy.**

When Utena Tenjo arrives at Ohtori Academy, she soon finds herself caught up in mysterious duels over Anthy, the Rose Bride. As she attempts to defend Anthy, Utena must try to unravel the mysteries behind the Rose Bride and the duels.

Someday's Dreamers. **Geneon, 2003. 12 25-Min. Episodes. 3 Discs. T Genre: Drama, Fantasy, Romance.**

Yume has moved to Tokyo for the summer in order to continue her training as a mage. Mages can only use there powers with special permission, and trainee mages must complete an apprenticeship under another mage. Yume's apprenticeship has just begun.

Fantasy

Fushigi Yûgi: The Mysterious Play. **Geneon, 1995. 52 25-Min. Episodes. 8 Dics. T Genre: Fantasy, Romance.**

When Miaka and her friend Yui get sucked into a world contained inside the book *The Universe of the Four Gods*, she finds herself named the Priestess of Suzaku.

Miaka will have to face friends who have become enemies and find new allies if she wishes to return home, and even so, she may not be able to leave before losing her heart to the enigmatic martial artist, Tamahome.

Princess Tutu. ADV, 2004. 26 25-Min. Episodes. 6 Discs. **T** Genre: Drama, Fantasy, Romance.

> Duck was actually once a duck, not a young girl in ballet school. After seeing a boy named Mytho dance, she has wanted nothing more than to help him, for he seems so sad and alone. Learning that he has a shattered heart, Duck is given the ability to transform into Princess Tutu, who can find and return the missing shards to him. But there is more to this story than there appears, and Mytho's heart may not be the only thing at stake.

Save Me! Lollipop. Funimation, 2006. 13 25-Min. Episodes. 2 Discs. **Y** Genre: Fantasy, Romantic Comedy.

> When Nina accidentally swallows the Crystal Pearl (she thought it was a piece of candy), she finds herself the target of a sorcery exam with a number of student wizards coming after her. Thankfully, two of the wizards have agreed to protect her until they can make a magic potion to recover the Crystal Pearl. However, the potion will take six months to make, so Nina's life is going to be interesting for awhile. On the plus side, she just might fall in love as well.

The Twelve Kingdoms. Anime Works, 2002. 45 25-Min. Episodes. 10 Discs. **T** Genre: Fantasy.

> Youko's life is pretty mundane. She feels rather out of place, but other than that, she doesn't think she's anything special. Then she gets pulled into another world with two of her classmates. In over her head and out of her element, Youko must figure out just who she is and what she can do. For Youko is the Empress of Kei and claiming her title will be only one of the challenges she faces.

Historical Fiction

Le Chevalier D'Eon. Funimation, 2006. 24 25-Min. Episodes. 6 Discs. **O** Genre: Historical, Horror, Mystery.

> When his older sister, Lia, shows up dead and floating in the river Seine, d'Eon decides that someone needs to get to the bottom of her murder. He joins the French secret police, and soon d'Eon finds that he had only scratched the tip of the iceburg.

Horror

Pet Shop of Horrors. 4 25-Min. Episodes. 1 Disc. **T** Genre: Horror, Mystery.

> At Count D's shop, one can find the most perfect pet ever imagined. However, there is a strict contract that comes with each pet, and if it it is broken, the consequences can be dire. Even as a police detective tries to figure out the mysteries behind Count D, people continue to purchase pets, and each has his or her own story.

Romance

Fruits Basket. Funimation, 2001. 26 21-Min. Episodes. 4 Discs. **Y** Genre: Drama, Fantasy, Romance.

> Tohru Honda has been orphaned and lives in a tent until her neighbors stumble across her and offer her a home with them, the Sohma family. However, the Sohmas have their own secrets, and while living with them puts a roof over her head, it has also made her life much more complicated. Tohru will find herself fighting for her new friends and maybe falling in love along the way.

Romantic Comedy

Boys Over Flowers: Hana Yori Dango. VIZ Media, LLC, 2003. 51 26-Min. Episodes. 12 Discs. **T** Genre: Romantic Comedy.

> Makino Tsukusa is a working-class girl attending a school for the ultra-rich. She doesn't feel like she fits in, and it doesn't help that she makes enemies of the F4, the four richest boys at the school. But the fact that Makino won't back down impresses Domyoji Tsukasa, the leader of the F4. She may just find that enemies can turn into friends and love can come from unexpected directions.

Marmalade Boy. Tokyopop, 2002–2005. 76 25-Min. Episodes. 12 Discs in 4 Sets. **T** Genre: Romantic Comedy.

> Miki finds it hard enough to be a teenager, and when her parents drop a bombshell on her, her life just gets more difficult. Her parents are divorcing one another so they each can marry a member of another couple that's divorcing. Oh, and they're all going to share a house. To make matters worse, Miki learns that her new crush is now her stepbrother. Somehow, she needs to figure out her relationships, but they just seem to get more and more confusing.

Ouran High School Host Club. Funimation 2008–2010. 26 23-Min. Episodes. 4 Discs. **T** Genre: Drama, Romantic Comedy.

> Haruhi just happens to be the only scholarship student at Ouran High School, which is known for its exclusive and wealthy students. She is just looking for a quiet place to study when she stumbles upon the Host Club. The six members of the Host Club entertain and flatter the female population of the school for a price. When Haruhi accidentally breaks an expensive vase, the boys of the Host Club decide she must join the club in order to pay for it. However, there's one little problem: they seem to think that she is a he.

Science Fiction

The Girl Who Leapt Through Time. Bandai, 2008. 98 Min. 2 Discs. **T** Genre: Science Fiction.

> Makoto is not having a good day at all, but it inadvertently leads her to find that she can leap back through time. With the ability to go back and change things, Makoto can't resist. But doing so may have consequences that she can't imagine.

Supernatural

<u>Ceres, Celestial Legend</u>. VIZ Media, LLC, 2003. 24 30-Min. Episodes. 4 Discs in 2 Sets. **O** Genre: Romance, Supernatural.

> Aya's 16th birthday has not exactly been fun. During the party at her grandfather's she and her twin brother Aki are presented with a mummified hand. Aki gets injuries all over his body, and her family tries to kill her. Aya doesn't know why this is happening to her, but if she ever wants her life to be under her own control again, she will have to solve the mysteries surrounding her family.

<u>Hell Girl</u>. Funimation, 2010. 26 25-Min. Episodes. 4 Discs. **T** Genre: Horror, Mystery, Supernatural.

> Hell Girl will get your revenge for you, but there is a price to her services: your soul. Ai Enma is not your ordinary schoolgirl at all. To contact her, you must go to the Hell Correspondence website and type in the name of the one you wish revenge on. But remember, revenge always comes with a price, and Ai is a messenger you might not want to meet.

<u>Trinity Blood</u>. Funimation, 2005. 24 25-Min. Episodes. 6 Discs. 4 Discs in Viridian Collection Ed. **O** Genre: Action, Supernatural.

> After Armageddon, two powers have risen in the world: the vampires and the humans. They seem to be constantly in a stalemated war with one another. Abel Nightroad is a traveling priest from the Vatican who works to protect humans from dangerous vampires and hopes for a path of peace between the two races. But while the forces of evil might be against him, Abel has a secret of his own up his sleeve, and since it looks like events are moving toward a choice between all-out war or peace, that's a very good thing.

Chapter 3

Seinen Manga and Anime

Seinen manga is marketed toward adult men and is similar to Shonen manga in many ways. While they do have many themes and conventions in common, Seinen manga often has a grittier and more realistic feel to it. Seinen manga tends to have more violence and is a little more explicit than Shonen manga, and it also sometimes has a darker tone than both Shonen and Shojo manga. Like the other types of manga, Seinen has a range of material fitting into many genres. Science fiction and action are the most common genres, but are by no means the only ones. The titles in this section are organized by their main genre, though all of the genres that a title fits into are included in the entry.

Seinen Manga

- From Japan

- Marketed toward adult men

- Reads right to left

- Often has a gritty and realistic feel

- Can be more violent and explicit than other manga

Seinen Manga

Action

Black Lagoon. Written and Illustrated by Rei Hiroe. VIZ Media, LLC, 2008–. Ongoing Series. 9 Vol. **M** Genre: Action, Adventure, Crime. Related Anime: *Black Lagoon, Black Lagoon: The Second Barrage, Black Lagoon: Roberta's Blood Trail.*
Rokuro was just a normal salaryman up until he got taken hostage by the crew of the Black Lagoon. They are a group of mercenaries who roam the seas of

Southeast Asia. Rokuro doesn't know if he will survive his encounter with these people, but he does know that his life is no longer normal in any way.

Full Metal Panic!. **Written by Shouji Gatou. Illustrated by Retsu Tateo. ADV, 2003–2006. 9 Vol.** T **Genre: Action, Mecha, Romantic Comedy.**

Sousuke Sagara is a former child soldier and a member of Mithril, a mercenary group. The 16-year-old can handle just about any battle situation thrown at him with ease and aplomb; at least, until his latest assignment. Sousuke and his team have been assigned to protect Kaname Chidori, a high school student. Sousuke may be the ultimate warrior, but he has no experience with normal life or high school. And given that no one is to learn he's Kaname's bodyguard, his life just got a lot more complicated, and so did his new classmates'.

Gimmick!. **Written by Youzaburou Kanari. Illustrated by Kuroko Yabuguchi. VIZ Media, LLC, 2008–2009. 9 Vol.** T **Genre: Action, Drama, Thriller.**

Studio Gimmick specializes in makeup and special effects, but that is not all they do. In fact, they had been known to fight crime among other things. If you don't want someone to recognize you, these are the guys to go to. And one thing is for sure, there is nothing boring about working at Studio Gimmick.

House of Five Leaves. **Written and Illustrated by Natsume Ono. VIZ Media, LLC, 2010–. 7 Vol.** O **Genre: Action. Related Anime:** *House of Five Leaves.*

Akitsu is a masterless samurai. Skilled and loyal, his shyness and naiveté has caused him to be fired more than once. But while he is desperate for work, Akitsu is a little wary when Yaichi, the leader of a group called the Five Leaves, approaches him. Still, he takes the job, and soon finds that there's something special about the group, even if they quite possibly may be outlaws.

Jormungand. **Written and Illustrated by Keitaro Takahashi. VIZ Media, LLC, 2009–. Ongoing Series. 8 Vol.** M **Genre: Action, Adventure.**

Jonah is a child soldier, and while he may not like weapons or violence, he's determined to get revenge for his family, killed when war raged through their home. Now he works for Koko Hekmatyar, a weapons dealer. War is her business, and she's not about to let a little thing like danger or her shipments getting held up stop her. Jonah is the newest member of her band of troubleshooters, and they definitely have some work to do.

Rose Hip Zero. **Written and Illustrated by Tohru Fujisawa. Tokyopop, 2006–2008. 5 Vol.** O **Genre: Action, Adventure, Police.**

The ALICE terrorist organization has declared war on Tokyo's police. Kyoji Kido, a police officer, finds himself teamed up with Kasumi Asakura. Kasumi just happens to be a teenage schoolgirl. But this innocent-looking young woman was raised as an assassin by ALICE itself, and she's more than determined to bring them down.

<u>Wild Adapter</u>. Written and Illustrated by Kazuya Minekura. Tokyopop, 2007–. Ongoing Series. 6 Vol. **M** Genre: Action, Drama, Film Noir, Mystery.

> Makoto Kabuta's rather ordinary criminal life as a head of a gang takes an interesting turn when he stumbles upon a drug called Wild Adapter. It seems to cause death as well as odd animalistic mutations. He also runs across Tokito Minoru, a man with no memory and an arm like a beast's. There's a mystery behind Wild Adapter, and these two may just find out what it is.

Adventure

<u>Orphen</u>. Written by Yoshinobu Akita. Illustrated by Hajime Sawada. ADV, 2005–2006. 6 Vol. **T** Genre: Adventure, Comedy, Fantasy. Related Anime: *Sorcerous Stabber Orphen: Begins, Sorcerous Stabber Orphen: Revenge.*

> Orphen is a sorcerer for hire with a habit of getting himself into trouble. But he is also searching for a way to save a friend of his, a girl named Azalie who made one mistake and is now wanted dead by the rest of the sorcerers from their school. But Orphen isn't about to let that happen even if he doesn't yet know how to help her.

<u>Slayers Premium</u>. Written by Hajime Kanzaka. Illustrated by Tommy Ohtsuka. CPM, 2005. 1 Vol. **T** Genre: Action, Adventure, Comedy, Fantasy. Related Anime: *Slayers Premium.*

> Lina and Gourry are off to a town famous for its octopus dishes. As usual, the main thing they are interested in is filling their stomachs. However, there just happens to be a little more going on than that. The octopi are out for revenge, and Lina's going to find her skills as a sorceress in demand once again.

<u>Trigun</u>. Written and Illustrated by Yasuhiro Nightow. Dark Horse, 2003–2004. 2 Vol. **T** Genre: Adventure, Science Fiction, Western.

> Vash the Stampede has a price on his head: $60 billon dollars, to be precise, which is only part of his problem. For one thing, he can't remember the incident that got him a price on his head, and for another, the bounty hunters that follow him cause quite a bit of damage. In fact, he has to be followed by Bernardelli Insurance Society agents in order to try and mitigate the damage he does, because wherever Vash goes, adventure definitely follows.

<u>Trigun Maximum</u>. Written and Illustrated by Yasuhiro Nightow. Dark Horse, 2004–2009. 14 Vol. **T** Genre: Adventure, Science Fiction, Western.

> A continuation of *Trigun, Trigun Maximum* is set two years later. Vash the Stampede is still on the loose, though in hiding. A friend in danger brings him back into the open and following him come his enemies, along with Meryl and Millie, in order to help clean things up. The adventure is not about to end anytime soon for the gang, once they are back together. Winner of the Sieun Award.

Comedy

Chi's Sweet Home. Written and Illustrated by Konami Kanata. Vertical, 2010–. Ongoing Series. 7 Vol. **A** Genre: Comedy.

> When the kitten, Chi, wanders away from her mother siblings, a kind family ends up adopting her. However, as much as they like Chi, pets are not allowed in their apartment building. Still, Chi makes herself at home, and everyone finds that adjusting to Chi's presence in their life makes for an interesting experience.

Comic Party. Written and Illustrated by Sekihiko Inui. Tokyopop, 2004–2006. 5 Vol. **T** Genre: Comedy, Drama, Harem. Related Anime: *Comic Party, Comic Party Revolution.*

> Kazuki is an artist, and his talent for it draws him into the world of otaku and doujinshi. But his friends and family, especially his best friend Mizuki, don't know what to make of this. Kazuki doesn't know where his talent will take him, but each step along the road proves to be an interesting one.

Crayon Shin-Chan. Written and Illustrated by Yoshito Usui. CMX, 2008–2010. 11 of 50 Vol. **M** Genre: Comedy. Related Anime: *Crayon Shin-Chan.*

> Shinnosuke Nohara, known as Shin-chan to his friends and family, is not exactly your average five-year-old. He's not very polite at times, and he is forever causing problems for everyone around him. However, he is big on laughs, and his adventures are more than just a little amusing. This series has been discontinued with 11 of the 50 volumes released.

Excel Saga. Written and Illustrated by Rikdo Koshi. VIZ Media, LLC, 2003–. Ongoing Series. 25 Vol. **T** Genre: Action, Comedy, Science Fiction. Related Anime: *Excel Saga.*

> Because they believe the world has become corrupt, the organization ACROSS is planning on taking over the world. Unfortunately for them, right now they consist of a director, two unpaid teenagers, and a dog. Excel is determined to help Director Il Palazzo with his goals, but enthusiasm isn't always exactly what is needed.

Kujibiki ♥ Unbalance. Written by Kio Shimoku. Illustrated by Koume Keito. Del Rey, 2008. 2 Vol. **O** Genre: Action, Comedy, Romance. Related Anime: *Kujibiki ♥ Unbalance.*

> Chihiro has the worst of luck, but it finally seems about to change when he reaches high school. He wins the lottery to get into the elite Rikkyoin High School and wins the lottery to be the student council president. However, the student council at Rikkyoin must undertake tasks set on them by the previous student council, and if they fail, they're expelled. Chihiro's luck is definitely going to be tested this year.

Maria Holic. Written and Illustrated by Minari Endou. Tokyopop, 2009–. Ongoing Series. 7 Vol. **O** Genre: Comedy, Romance. Related Anime: *Maria Holic.*

> Due to her phobia of men, Kanako decides to go to an all-girls school, and one of her classmates, Mariya, just could be her ideal mate. However, Mariya also hap-

pens to be a boy who enjoys cross-dressing. Could it still be love for the two of them?

Neko Ramen. **Written and Illustrated by Kenji Sonishi. Tokyopop, 2010–. 4 Vol.** ▣ **Genre: Comedy. Related Anime:** *Neko Ramen.*

> Taisho owns and runs the ramen shop Neko Rahmen. He also happens to be the only cat running a restaurant in Tokyo. With that sort of combination, there are all sorts of adventures to be had.

Crime

Crying Freeman. **Written by Kazuo Koike. Illustrated by Ryoichi Ikegami. Dark Horse, 2006–2007. 5 Vol.** ▣ **Genre: Crime, Martial Arts. Related Anime:** *Crying Freeman.*

> Yo Hinomura was once a simple potter. Now he is the Crying Freeman, an assassin for a Chinese Mafia group known as the 108 Dragons. When he is assigned to kill Emu, a young woman who witnessed an assassination, suddenly everything begins to change. If he survives, he may become something more than a pawn for a change.

Gunsmith Cats: Revised Edition. **Written and Illustrated by Kenichi Sonoda. Dark Horse, 2007. 4 Vol.** ▣ **Genre: Action, Crime. Related Anime:** *Gunsmith Cats.*

> Gunsmith Cats happens to be a gun shop in Chicago. Run by Minnie-May and Rally, they supplement their income by working as bounty hunters. Of course, with Minnie-May being a demolitions expert and Rally being skilled with just about every firearm known to man, things can very interesting at times.

Gunsmith Cats Burst. **Written and Illustrated by Kenichi Sonoda. Dark Horse, 2007–2010. 5 Vol.** ▣ **Genre: Action, Crime.**

> A sequel to *Gunsmith Cats, Gunsmith Cats Burst* brings back Minnie-May and Rally. As usual they are finding trouble all over the place, and they are still running their weapons shop and doing freelance work as bounty hunters. With these two the excitement and the action is never far behind.

Lupin III. **Written and Illustrated by Monkey Punch. Tokyopop, 2002–2004. 14 Vol.** ▣ **Genre: Adventure, Comedy, Crime, Drama. Related Anime:** *Lupin the 3rd, Mystery of Mamo, The Castle of Cagliostro, Farewell to Nostradamus, Dead or Alive.*

> Arsene Lupin III is the grandson of the gentleman thief, Arsene Lupin, and is considered the greatest thief in the world. With his gang, he roams around the world pulling heists. They are pursued by one Inspector Zenigata who has made it his mission to catch Lupin. Adventure and excitement are never far behind when Lupin arrives in town.

Old Boy. Written by Garon Tsuchiya. Illustrated by Nobuaki Minegishi. Dark Horse, 2006–2007. 8 Vol. **M** Genre: Crime.

> After spending 10 years in a private jail with only a television for company, Goto is suddenly released. He doesn't know why he was in jail or who put him there, but the man aims to find out. After all, he's had 10 years to consider revenge. Winner of the Eisner Award.

Cyberpunk

Akira. Written and Illustrated by Katsuhiro Otomo. Dark Horse, 2000–2002. 6 Vol. Kodansha, 2009–2011. 6 Vol. **O** Genre: Cyberpunk. Related Anime: *Akira*.

> Neo-Tokyo has risen out of the ashes of Tokyo after World War III, but it has become a harsh place. Struggling for survival are Tetsuo and Kaneda, a pair of teenagers. When psychic powers begin to awaken in Tetsuo, their lives will change in ways neither of them imagine. Considered a classic. Winner of the Kodansha Award, the Eisner Award, and the Harvey Award.

Appleseed. Written and Illustrated by Shirow Masamune. Dark Horse, 2007–2009. 4 Vol. **T** Genre: Cyberpunk. Related Anime: *Appleseed, Appleseed Ex Machina, Appleseed (OVA)*.

> Deunan and her cyborg partner, Briareos, have survived World War III and its aftermath, but it hasn't been easy. When they are invited to come live in Olympus, the closest thing to a Utopia there is, everything changes. They both join the police force there and find that Olympus's perfect city isn't quite as perfect as it seems. The two of them are soon embroiled in a struggle that may just lead to another war. Winner of the Shogakukun Award.

Battle Angel Alita. Written and Illustrated by Yukito Kishiro. VIZ Media, LLC, 2003–2005. 9 Vol. **O** Genre: Action, Cyberpunk, Science Fiction. Related Anime: *Battle Angel*.

> The cyborg Alita has no memory of her previous life when Daisuke wakes her up in the Scrapyard. However, she does have a talent for fighting and martial arts. In search of her past, Alita decides to use those skills. But there are dark secrets both in Alita's past and in the world that she will now be caught up in, and survival isn't always easy.

Battle Angel Alita: Last Order. Written and Illustrated by Yukito Kishiro. VIZ Media, LLC, 2003–. Ongoing Series. 15 Vol. **O** Genre: Action, Cyberpunk, Science Fiction.

> Alita thought her battles were over. But she awakes in a new cyborg body and with more power than before. As she searches both for an old friend and for answers about her past, Alita gets caught up in power struggles beyond her control. This story can be seen as either a sequel or an alternate version of the original *Battle Angel Alita*. The series is currently on hiatus in Japan.

<u>Biomega</u>. **Written and Illustrated by Tsutomu Nihei. VIZ Media, LLC, 2010– 2011. 6 Vol. M Genre: Action, Cyberpunk, Horror, Science Fiction.**

In the future, the N5S virus has swept across the world, turning people into zombie-like drones. Zoicichi Kanoe searches the world rescuing those who can resist this disease with the help of his motorcycle, an AI named Fuyu. They may just be humanity's best hope of survival.

<u>Blame!</u>. **Written and Illustrated by Tsutomu Nihei. Tokyopop, 2005–2007. 10 Vol. O Genre: Action, Cyberpunk, Science Fiction. Related Anime:** *Blame!*

Killy roams around the city searching for Net Terminal Genes, which hold some sort of power. No one quite knows what sort of power, but that doesn't stop them for searching for them. There is always danger as well from the silicate creatures. Survival isn't easy, especially with the Safeguard out to kill all humanity, but if he can survive, Killy might be able to find the answer that could save everyone

<u>Noise</u>. **Written and Illustrated by Tsutomu Nihei. Tokyopop, 2007. 1 Vol. O Genre: Cyberpunk, Science Fiction.**

Susono Musubi, a young police officer, stumbles into a dangerous plot and makes discoveries that may change her life forever, if she does not lose it. Considered a prequel to Blame!.

Detective

<u>MPD—Psycho</u>. **Written by Eiji Otsuka. Illustrated by Sho-u Tajima. Dark Horse, 2007–. Ongoing Series. 14 Vol. M Genre: Detective, Psychological Thriller.**

Yousuke Kobayashi was a police detective. Unfortunately for him, Yousuke may not be the only personality in his mind. Even as he seeks out murderers for his job, Yousuke finds himself also drawn into madness, and perhaps the realization that he might be what he hunts.

<u>Pluto: Urasawa x Tezuka</u>. **Written by Naoki Urasawa, Osamu Tezuka, and Takashi Nagasaki. Illustrated by Naoki Urasawa. VIZ Media, LLC, 2009– 2010. 8 Vol. O Genre: Detective, Science Fiction.**

Based on Osamu Tezuka's *Astro Boy*, Pluto is the tale of a robot detective. Gesicht is a German detective working for Europol. He is on the trail of a murderer who has left a string of bodies, both human and robot, behind him. The case is a puzzling one and it just keeps getting stranger. Winner of the Seiun Award and the Tezuka Osamu Cultural Award.

Drama

<u>Initial D</u>. **Written and Illustrated by Shuichi Shigeno. Tokyopop, 2002– 2009. 33 of 41 Vol. Ongoing Series. T Genre: Action, Drama, Racing. Related Anime:** *Initial D, Initial D Second Stage, Initial D Extra Stage 1.0 &*

1.5, Initial D Third Stage, Initial D Battle Stage 1, Initial D Fourth Stage, Initial D Battle Stage 2, Initial D Extra Stage 2.

Tak does a lot of driving for his job, but when a local street racing group comes into town, he finds himself getting drawn into the world of racing. However, the first race is only the beginning.

Oishinbo A la Carte. Written by Tetsu Kariya. Illustrated by Akira Hanasaki. VIZ Media, LLC, 2009–2010. 7 Vol. T Genre: Drama, Cooking.

This series actually consists of seven volumes that are not numbered and can each stand alone. They are collected by subject and can be read in any order. Each volume has been given its own annotation as the volumes are mostly connected through the characters that appear in them, and each volume has its own theme. They have been listed in the reading order suggested by the publisher. Winner of the Shogakukun Award.

Oishinbo A la Carte: Fish, Sushi, and Sashimi. Written by Tetsu Kariya. Illustrated by Akira Hanasaki. VIZ Media, LLC, 2009. 1 Vol. T Genre: Drama, Cooking.

Fish, of course, is a staple of the Japanese diet and so is a must for the Ultimate Menu. But what fish provide the best dishes and which are worthy to be included in the Ultimate Menu? The volume also features illustrated recipes.

Oishinbo A la Carte: Izakaya: Pub Food. Written by Tetsu Kariya. Illustrated by Akira Hanasaki. VIZ Media, LLC, 2010. 1 Vol. T Genre: Drama, Cooking.

In this volume, Shiro and Yuka tackle Japanese bar food. A favorite for after-work snacks or just hanging out, Izakaya food is a staple of life. From old standards to new innovations, the pair delve into Japanese pub food in order to find the best of it. The volume also features illustrated recipes.

Oishinbo A la Carte: Japanese Cuisine. Written by Tetsu Kariya. Illustrated by Akira Hanasaki. VIZ Media, LLC, 2009. 1 Vol. T Genre: Drama, Cooking.

Shiro Yamaoka is a journalist with zero initiative but a love of food. He and his partner, Yuka, have embarked on a quest for the Ultimate Menu. In *Japanese Cuisine*, they introduce and explore the main staple ingredients of Japanese food with comedy and detail. The volume also features illustrated recipes.

Oishinbo A la Carte: The Joy of Rice. Written by Tetsu Kariya. Illustrated by Akira Hanasaki. VIZ Media, LLC, 2009. 1 Vol. T Genre: Drama, Cooking.

Rice, of course, is one of the most important ingredients in Japanese cooking and is a must for the Ultimate Menu. In *The Joy of Rice*, Yamaoka searches for new rice dishes and explores the various ways rice is used in Japanese cooking. The volume also features illustrated recipes.

Oishinbo A la Carte: Ramen and Gyoza. Written by Tetsu Kariya. Illustrated by Akira Hanasaki. VIZ Media, LLC, 2009. 1 Vol. T Genre: Drama, Cooking.

Ramen is a dish that can cause fights. It exists in every form from the simple and traditional to the new and innovative. And one can't have ramen without gyoza, dumplings served as a side dish. While ramen may seem like a simple enough dish, but Shiro will find that the simple things can sometimes be the most difficult to master. The volume also features illustrated recipes.

Oishinbo A la Carte: Sake. Written by Tetsu Kariya. Illustrated by Akira Hanasaki. VIZ Media, LLC, 2009. 1 Vol. **T** Genre: Drama, Cooking.

In *Sake*, Yamaoka focuses on the sake, Japan's main alcoholic drink. Exploring the various varieties and the process of making the drink, he also seeks which food pairings with sake work the best and which ones are belong on the Ultimate Menu.

Oishinbo A la Carte: Vegetables. Written by Tetsu Kariya. Illustrated by Akira Hanasaki. VIZ Media, LLC, 2009. 1 Vol. **T** Genre: Drama, Cooking.

This time they are tackling vegetables. Between a contest using cabbages and turnips, hatred of eggplant, and asparagus as a fix-it for a relationship, these two will have their hands full. The volume also features illustrated recipes.

Tanpenshu. Written and Illustrated by Hiroki Endo. Dark Horse, 2007. 2 Vol. **O** Genre: Drama, Psychological.

A two-volume collection of short stories by Hiroki Endo. Most of the stories focus on exploring the challenges and complications that life brings as well as the struggle to make meaning of one's life.

Fantasy

Baby Birth. Written by Sukehiro Tomita. Illustrated by Haruhiko Mikimoto. Tokyopop, 2003. 2 Vol. **T** Genre: Action, Adventure, Fantasy, Science Fiction.

Hizuru and Takuya are both students at a prestigious art school in Tokyo. While at first glance they don't seem to have much in common, these two may be the only ones who can protect the world—if. they can get along long enough to do so, that is.

Bastard!!: Heavy Metal Dark Fantasy. Written and Illustrated by Kazushi Hagiwara. VIZ Media, LLC, 2002–. Ongoing Series. 26 Vol. **M** Genre: Fantasy, Postapocalyptic, Supernatural. Related Anime: *Bastard!!*.

The powerful wizard, Dark Schneider, was finally defeated a generation ago by the High Priest of Metallicana. However, now the Kingdom of Metallicana is under attack, and its only hope may rest in the hands of a 14-year-old boy. Lucien has the spirit of Dark Schneider restrained inside him, controlled by the High Priest's daughter Yoko, and he may be able to save them, but will Dark Schneider save the kingdom or simply conquer the world?

Berserk. Written and Illustrated by Kentaro Muira. Dark Horse, 2003–. Ongoing Series. 35 Vol. **M** Genre: Action, Dark Fantasy, Drama, Horror. Related Anime: *Berserk.*

> Guts is known as the black swordsman and is a legendary mercenary. Griffith is the leader of the mercenary band, Band of the Hawk. Their lives seem intertwined in the dark tale of fantasy and horror that will leave a trail of bodies in its wake. Winner of the Tezuka Osamu Cultural Award.

Spice and Wolf. Written by Isuna Hasekura. Illustrated by Keito Koume. Yen Press, 2009–. Ongoing Series. 5 Vol. **M** Genre: Fantasy, Romance, Thriller. Related Anime: *Spice and Wolf, Spice and Wolf (OVA.), Spice and Wolf (OVA.), Spice and Wolf II.*

> A merchant and a harvest goddess make for an odd pair of traveling companions, but it seems to work for Kraft Laurence and Holo the Wisewolf. As the two of them travel and begin to head toward Holo's homeland, they will find perhaps both profit and adventure.

Historical Fiction

Adolf. Written and Illustrated by Osamu Tezuka. Cadence, 1996–1997. 5 Vol. **O** Genre: Drama, Historical Fiction.

> Adolf is the weaving together of several different stories during World War II. There is Sohei Togo, a Japanese reporter sent to Germany to cover the Olympics. His brother was an exchange student in Germany, but he was murdered after he discovered something, though what is unknown. Adolf Kamil is a young Jew living in Japan, as is Adolf Kaufmann, a young man who is both German and Japanese. And then there is the dictator himself, Adolf Hitler. Winner of the Kodansha Award.

Basilisk: The Koga Ninja Scrolls. Written and Illustrated by Masaki Segawa. Del Rey, 2006–2007. 5 Vol. **M** Genre: Action, Fantasy, Historical Fiction. Related Anime: *Basilisk.*

> The feud between the Kouga and Iga clans was halted once before when they both served the same master, Ieyasu Tokugawa. But now that truce has been dissolved as 10 ninja from each clan must fight to the death in order to choose the next shogun. However, the heirs to both clans just happen to be in love with one another, and neither of them wishes to kill the other. Whether they'll be able to have a happy ending is unknown, but they both are willing to try. Winner of the Kodansha Award.

Emma. Written and Illustrated by Kaoru Mori. CMX, 2006–2010. 10 Vol. **T** Genre: Historical Fiction, Romance. Related Anime: *Emma—A Victorian Romance, Emma—A Victorian Romance: Second Act.*

> William Jones was not supposed to fall in love with Emma. He is the eldest son of a family with new money in Victorian England, and she is his former governess' maid. The two of them struggle to find a future together with the help and the hindrance of a large cast of characters.

Lady Snowblood. Written by Kazuo Koike. Illustrated by Kazuo Kamimura. Dark Horse, 2005–2006. 4 Vol. **M** Genre: Historical Fiction, Samurai.

> Oyuki is the assassin known as Lady Snowblood. For a high price, she will kill. But besides being her work, her job is personal. Oyuki was born for the purpose of revenge. Her mother passed a task on to her in order to avenge their family, and Lady Snowblood will carry it out.

Me and the Devil Blues: The Unreal Life of Robert Johnson. Written and Illustrated by Akira Hiramoto. Del Rey, 2008. 2 Vol. **T** Genre: Drama, Historical Fiction, Horror, Psychological, Supernatural.

> A reimagining of Robert Johnson's life, Me and the Devil Blues tells the story of a young man who may have sold his soul to the devil in order to play the blues.

Path of the Assassin. Written by Kazuo Koike. Illustrated by Goseki Kojima. Dark Horse, 2006–2009. 15 Vol. **M** Genre: Historical Fiction, Martial Arts.

> Hanzo Hattori was known as the master ninja who protected the shogun, Ieyasu Tokogawa. But before he was a legend, Hanzo was a young man learning the many skills and talents he would use as a ninja. Furthermore, he began to form a friendship with the young Tokogawa. The two friends shared dreams that would one day change their nation, and this is their story.

Town of Evening Calm, Country of Cherry Blossoms. Written and Illustrated by Fumiyo Kouno. Last Gasp, 2007. 1 Vol. **T** Genre: Drama, Historical Fiction.

> *Town of Evening Calm, Country of Cherry Blossoms* tells two interconnected stories about life after the atomic bomb was dropped on Hiroshima and provides a glimpse into the lives of survivors of that event. Winner of the Tezuka Osamu Cultural Award.

Vagabond. Written and Illustrated by Takehiko Inoue. VIZ Media, LLC, 2008–. Ongoing Series. 33 Vol. 9 VIZ Big Vol. **M** Genre: Historical Fiction, Samurai.

> Set in 16th-century Japan, *Vagabond* is a fictional version of the life of Miyamoto Musashi, a legendary swordsman. From his beginnings as Shinmen Takezo, the story follows his life and adventures. Musashi's life happens to be legendary for a reason. Winner of the Kodansha Award.

Horror

Dragon Head. Written and Illustrated by Minetaro Mochizuki. Tokyopop, 2006–2008. 10 Vol. **O** Genre: Horror, Psychological.

> When disaster strikes on the way home from a school field trip, Teru finds himself one of only three survivors. Trapped in darkness and with very few resources, they must try to survive and escape, but the greatest danger may come from one of his fellow survivors.

The Kurosagi Corpse Delivery Service. Written by Eiji Otsuka. Illustrated by Housui Yamazaki. Dark Horse, 2006–. Ongoing Series. 13 Vol. NR Genre: Horror.

The members of the Kurosagi Corpse Delivery Service all have talents that aren't really much in demand from the living for the most part. From hearing dead spirits' voices to embalming to channeling, the group has some odd skills. But they're finding a way to put them to good use by helping the dead find peace. They'll take a body where it needs to go in order to pass on.

Lament of the Lamb. Written and Illustrated by Kei Toume. Tokyopop, 2004–2005. 7 Vol. **O** Genre: Drama, Horror.

When his mother died, Kazuna's father left, taking with him Chizuna, Kazuna's sister. But now, Kazuna finds himself losing control at the sight of blood. It is his long-lost sister who has the answer. Both of them have an illness that is turning them into vampires, and neither of them know just what they may become as it progresses.

Parasyte. Written and Illustrated by Hitoshi Iwaaki. Del Rey, 2007–2009. 8 Vol. **O** Genre: Horror, Science Fiction.

Shinichi Izumi was an ordinary teenager until the aliens invaded. The aliens called parasytes can infest people's bodies and possess them. However, Shinichi's parasyte ended up controlling his hand, rather than his brain. As Shinichi is one of the few people who know about the parasytes, he must not only learn to coexist with his own but also figure out how to protect humanity from them. Winner of the Kodansha Award.

Tokko. Written and Illustrated by Tohru Fujisawa. Tokyopop, 2008–2009. 3 Vol. **M** Genre: Action, Horror, Police. Related Anime: *Tokko*.

Tokko's job is to deal with the demons that prey upon the world—not that this is common knowledge. Ranmaru doesn't know it at first, but as a survivor of the Machida Massacre, he is linked to the organization, especially to Sakura Rokujo, whom he has been dreaming about for years. Now that he has finally met her, he may find that his nightmares are far more real than he likes.

Uzumaki. Written and Illustrated by Junji Ito. VIZ Media, LLC, 2007–2008. 3 Vol. **O** Genre: Horror.

In the small town of Kurôzu-cho, spirals are ominous harbingers. They can lead to insanity and death, and it seems that no one is safe.

Vampire Hunter D. Written by Hideyuki Kikuchi. Illustrated by Saiko Takaki. DMP, 2007–. Ongoing Series. 4 Vol. **O** Genre: Action, Fantasy, Horror. Related Anime: *Vampire Hunter D, Vampire Hunter D: Bloodlust*.

In the year 12,090 A.D., things are not looking good for humanity. There are very few survivors of the human race, and the world has been torn apart by war and destruction. Furthermore, there are vampires called the Nobility roaming around. Once you are bitten by a Nobility, you are cursed to be undead. Humanity's only hope is a Vampire Hunter.

Martial Arts

<u>Battle Vixens</u>. Written and Illustrated by Yuji Shiozaki. Tokyopop, 2004–. Ongoing Series. 16 Vol. **M** Genre: Comedy, Harem, Martial Arts. Related Anime: *Ikkitōsen: Battle Vixens (B.V.), Ikkitōsen: Dragon Destiny (D.D.), Ikkitōsen: Great Guardians (G.G.).*

> Hakufu has always enjoyed fighting, but a chance fight with a stranger changes her life. Now she's off to Tokyo with an earring that contains a spirit. That spirit will lend Hakufu its power, but the real question is, will they share the same fate?

<u>Tenjho Tenge</u>. Written and Illustrated by Oh!great. CMX, 2005–2008. 18 of 22 Vol. **T** Genre: Action, Martial Arts, Romance. Related Anime: *Tenjho Tenge, Ultimate Fight.*

> Toudou Academy isn't your normal high school. Fights are par for the course, and only the best fighters end up in the Juken Club. The Juken Club just happens to be in opposition to the Executive Council, and two new students are going to find themselves involved in the fight of their lives.

Mecha

<u>Bokurano Ours</u>. Written and Illustrated by Mohiro Kitoh. VIZ Media, LLC, 2010–. 11 Vol. **O** Genre: Drama, Deconstruction, Horror, Mecha, Psychological, Science Fiction.

> During a summer camp, 15 children are approached by a man calling himself Kokopelli who claims he is a game designer and asks them to test the game. All but one agree, and so the game begins. But it soon becomes clear that there are hidden costs to this game, and that their very lives are at stake.

<u>The Candidate for Goddess</u>. Written and Illustrated by Yukiru Sugisaki. Tokyopop, 2004–. Ongoing Series. 5 Vol. **T** Genre: Action, Adventure, Mecha, Military. Related Anime: *Pilot Candidate.*

> The year is 4048. A thousand years ago an alien force completely wiped out Earth's planetary systems. Since then, humanity has developed weapons called Goddesses to protect themselves. Five young men have entered the Goddess Operation Academy hoping to learn to pilot these weapons, but they may have more work ahead of them than they expect.

<u>Neon Genesis Evangelion</u>. Written and Illustrated by Yoshiyuki Sadamoto. VIZ Media, LLC, 2004–. Ongoing Series. 12 Vol. **O** Genre: Drama, Horror, Mecha, Psychological. Related Anime: *Neon Genesis Evangelion, Evangelion: Death and Rebirth, The End of Evangelion, Rebuild of Evangelion.*

> In the year 2015, Shinji Ikari finds himself caught up in the struggle to save humanity. Angels (giant aliens) have been attacking Earth for years now,

and it seems that the only effective defense against them are Evangelions or Evas. Shinji had been designated as a pilot for one of these Evas, but actually piloting the Evas maybe more difficult than Shinji ever imagined. This is considered a classic by many.

The Voices of a Distant Star. Written and Illustrated by Mizu Sahara. Tokyopop, 2006. 1 Vol. T Genre: Drama, Mecha, Romance. Related Anime: *Voices of a Distant Star.*

Mikako has joined a research team to explore space. She leaves behind Noboru, her best friend and perhaps something more. The two of them send messages to one another via their cell phones, but the farther away they get from one another, the longer the messages take to arrive. Separated by time and space, can a love truly form between them or is their relationship doomed instead?

Mystery

Children of the Sea. Written and Illustrated by Daisuke Igarashi. VIZ Media, LLC, 2009–. Ongoing Series. 4 Vol. O Genre: Action, Mystery.

One summer vacation Ruka meets Umi and Sora. All three of them are drawn to the ocean, and there is the mysterious disappearance of much of the fish from the world's oceans. Together these three may find the answers, and may change the world.

R.O.D. Read or Dream. Written by Hideyuki Kurata. Illustrated by Ran Ayanaga. VIZ Media, LLC, 2006–2007. 4 Vol. O Genre: Adventure, Comedy, Mystery.

Anita, Michelle, and Maggie run the Paper Sisters Detective Company. It's not your typical sort of agency. For one thing, all three girls have the ability to manipulate and control paper. For another, most of their cases have to do with books. However as it turns out, books can make for the most interesting adventures.

Swallowing the Earth. Written and Illustrated by Osamu Tezuka. DMP, 2009. 1 Vol. O Genre: Action, Mystery, Science Fiction.

Zephyrus is a mysterious woman who is said to seduce men to their doom. A drunk named Gohonmatsu Seki is the only man who seems to be able to resist her. He is employed to find out what he can about Zephyrus and to see if he can stop her plans. But what are her plans and can they really be stopped?

Romance

Oh My Goddess!. Written and Illustrated by Kosuke Fujishima. Dark Horse, 2005–. Ongoing Series. 41 Vol. T Genre: Comedy, Fantasy, Romance. Related Anime: *Ah! My Goddess, Ah! My Goddess: The Movie.*

When Keiichi accidentally dials the wrong phone number in his dorm one night, he gets Goddess Technical Help Line. When the goddess Belldandy offers him one wish, Keiichi wishes for a goddess like her to stay with him forever. However, Belldandy's companionship gets Keiichi kicked out of his all-male dorm.

Now he has to find a new home and learn to live with a goddess, permanently. Winner of the Kodansha Award.

Train_Main: Densha Otoko. Written and Illustrated by Hidenori Hara. VIZ Media, LLC, 2006–2007. 3 Vol. T Genre: Comedy, Romance.

When an ordinary geek on the train stands up to a guy hassling a pretty girl, he finds that his life changes. She wants to thank him. He has no problem with that, but he's not used to interacting with girls, especially pretty ones. What is a geek to do except post online asking for help? With a cadre of online friends giving advice, does he have a chance with this girl?

Romantic Comedy

Ai Yori Aoshi. Written and Illustrated by Kou Fumizuki. Tokyopop, 2004–2007. 17 Vol. O Genre: Drama, Romantic Comedy. Related Anime: *Ai Yori Aoshi, Ai Yori Aoshi: Enishi, Ai Yori Aoshi Enishi X-mas Special.*

Kaoru has been living the life of an ordinary college student on his own. However, everything changes when a face from his past returns. Her name is Aoi, and she is there to be his wife. And that's only the beginning of the changes in Kaoru's life.

Maison Ikkoku. Written and Illustrated by Rumiko Takahashi. VIZ Media, LLC, 2003–2006. 15 Vol. O Genre: Romantic Comedy. Related Anime: Maison Ikkoku.

Yusaku is more than ready to move out of his apartment building, Maison Ikkoku. He finds himself completely unable to study with all the hijinks going on with the other tenants. However, when the beautiful Kyoko arrives to be the new building manager, he decides to stick around. But the course of love has never run smoothly, and it certainly won't in a place like Maison Ikkoku.

Ohikkoshi. Written and Illustrated by Hiroaki Samura. Dark Horse, 2006. 1 Vol. T Genre: Humor, Romantic Comedy.

Ohikkoshi is a collection of short stories by the author, mostly focusing on romantic comedies.

Sumomomo Momomo. Written and Illustrated by Shinobu Ohtaka. Yen Press, 2009–. 13 Vol. O Genre: Martial Arts, Romantic Comedy.

Momoko Kuzuryuu is the heir to her clan and its martial arts tradition. The only problem is her father isn't so sure a girl can preserve their strongest techniques. His solution is to betroth her to the heir to another martial arts clan, Koushi Inuzaka. However, Koushi has no interest in fighting at all; he's immersed in his own legal studies. But he may not have a choice in the matter. Not everyone is happy about Momoko and Koushi's impending marriage, and they may have to fight for their lives.

Samurai

Afro Samurai. Written and Illustrated by Takashi Okazaki. Seven Seas, 2008–2009. 2 Vol. **O** Genre: Comedy, Drama, Fantasy, Samurai, Science Fiction. Related Anime: *Afro Samurai, Afro Samurai: Resurrection.*

> Only the Number Two samurai can challenge the Number One samurai. When a young Afro witnesses his father, the Number One samurai, killed the Number Two, a man named Justice, he swears revenge. But if he wants to kill Justice, first he'll have to become the Number Two samurai himself.

Blade of the Immortal. Written and Illustrated by Hiroaki Samura. Dark Horse, 1997–. Ongoing Series. 26 Vol. **O** Genre: Samurai, Supernatural. Related Anime: *Blade of the Immortal.*

> Manji cannot die. Cursed with immortality, the only way for him to end his life is to kill a thousand evil men in atonement for his past deeds. When a young girl asks for his help in gaining revenge for her family, his quest begins. Winner of the Eisner Award.

Lone Wolf and Cub. Written by Kazou Koike. Illustrated by Goseki Kojima. Dark Horse, 2000–2002. 28 Vol. **M** Genre: Samurai.

> Itto Ogami has been the Shogun's executioner. However, when he returns home to find everyone in his household dead save for his young son, Itto vows revenge and turns all his attention to this endeavor. Traveling alone with his one-year-old son, Daigoro, he embarks on his quest for vengeance. Winner of the Eisner Award and the Harvey Award.

Samurai Executioner. Written by Kazuo Koike. Illustrated by Goseki Kojima. Dark Horse, 2004–2006. 10 Vol. **M** Genre: Drama, Historical, Samurai.

> Yamada Asamon is executioner for the Shogun. It is his job to kill criminals once they have been caught. But first they have to be caught, and each has his or her own story.

Science Fiction

Afterschool Charisma. Written and Illustrated by Kumiko Suekane. VIZ Media, LLC, 2010–. Ongoing Series. 4 Vol. **O** Genre: School, Science Fiction.

> To enroll at St. Kleio Academy, one must be a clone of a famous figure. All of the students are clones save for one: Shiro Kamiya. Shiro is the son of Dr. Kamiya, one of the professors at the school, and no one quite knows why he's attending since he's a normal teenager. And there seems to be something mysterious going on with the clones as well. There are a lot of secrets at this school, and some of them are coming to light.

Alien Nine. Written and Illustrated by Hitoshi Tomizawa. CMP, 2003. 3 Vol. **O** Genre: Science Fiction. Related Anime: *Alien Nine.*

> When Yuri's elementary school class votes her to be this year's alien fighter for the class, she is not very happy. Sure the alien fighters get to miss class, don't have

to always complete their homework, and get to skip cleaning duty, but it's a hard job and not really a fun one, in Yuri's opinion. This year, however, Yuri may just make some new friends as well as fight aliens.

Chobits. Written and Illustrated by CLAMP. Tokyopop, 2002–2003. 8 Vol. **O** Genre: Romantic Comedy, Science Fiction. Related Anime: *Chobits.*

Hideki hasn't had much luck lately. He's trying to pass his exams to get into university, and he can't afford a persocom, an android that acts as a personal computer. When he stumbles across an abandon persocom, he ends up taking her home. However, Chi may be more than an ordinary persocom, and Hideki finds himself rather fond of her. But she's just a computer, isn't she?

Deus Vitae. Written and Illustrated by Takuya Fujima. Tokyopop, 2004. 3 Vol. **O** Genre: Science Fiction.

Androids have created an almost perfect society. There is just one problem for them to wipe out: humans. Ash Ramy is a human survivor, and he and other humans are willing to fight to take back their world.

Eden: It's the Endless World!. Written and Illustrated by Hiroki Endo. Dark Horse, 2005–. 18 Vol. **M** Genre: Science Fiction.

In the future, after a global pandemic that left much of the population dead with more crippled, things are mostly controlled by a group called Propater. Elijah is a 15-year-old on his own after his mother and sister were captured by Propater. He must try to survive in the world and maybe rescue his family.

FLCL. Written by Gainax. Illustrated by Hajime Ueda. Tokyopop, 2003. 2 Vol. **T** Genre: Action, Comedy, Romance, Science Fiction, Surreal. Related Anime: *FLCL.*

Naota is living a lonely life in the midst of utter chaos. Then throw in alien robots bent on Earth's destruction and a new girl in town determined to stop them, and things really begin to get interesting.

Heat Guy J. Written and illustrated by Chiaki Ogishima. Tokyopop, 2005. 1 Vol. **T** Genre: Science Fiction. Related Anime: *Heat Guy J.*

Daisuke works for the Special Services Department. His partner is the android known as Heat Guy J. Together the two of them work toward keeping Jewde City safe, even when faced with an organized crime ring that wants them very dead.

King of Thorn. Written and Illustrated by Yuji Iwahara. Tokyopop, 2007–2008. 6 Vol. **O** Genre: Action, Science Fiction, Survival Horror.

Kasumi and Shizuka are separated by an experimental treatment for the Medusa virus with which they both are infected. Kasumi is cryogenically frozen while her sister is left behind. When she awakens, she finds the world covered by giant thorny plants and monstrous creatures. She and the others who have awakened must try to survive and find out how long they have been asleep and what has happened to the world since.

Planetes. Written and Illustrated by Makoto Yukimura. Tokyopop, 2003–2005. 5 Vol. T Genre: Drama, Science Fiction. Related Anime: *Planetes.*

Set in the near future, Planetes follows the lives and adventures of the crew of the DS-12 Toy Box. Their job is to collect space debris and by doing so protect space stations, shuttles, the Earth and the moon from danger. But there is more to space than simply picking out trash, and the members of the crew each have their own story. Winner of the Seiun Award.

Sakura Taisen. Written by Ohji Hiroi. Illustrated by Ikku Masa. Tokyopop, 2005–2008. 7 Vol. T Genre: Action, Historical, Romance, Science Fiction. Related Anime: *Sakura Wars (OVA), Sakura Wars 2 (OVA), Sakura Wars (TV Series), Sakura Wars: the Movie, Sakura Taisen: Sumire, Sakura Taisen: Ecole de Paris.*

Ensign Ichiro Ogami isn't quite sure what to make of his new assignment. It certainly feels like a demotion. He is now a ticket collector at the Imperial Theater in Tokyo. However, some of his new coworkers have some interesting abilities, and when demons attack, Ichiro will find out that this assignment may be far more interesting than he could have imagined.

20th Century Boys. Written and Illustrated by Naoki Urasawa. VIZ Media, LLC, 2009–. 22 Vol. O Genre: Mystery, Science Fiction.

When Kenji's friend, Donkey, commits suicide, memories of the past come to mind as familiar symbols reappear. When they had been children, Kenji and his friends had imagined they could save the world. Now, Kenji begins to reunite with his old friends, and he can't help but wonder if saving the world is really what they were meant to do. Winner of the Kondasha Award, the Shogakukun Award, and the Seiun Award.

Wolf's Rain. Written by Bones and Keiko Nobumoto. Illustrated by Toshitsugu Iida. VIZ Media, LLC, 2004–2005. 2 Vol. T Genre: Action, Adventure, Science Fiction, Supernatural. Related Anime: *Wolf's Rain, Wolf's Rain (OVA).*

Wolves are supposed to lead the way to paradise, but they are now extinct—or so humans think. Some wolves still live. Kiba is one of them, and as he searches for the Lunar Flower that will lead him to paradise, he will come across both friends and enemies.

Slice of Life

Genshiken. Written and Illustrated by Kio Shimoku. Del Rey, 2005–2007. 9 Vol. O Genre: Comedy, Slice of Life. Related Anime: *Genshiken, Genshiken 2, Genshiken (OVA.).*

Kanji Sasahara has decided to finally join a school club that he will enjoy, the otaku club. His girlfriend, Saki, is determined to get her anime fan boyfriend to lead a normal life. However, Kanji manages to drag Saki into joining Genshiken:

The Society for the Study of Modern Visual Culture. Saki is about to get a crash course in the world of Japanese otaku, and she might even learn to enjoy it.

K-On!. Written and Illustrated by Kakifly. Yen Press, 2010–. 4 Vol. O Genre: Music, Slice of Life.

With their high school's pop music club in trouble, four girls step up to keep it from disbanding. The only problem is none of them actually know how to play music it. It's going to take time and practice if they want be a band, but with all four of them determined to make it work, their club just might produce the greatest band their high school has seen.

Kingyo Used Books. Written and Illustrated by Seimu Yoshizaki. VIZ Media, LLC, 2010–. Ongoing Series. 10 Vol. O Genre: Slice of Life.

Kingyo Used Books specializes in old and rare manga. They have the books that you've been looking for or the ones you wanted but didn't know you were looking for, and their books can change one's life.

Solanin. Written and Illustrated by Inio Asano. VIZ Media, LLC, 2008. 1 Vol. O Genre: Music, Romance, Slice of Life.

Meiko has graduated from college and now works a job she hates. Her boyfriend crashes at her place almost permanently, and she doesn't know what she wants from life. As she tries to figure out life as an adult, music becomes something of a solace, and Meiko finds that life, while not easy, is something special.

Twin Spica. Written and Illustrated by Kou Yaginuma. Vertical, 2010–. 16 Vol. T Genre: Drama, Science Fiction, Slice of Life, Supernatural.

Asumi would like to be an astronaut, and she is determined to get into the Tokyo Space School. It isn't going to be easy, and first she is going to have to convince her father that space is where she belongs. Even if she manages that, Asumi had a long hard road ahead of her.

Sports

One Pound Gospel. Written and Illustrated by Rumiko Takehashi. VIZ Media, LLC, 2008. 4 Vol. O Genre: Sports, Romantic Comedy.

Kosaku is the pride of his boxing gym. However, his appetite may just do him in. He can't seem to stop eating and has already moved up a weight class. Enter Sister Angela, a novice nun, who is determined to help Kosaku get over his gluttony. But will Angela prove to be more of a distraction than food?

Real. Written and Illustrated by Takehiko Inoue. VIZ Media, LLC, 2008–. Ongoing Series. 9 Vol. O Genre: Drama, Sports.

Togawa, Nomiya, and Takahashi have only two things in common: they are all now in wheelchairs, and they want to play basketball. But those two things are enough for them to have a common goal to break past their problems and difficulties.

Supernatural

<u>Dance in the Vampire Bund</u>. **Written and Illustrated by Nozomu Tamaki. Seven Seas, 2008–. Ongoing Series. 10 Vol. O Genre: Romance, Supernatural. Related Anime:** *Dance in the Vampire Bund.*

> After spending years in hiding, the vampire Mina Tepes wants changes. Using her family's wealth, she pays off the country of Japan's debt in exchange for permission to create a haven for her kind. Then she goes on to announce the existence of vampires to the world at large. However, not everyone is happy about Mina's plans for peace between vampires and humans, and if she wants her dreams to become reality, Mina is going to have to stay alive somehow.

<u>Hellsing</u>. **Written and Illustrated by Kohta Hirano. Dark Horse, 2003–2010. 10 Vol. T Genre: Action, Horror, Supernatural. Related Anime:** *Hellsing, Hellsing Ultimate.*

> England has a secret organization to protect the country from vampires and other supernatural threats. Hellsing has secretly protected the country for years now, and its current head, Sir Integra Hellsing, continues the tradition. Integra also has a secret weapon in her arsenal: Alucard. An ancient vampire armed with silver bullets is just the thing for dealing with any problems one might have, which is a good thing because the war against the evil in the world has just stepped into high gear.

<u>Mushishi</u>. **Written and Illustrated by Yuki Urushibara. Del Rey, 2007–2010. 10 Vol. O Genre: Detective, Occult, Supernatural. Related Anime:** *Mushishi.*

> Mushi are creatures of the supernatural, and most humans can't see them. However, that doesn't stop mushi from causing trouble for humans. Ginko, however, can see mushi as well as attract them. As he wanders around the countryside, he deals with the various mushi he meets. Winner of the Kodansha Award.

<u>Oninagi</u>. **Written and Illustrated by Akira Ishida. Yen Press, 2009–. Ongoing Series. 4 Vol. O Genre: Action, Comedy, Supernatural.**

> Nanami was looking forward to the beginning of the school year and getting closer to her crush, Kazuto. However, on her first day of school she gets attacked by a swordswoman claiming that Nanami is a demon. Nanami isn't a demon, but she is descended from one and has some powers, and those powers may just threaten her life.

<u>Translucent</u>. **Written and Illustrated by Kazuhiko Okamoto. Dark Horse, 2007–. 5 Vol. T Genre: Romance, School, Supernatural.**

> Shizuka is sick. She had the mysterious Translucent Syndrome, a disease that makes her turn invisible or just semitransparent at times. There is no cure. But that doesn't stop Mamaru from being her friend and maybe even falling for her. High school is never exactly easy, but for these two it may be far more than either expected.

XXXHolic. **Written and Illustrated by CLAMP. Del Rey, 2004–. 18 Vol.** T
Genre: Comedy, Psychological, Supernatural. Related Anime: *A Midsummer Night's Dream, XXXHolic.*

> Kimihiro Watanuki is not your normal high school student. He sees ghosts and spirits. When he stumbles upon a witch named Yuko, it seems like a godsend. Yuko grants wishes, for a price. In return for taking away his abilities to see the supernatural, Watanuki has to work for Yuko at her shop. It will be a job like nothing he has ever experienced before. This series at times crosses over with the series *Tsubasa Reservoir Chronicle.*

Thriller

Battle Royale. **Written by Koushen Takami and Masayuki Taguchi. Illustrated by Masayuki Taguchi. Tokyopop, 2009–2009. 15 Vol. 5 Ultimate Edition Vol.** M **Genre: Action, Horror, Romance, Science Fiction, Thriller.**

> Shuya Nanahara has been stranded on an island with 41 of his classmates. They are each given a survival kit that includes a weapon of some sort and the information that only one student can be alive in three days or they will all die. Only one of them can survive this sinister game. The question is, which one will it be?

ES Eternal Sabbath. **Written and Illustrated by Fuyumi Soryo. Del Rey, 2006–2007. 8 Vol.** O **Genre: Drama, Science Fiction, Thriller.**

> Ryousuke is not a normal young man—not when he is immune to all diseases and has psychic abilities, and knows it. But nobody besides him seems to notice this until he meets one Dr. Mine Kujo, a researcher who is one of the few people whose mind he can't get into. Mine has questions as does Ryousuke, and their paths in finding answers might lead them to help one another out. But Ryousuke may not be the only one like him in the world, and his counterpart may be far more dangerous.

Gantz. **Written and Illustrated by Hiroya Oku. Dark Horse, 2008–. Ongoing Series. 30 Vol.** M **Genre: Action, Psychological, Science Fiction, Thriller. Related Anime:** *Gantz.*

> Saving the life of a bum, Kei and Maaru get hit by a subway train. However, when they wake up, they find themselves alive and taking orders from some sort of alien orb called Gantz. Soon they find themselves caught up in hunts with other ordinary people who also may have died. But the real question is, what is all this about and will they ever escape?

Ikigami: the Ultimate Limit. **Written and Illustrated by Motoro Mase. VIZ Media, LLC, 2009–2011. 7 Vol.** M **Genre: Thriller.**

> In Japan, when you are ages 18 to 24, you may receive noticed that you have been selected to be killed in the next 24 hours. These notices are called ikigami, and it is Kengo Fujimoto's job to deliver them. As he does so, he meets a number of individuals who are going to die and learns that this national policy is meant to increase productivity. Prosperity definitely has a darker side.

Monster. Written and Illustrated by Naoki Urasawa. VIZ Media, LLC, 2006–2008. 18 Vol. **O** Genre: Detective, Drama, Horror, Psychological, Thriller. Related Anime: *Monster*.

> Dr. Kenzo Tenma seems to have everything. He is a talented brain surgeon with an upcoming promotion as well as a fiancée. But when he stays true to his belief that all patients are equal and operates on a young boy instead of Mayor Roddecker, his life turns into a downward spiral. And what he doesn't know is that he may have created a monster that only he can stop. Winner of the Shogakukun Award and the Tezuka Osamu Cultural Award.

MW. Written and Illustrated by Osamu Tezuka. Vertical, 2007. 1 Vol. **O** Genre: Thriller.

> Michio Yuki is not the man he appears to be. He hides behind the mask of a young, wealthy banker, but he also has carried out a number of murders and kidnappings. The only one who knows what Michio has done is Father Garai. Garai knows that as a child Michio was exposed to a chemical agent called MW that drove the young man insane. Michio has a plan, however, and the real question has become, can anyone stop him?

Sanctuary. Written by Sho Fumimura. Illustrated by Ryoichi Ikegami. VIZ Media, LLC, 1995–1998. 9 Vol. **O** Genre: Crime, Thriller. Related Anime: *Sanctuary*.

> Akira Hojo and Chiaki Asami are childhood friends. They survived the killing fields of Cambodia when they were young, and are now determined to change Japan. Now Hojo is a member of the Yakuza while Asami is a rising politician. Both have plans to rise to the top, but the question remains: will either of them succeed?

Seinen Anime

Action

Black Lagoon. Geneon, 2009. 12 25-Min. Episodes. 8 Discs. **M** Genre: Action, Adventure, Comedy, Crime.

> Rokuro was just a normal salaryman making a delivery for his company up until he got taken hostage by the crew of the Black Lagoon. They are a group of mercenaries who roam the seas of Southeast Asia. Rokuro, now nicked named Rock, gets swept up in their business. He doesn't know if he will survive his encounter with these people, but he does know that his life is no longer normal in any way.

Full Metal Panic!. ADV, 2002. 24 24-Min. Episodes. 7 Discs. **T** Genre: Action, Mecha, Romantic Comedy.

> Sousuke Sagara is a former child soldier and a member of Mithril, a mercenary group. The 16-year-old can handle just about any battle situation thrown at him

with ease and aplomb—at least, until his latest assignment. Sousuke and his team have been assigned to protect Kaname Chidori, a high school student. Sousuke may be the ultimate warrior, but he has no experience with normal life or high school. And given that no one is to learn he's Kaname's bodyguard, his life just got a lot more complicated, and so did his new classmates'.

Full Metal Panic!?: Fumoffu. ADV, 2005. 12 25-Min. Episodes. 4 Discs. **2 Discs for Complete Collection Ed.** **T** Genre: Action, Comedy, Romance.

> Sousuke's mission to protect Kaname continues. However, he may be facing his biggest foe yet: a fairly normal high school existence. Sousuke may be ready to tackle just about any battlefield, but between high school and romance, he may be out of his league.

Full Metal Panic!: The Second Raid. Funimation, 2005. 12 24-Min. Episodes. 4 Discs. **T** Genre: Action, Mecha, Romantic Comedy.

> With a new threat on the horizon, Sousuke ends up getting pulled off his mission to protect Kaname. However, that doesn't necessarily mean that Kaname is out of danger and Mithril may be falling into a trap its enemies set.

Trigun. Funimation, 2010. 26 25-Min. Episodes. 4 Discs. **T** Genre: Action, Western.

> Vash the Stampede has a price on his head: $60 billon, to be precise, which is part of his problem. For one thing, he can't remember the incident that got him a price on his head, and for another, the bounty hunters that follow him cause quite a bit of damage. In fact, he has to be followed by Bernardelli Insurance Society agents in order to try and mitigate the damage he does, because wherever Vash goes, adventure definitely follows.

Cyberpunk

Akira. Geneon, 2004. 125 Min. 1 Disc. **M** Genre: Cyberpunk.

> Neo-Tokyo has risen out of the ashes of Tokyo after World War III, but it has become a harsh place. Struggling for survival are Tetsuo and Kaneda, a pair of teenagers. When psychic powers begin to awaken in Tetsuo, their lives will change in ways neither of them imagine, for Tetsuo's powers are very similar to Akira's, a psychic who when he lost control just may have destroyed Tokyo the first time. Considered a classic.

Appleseed. Geneon, 2005. Section 23, 2009. 106 Min. 1 Disc. **O** Genre: Cyberpunk.

> Deunan has spent most of her life immersed in war. When she gets rescued and taken to Olympus, it seems like a paradise. Reunited with her old partner Brioareos, Deunan will soon find that her past holds keys to the future of Olympus, and she will have to make some decisions about what part she will play in that future.

Serial Experiments Lain. Geneon, 1999. 13 24-Min. Episodes. 4 Discs. **O** Genre: Cyberpunk, Psychological, Thriller.

> After Lain's friend, Chisa, dies, Lain gets a strange message from her. It claims that Chisa isn't dead but that she had simply "abandoned her flesh." This draws Lain into the world of the Wired, a communications network. Lain searches for answers and explores the Wired, all the time being drawn deeper and deeper into a world that may not be real.

Historical Fiction

Emma: A Victorian Romance. Nozomi, 2008. 24 25-Min. Episodes. 8 Discs. **T** Genre: Historical Fiction, Romance.

> William Jones was not supposed to fall in love with Emma. He is the eldest son of a family with new money in Victorian England, and she is his former governess's maid. The two of them struggle to find a future together with the help and the hindrance of a large cast of characters.

Horror

Le Portrait de Petite Cossette. Geneon, 2004. 3 37-Min. Episodes. 1 Disc. **O** Genre: Horror, Psychological, Romance.

> Eiri's life changes when he starts seeing visions of a beautiful young woman who haunts a Venetian glass. Eiri quickly falls in love with Cossette and soon makes a pact with her to help her achieve the revenge she wants. But as Eiri undertakes this task, his friends and family begin to worry about him. Will his love for Cossette mean the end of him?

Mecha

The Big O. Bandai, 2001–2003. 26 25-Min. Episodes. 8 Discs in 2 Sets. **T** Genre: Mecha, Science Fiction.

> Forty years ago, everyone in Paradigm City lost their memory. Now, Roger Smith works there as a negotiator. He handles all sorts of transactions even as he searches for some answers about all those lost memories, which proves to be dangerous at times. Roger has an ace up his sleeve called the Big O for just such occasions.

RahXephon. ADV, 2005. 26 25-Min. Episodes. 7 Discs. **T** Genre: Drama, Mecha, Romance.

> The Mu are invaders, but they looked and act exactly like humans for the most part. When they attack with their Doloms (giant animated machines), Tokyo is cut off from most of the rest of the world and kept under the Mu's control. Ayato is a teenager haunted by a young woman who keeps appearing in his art. When she appears in his life, though, Ayato finds himself learning things he never would have imagined. Haruka has a connection with him even though he doesn't recognize her at first. With her help, Ayato will find

himself in a role where he can change the world and may even be able to save it.

Romantic Comedy

Ai Yori Aoshi. Geneon, 2002. 24 25-Min. Episodes. 5 Discs. T Genre: Drama, Romantic Comedy.

Kaoru has been living the life of an ordinary college student on his own. However, everything changes when a face from his past returns. Her name is Aoi, and she is there to be his wife. And that's only the beginning of the changes in Kaoru's life. Now living in a mansion that's doubling as a boarding house with Aoi as the landlady, Kaoru finds himself surrounded by women, and most of them are interested in Kaoru.

Ai Yori Aoshi: Enishi. Geneon, 2004. 12 27-Min. Episodes. 3 Discs. T Genre: Drama, Romantic Comedy.

It's been two years since Kaoru and Aoi were reunited, and things haven't changed too much. Aoi is still acting as landlady, and Kaoru is now in graduate school. Life has gone back to normal—or as normal as things ever get for these two.

Science Fiction

Darker than Black. Funimation, 2009–2010. 26 25-Min. Episodes. 6 Discs. Also Available in 4-Disc Set. O Genre: Science Fiction, Supernatural.

Ten years ago, Hell's Gate appeared in Tokyo, and the stars were replaced with false ones. Now each star represents a Contractor. Contractors have special abilities; however, they come at the cost of the contractor's humanity. But Hei is not your typical contractor. He has the powers, but he also retains his humanity. Hei works for the Syndicate, a mysterious organization, but he has started to question just what his role in the world is, and that might change the fate of more than one person.

The Galaxy Railways. Funimation, 2008. 26 25-Min. Episodes. 6 Discs. T Genre: Action, Science Fiction.

People travel the stars on the Galaxy Railways, and the Space Defense Force protects those who ride. Manabu follows his brother and his father into the SDF and races towards his destiny.

Outlaw Star. Bandai, 1999. 26 25-Min. Episodes. 6 Discs. O Genre: Science Fiction.

Gene Starwind is a bounty hunter with dreams. When a job lands him and his partner, Jim, with an experimental space ship and a strange girl named Melfina, they find they might be in over their heads. But these outlaws aren't about to let that stop them.

Slice of Life

Shrine of the Morning Mist. Anime Works, 2002. 26 12.5-Min. Episodes. 3 Discs. **T** Genre: Comedy, Magical Girl, Slice of Life.

Yuzu has been looking forward to her cousin Hiro's return to her life. The catch is that Hiro just happens to be the target of demons, and Yuzu comes from a family of priestesses. In order to protect Hiro, a club forms at school to fight demons. But can Yuzu manage school, demons, and a crush on Hiro?

Supernatural

Devil May Cry. Funimation, 2008. 12 25-Min. Episodes. 3 Discs. **O** Genre: Action, Horror, Supernatural.

Dante is a particular sort of bounty hunter. He's the man you go to if you have problems that can't be dealt with by normal means. Dante hunts demons, and if he can't deal with them, then the world is definitely in trouble.

Hellsing. Geneon, 2005. 13 23-Min. Episodes. 4 Discs. **O T** Genre: Action, Supernatural.

England has a secret organization to protect the country from vampires and other supernatural threats. Hellsing has secretly protected the country for years now, and its current head, Sir Integra Hellsing, continues the tradition. Integra also has a secret weapon in her arsenal: Alucard. An ancient vampire armed with silver bullets is just the thing to deal with any problems one might have. Seras Victoria is a stray that Alucard has just happened to turn into a vampire. Now she finds herself in a world she doesn't understand. But Seras will have to learn quickly if she wishes to survive.

Hellsing Ultimate. Geneon, 2006–2008. Funimation, 2008–. Ongoing Series. 10 50-Min. Episodes. **M** Genre: Action, Supernatural.

It is Hellsing's sworn duty to protect England and its people from supernatural threats. Run by Sir Integra Hellsing, the organization has one major ace up its sleeve: Alucard. Alucard is an ancient vampire now bound to Integra's will. And the two of them take threats from vampires, other supernatural creatures, and foreign agencies very seriously. This is a good thing as the war against the evil in the world has just stepped up into high gear. This OVA series is still in production with 10 volumes planned. Episodes 5 through 7 are slated to be released by Funimation in 2011.

Read or Die. Aniplex USA, 2003. 90 Min. 1 Disc. **O** Genre: Action, Comedy, Spy, Supernatural.

Yomiko, a young book lover, is also known as Agent Paper. She has the ability to manipulate paper and use it as a weapon. She is among an elite group of agents, and this time, the assignment is personal. A rare Beethoven manuscript has been stolen right out of Yomiko's hands. To make matters worse, that particular manuscript contains a piece of music that could kill whoever hears it. But friends may actually be foes, and Yomiko will have her work cut out for her if she wants to save the world.

Witch Hunter Robin. Bandai, 2006. 26 25-Min. Episodes. 6 Discs. **O** Genre: Detective, Mystery, Supernatural.

The STN-J is the Japanese branch of an organization that hunts witches. Using craft users who have unusual powers, they protect the unknowing public from danger. When young Robin is sent to the STN-J to replace an agent, however, things begin to take an interesting turn. Robin commands the power of fire, and since she has arrived events are taking some interesting turns.

XXXHolic. Funimation, 2010. 24 25-Min. Episodes. 4 Discs. **T** Genre: Comedy, Psychological, Supernatural.

Kimihiro Watanuki is not your normal high school student. He sees ghosts and spirits. When he stumbles upon a witch named Yuko, it seems like a godsend. Yuko grants wishes, for a price. In return for taking away his abilities to see the supernatural, Watanuki has to work for Yuko at her shop. It will be a job like nothing he has ever experienced before.

1

2

3

4

5

6

7

Chapter 4

Josei Manga and Anime

Josei manga were originally marketed toward adult women. They tend to deal with more mature topics and issues than Shojo manga and often have older characters. Josei manga most often have an emphasis on romance. While they are a smaller market than some of the other demographics in Japan, Josei manga has a wide variety of titles. Currently Josei manga are the least available of the types of manga published in North America. While there have been a number of titles published, there is a far more limited selection than is found from the other categories of manga. The titles in this section are organized by their main genre, though all of the genre that a title fits into are included.

Josei Manga

- From Japan

- Marketed toward adult women

- Read right to left

- Often have an emphasis on romance

Josei Manga

Action

<u>Maiden Rose</u>. **Written and Illustrated by Fusanosuke Inariya. DMP, 2010–. Ongoing Series. 4 Vol. M Genre: Action, Adventure, Drama, Romance, War, Yaoi.**
The young aristocrat, Taki, is caught between duty and love just as war breaks out. Claus has sworn himself to be Taki's knight, binding the two of them together. Now they must survive both war and their own relationship, with both the fate of countries and their own hearts on the line.

Vassalord. Written and Illustrated by Nanae Chrono. Tokyopop, 2008–. Ongoing Series. 4 Vol. **O** Genre: Action, Fantasy, Supernatural, Yaoi.

> Charley just happens to be a cyborg vampire who works for the Vatican. His master, Johnny, is something of a playboy. The two of them don't exactly get along, but together they fight crime, mysterious enemies, and their own feelings.

Yellow. Written and Illustrated by Makoto Tateno. DMP, 2005–2006. 4 Vol. 2 Omnibus Vol. **M** Genre: Action, Romance, Yaoi.

> Taki and Goh share an apartment as well as the job of being elite drug curriers. However, Goh's falling for his partner, and that might cause some problems for the two of them. Not to mention the fact that Taki's past just might cause them both some problems when it catches up with him. This series is also available in omnibus form.

Adventure

Legend of Chun Hyang. Written and Illustrated by CLAMP. Tokyopop, 2004. 1 Vol. **T** Genre: Adventure, Fantasy, Historical.

> Chun Hyang is a young woman skilled in martial arts. When corrupt officials take advantage of her family, Chun Hyang is determined to save her mother, and with her actions, a legend will begin.

Comedy

Bunny Drop. Written and Illustrated by Yumi Unita. Yen Press, 2010–. Ongoing Series. 8 Vol. **T** Genre: Comedy, Drama.

> When he goes home for his grandfather's funeral, Daikichi is shocked to find that his grandfather has an illegitimate daughter named Rin, and no one knows who her mother is. And when no one else in the family is willing to take the girl in, Daikichi decides that he'll raise Rin, despite the fact that he is a bachelor and has no experience with children.

Camera, Camera, Camera. Written and Illustrated by Kazura Matsumoto. DMP, 2007–2008. 2 Vol. **O** Genre: Comedy, Romance, Yaoi.

> Akira's a pretty average teenager who's in love with his stepbrother, Satoru. However, when a photographer takes a job at his school, Akira finds himself drawn to the man. But romantic complications abound, and Akira might not be ready to give up on Satoru and move on to someone new.

Drama

All My Darling Daughters. Written and Illustrated by Fumi Yoshinaga. VIZ Media, LLC, 2010. 1 Vol. **O** Genre: Drama.

> All My Darling Daughters is a collection of five short stories exploring the relationship of Yukiko, business woman in her 30s, and her mother, with whom she still lives.

Antique Bakery. Written and Illustrated by Fumi Yoshinaga. DMP, 2005–2006. 4 Vol. **O** Genre: Comedy, Drama.

> When a new bakery opens in a former antique shop, there's more than just baking going on. There is a variety of chemistry between the staff, and it is unclear what the results will be. Winner of the Kodansha Award.

Don't Blame Me. Written and Illustrated by Yugi Yamada. DMP, 2008. 1 Vol. **M** Genre: Drama, Romance, Yaoi.

> Makoto idolizes his cousin Toshi. But it seems now that Toshi has given up his aspirations to make movies. Makoto gets a glimpse into his cousin's past through Toshi's old high school film club movies, and the story of friendship and love there might not be over with quite yet.

FAKE. Written and Illustrated by Sanami Matoh. Tokyopop, 2003–2004. 7 Vol. **O** **T** Genre: Drama, Yaoi. Related Anime: *FAKE*.

> Ryo and Dee are New York cops with rather opposite personalities. Still, the pair have chemistry, and they seem to have success as crime fighting partners. Is that all they are, or is there something more brewing between the pair?

Nana. Written and Illustrated by Ai Yazawa. VIZ Media, LLC, 2005–. Ongoing Series. 21 Vol. **O** Genre: Drama, Romance. Related Anime: *Nana*.

> When two women with the same first name on the train meet, it is the beginning of a friendship. Both Nana Komatsu and Nana Osaki are heading to Tokyo, and while they are opposites in many ways, they hit it off. They end up sharing an apartment together, and with one another's support, they face life and its challenges as they search for fame, love, and happiness. This series is currently on hiatus. Winner of the Shogakukun Award.

Necratoholic. Written and Illustrated by Maguro Wasabi. DMP, 2008. 1 Vol. **M** Genre: Drama, Romance, Supernatural, Yaoi.

> Sakuya is a vampire with a problem. He can no longer drink blood. Ever since the vampire hunter, Atsumi, forced Sakuya to drink his blood, Sakuya has been unable to drink human blood. Atsumi enjoys playing cat and mouse with Sakuya, but is there something more between the two of them than just hunter and hunted.

Suppli. Written and Illustrated by Mari Okazaki. Tokyopop, 2007–. 7 Vol. **M** Genre: Drama, Romance.

> When Minami's boyfriend of seven years dumps her, she finds herself rather at a loss. As she begins to create a new life for herself, Minami gets a chance to rediscover love and her social life.

Truly Kindly. Written and Illustrated by Fumi Yoshinaga. Blu Manga, 2007. 1 Vol. **M** Genre: Drama, Romance, Yaoi.

> A collection of short romantic stories set in a number of different time periods. Characters from another of Yoshinaga's books appear in one of the stories.

Walkin' Butterfly. Written and Illustrated by Chihiro Tamaki. Aurora, 2007–2008. 4 Vol. **O** Genre: Drama.

Michiko has never really felt too comfortable in her own skin. She's too tall and has what's typically considered a guy's job. However, when she's mistaken for a model while delivering pizza to a fashion show, Michiko finds herself challenged to overcome her insecurities and really find a place of her own in the world.

White Brand. Written and Illustrated by Youka Nitta. DMP, 2008. 1 Vol. **M** Genre: Drama, Romance, Yaoi.

White Brand is a collection of short stories with characters challenging convention and expectations in order to have the lives they want and the relationships that are important to them.

With the Light: Raising an Autistic Child. Written and Illustrated by Keiko Tobe. Yen Press, 2007–. 8 Vol. **T** Genre: Drama.

Sachiko Azuma's newborn son had an auspicious start by being born at sunrise. However, soon it becomes clear that Hikaru is not quite the same as other children his age, and he is diagnosed with autism. But Sachiko is determined to raise Hikaru to be both happy and part of society despite the difficulties they face.

Historical Fiction

Garden Dreams. Written and Illustrated by Fumi Yoshinaga. DMP, 2007. 1 Vol. **T** Genre: Drama, Historical Fiction, Romance.

A pair of brothers who make their living as traveling bards come across a baron haunted by past memories. Can the brothers bring the baron peace and hope with their music or will they bring his painful memories to the surface?

Lovers in the Night. Written and Illustrated by Fumi Yoshinaga. Blu Manga, 2007. 1 Vol. **M** Genre: Historical Fiction, Romance, Yaoi.

As a young man Claude became a servant in the household of a French aristocrat. Now he serves the only remaining family member, a young man named Antoine. Claude finds himself responsible for taking care of Antoine and making sure he behaves as a gentlemen should. But as the two of them become closer, a forbidden love also begins to grow.

Ōoku: The Inner Chambers. Written and Illustrated by Fumi Yoshinaga. VIZ Media, LLC, 2009–. Ongoing Series. 5 Vol. **M** Genre: Historical Fiction, Romance.

In Edo period Japan, an epidemic has hit the country's men. Within 80 years, 75 percent of the male population was dead. Society has become matriarchal. Only the Shogun can afford to have a harem of handsome men at her beck and call. These are known as Ōoku. Winner of the Shogakukun Award and Tezuka Osamu Cultural Award.

Romance

<u>Don't Say Any More, Darling</u>. **Written and Illustrated by Fumi Yoshinaga. DMP, 2007. 1 Vol. M Genre: Drama, Romance, Yaoi.**

Don't Say Any More, Darling is a collection of several short stories exploring the bittersweet nature of relationships and love.

<u>Hero Heel</u>. **Written and Illustrated by Makoto Tateno. DMP, 2006–2008. 3 Vol. M Genre: Drama, Romance, Yaoi.**

An aspiring actor, Minami isn't really that thrilled about his latest job, the hero on a superhero TV show. However, his new coworker, Sawada, is making him much more interested in the role. But Minami can't tell if Sawada actually cares or if this is just a step on the show business ladder for him, and its clear that their relationship has started to affect their acting. Whatever the end result, it is a job that Minami will not soon forget.

<u>Honey and Clover</u>. **Written and Illustrated by Chica Umino. VIZ Media, LLC, 2008–2010. 10 Vol. O Genre: Comedy, Drama, Romance. Related Anime:** *Honey and Clover, Honey and Clover II.*

Life at art college is pretty typical for the students. They worry about getting to class on time, getting dinner, and getting their assignments done. Then Hagumi Hanamoto arrives, and things start getting complicated. Love, friendship, and life are never easy. Winner of the Kodansha Award.

<u>Ichigenme . . . The First Class Is Civil Law</u>. **Written and Illustrated by Fumi Yoshinaga. 801, 2007. 2 Vol. M Genre: Romance, Yaoi.**

When Tamiya starts his new seminar at university, he doesn't expect to be kissed by another guy at the launch party. But Tohdou, the guy who kisses him, proves to be intriguing, and Tamiya strikes up an odd friendship with him. Are they just friends as Tamiya insists, or perhaps is something more developing between the two of them?

<u>Little Butterfly</u>. **Written and Illustrated by Hinako Takanaga. DMP, 2006. 3 Vol. 1 Omnibus Vol. M Genre: Drama, Romance, Yaoi.**

When Kojima decides that he will befriend the loner, Nakahara, neither of them expects the friendship or the love that blossoms. However, Nakahara's family may just tear them apart if they can't find a way to spread their own wings and fly.

<u>The Moon and the Sandals</u>. **Written and Illustrated by Fumi Yoshinaga. DMP, 2007. 2 Vol. M Genre: Romance, Yaoi.**

Love is always complicated, especially when it involves a student and a teacher. But when Kobayashi confesses to his teacher Mr. Ida, it will cause both of them to take a look at their lives and where love fits in.

Paradise Kiss. Written and Illustrated by Ai Yazawa. Tokyopop, 2002–2004. 5 Vol. ◙ Genre: Drama, Romance. Related Anime: *Paradise Kiss.*

> Yukari's life is not much more than studying for her college entrance exams and doing well in school. However, the second they meet her, the fashion designers of Paradise Kiss want Yukari to be their model. It certainly would bring a little more excitement and color to her life, but balancing school and modeling may be a challenge she doesn't expect.

Solfege. Written and Illustrated by Fumi Yoshinaga. DMP, 2007. 1 Vol. ◙ Genre: Drama, Romance, Yaoi.

> Kugayama is a gifted teacher of music without much ambition. When he meets Azuma, a gifted student who needs some help preparing for entrance exams, he suddenly finds himself much more interested in life again. Both Azuma and Kugayama find themselves drawn to one another. But with a forbidden relationship and future plans that could tear them apart, what will become of either one of them is unknown.

Tramps Like Us. Written and Illustrated by Yayoi Ogawa. Tokyopop, 2004–2008. 14 Vol. ◙ Genre: Comedy, Romance.

> Sumire's life has gone downhill lately, from her fiancé leaving her to being demoted at work. When she stumbles across a homeless young man, Sumire ends up taking him in and calling him Momo. There's something about him that makes her feel better despite the chaos of the rest of her life, but when an old crush of Sumire's comes back into her life, things may change between them. Winner of the Kodansha Award.

Romantic Comedy

Butterflies, Flowers. Written and Illustrated by Yuki Yoshihara. VIZ Media, LLC, 2009–. 8 Vol. Ⓜ Genre: Romantic Comedy.

> Choko was born into a wealthy family who has lost just about everything, thanks to the downturn of the economy. So she has joined the work force. Unfortunately for her, Choko's new boss does not seem like a very kind person. However, Choko and Domoto have a shared past that Choko hasn't quite remembered. Their working relationship might be the first step into something more, or maybe Choko would be better off just finding a new job.

Slice of Life

Gente: The People of Ristorante Paradiso. Written and Illustrated by Natsume Ono. VIZ Media, LLC, 2010. 3 Vol. ◙ Genre: Slice of Life, Romance.

> A continuation of *Ristorante Paradiso, Gente* provides the stories of Casetta dell'Orso's staff. From to the beginning of the restaurant to its current day, these are its stories.

<u>Ristorante Paradiso</u>. **Written and Illustrated by Natsume Ono. VIZ Media, LLC, 2010. 1 Vol. O Genre: Romance, Slice of Life.**

> At age 21, Nicoletta sets off to Italy to reunite with her mother, Olga. She ends up working at the restaurant owned by Olga's new husband. Life working at Casetta dell'Orso is interesting, and it will provide Nicoletta the opportunity to learn both about herself and the mother she never really knew.

Josei Anime

Drama

<u>FAKE</u>. **Anime Works, 2006. 60 Min. 1 Disc. T Genre: Drama, Yaoi.**

> Ryo and Dee are New York cops with rather opposite personalities. Still, the pair have chemistry, and they seem to have success as crime fighting partners. The two of them are supposed to be having a relaxing vacation in England. However, when they stumble across a murder investigation, their vacation may not turn out to be so relaxing after all.

<u>Nana</u>. **VIZ Media, LLC, 2006. 47 24-Min. Episodes. 12 Discs in 4 Sets. O Genre: Drama, Romance.**

> When two women with the same first name on the train to Tokyo meet, it is the beginning of a friendship. Both Nana Komatsu and Nana Osaki are opposites in many ways, but they soon hit it off. They end up sharing an apartment together, and with one another's support, they face life and its challenges as they search for fame, love, and happiness.

Romance

<u>Honey and Clover</u>. **VIZ Media, LLC, 2005. 36 23-Min. Episodes. 9 Discs in 3 Sets. O Genre: Comedy, Drama, Romance.**

> Life at art college is pretty typical for the students. They worry about getting to class on time, getting dinner, and getting their assignments done. They're almost always broke and scraping together the means to survive, but with friends and classmates around, everyone tends to manage. Then Hagumi Hanamoto arrives, and things start getting complicated. Love, friendship, and life are never easy.

<u>Paradise Kiss</u>. **Geneon, 2005. 12 25-Min. Episodes. 3 Discs. O Genre: Drama, Romance.**

> Yukari's life is not much more than studying for her college entrance exams and doing well in school. However, the second they meet her, the fashion designers of Paradise Kiss want Yukari to be their model. It certainly would bring a little more excitement and color to her life, and Yukari may find that there's far more to life than she's been experiencing.

Chapter **5**

Manhwa

Manhwa (pronounced mahn-hwah) are Korean comics. While they are a more recent import than manga, they have quickly gained popularity and are now commonly found in the graphic novel sections of bookstores and libraries. They can sometimes be mistaken for manga and are even sometimes labeled as such according to the marketing practices of some publishers. While there are some similarities in format and style between manga and manhwa, they also each have their own particular style.

Like English works, manhwa read left to right. The art style is often a little more realistic than is found in manga, and the characters in manhwa often show more of an Asian ethnicity in their features rather than the more generic-looking manga characters. Probably the easiest way of differentiating between manga and manhwa, however, is looking at the name of the creator and the characters. Korean names and Japanese names look quite different. Like manga, manhwa encompass a variety of genres. Titles in this section are organized in alphabetical order and are tagged with all relevant genres.

Manhwa

- From Korea

- Read left to right

- Often realistic in art style

Angel Cup. Written by Dong Wook Kim. Illustrated by Jae-Ho Youn. Tokyopop, 2006–2007. 5 Vol. ▉T Genre: Action, Adventure, Sports.
So-jin sees Shin-bee as her rival, even if Shin-bee is more interested in coaching the boys' soccer team. In order to challenge her rival, So-jin decides to put together a girls' soccer team. However, putting together her own team may be more of a challenge than So-jin expects.

Angel Diary. Written by YunHee Lee. Illustrated by Kara. Yen Press, 2005–2010. 13 Vol. **T** Genre: Fantasy, Romance.

High school student Dong-Young isn't quite who he seems. In fact, he just happens to actually be the Princess of Heaven. Determined to avoid her arranged marriage to the King of Hell, she ran away to Earth and disguised herself as a boy. However, four guardians have been sent to find her and bring her back. There are dangers on Earth as well, and she might not be the only one with secrets.

The Antique Gift Shop. Written and Illustrated by Eun Lee. Yen Press, 2005–. Ongoing Series. 10 Vol. **T** Genre: Horror, Mystery, Romance.

Bun-Nyuh has become the new proprietor of an antique shop, thanks to her grandmother. But it's an interesting store where it almost seems as if the items choose the buyer rather than the other way around. Bun-Nyuh isn't sure what to make of this as she's not superstitious. Perhaps the question, is does she believe in destiny?

Banya: The Explosive Delivery Man. Written and Illustrated by Kim Young-Oh. Dark Horse, 2006–2007. 5 Vol. **T** Genre: Action, Adventure.

Banya's an unstoppable delivery man. He has no real loyalty except to the Gaya Desert Post Office motto: "Fast. Precise. Secure." If you need something delivered, he's your man. Nothing is going to stop him, and he'll do just about anything to make his deliveries.

Bird Kiss. Written and Illustrated by Eun Ah Park. Tokyopop, 2006–2007. 5 Vol. **T** Genre: Comedy, Romance.

Miyoul is in love with Guelin, probably the most popular boy at her school. However, her next-door neighbor, Heerack, just happens to be in love with her. In this retelling of "The Frog Prince," figuring out just who her prince is might be difficult. But Miyoul will have to figure out whom her heart belongs to before too long if she wants her happy ending.

Bride of the Water God. Written by Mi-Kyung Yun. Dark Horse, 2007–. Ongoing Series. 11 Vol. **T** Genre: Fantasy, Historical Fiction, Romance.

Desperate for an end to the drought, the people of her village sacrifice Soah to the Water God, Habaek. Soah finds herself saved by Habaek and taken to live in his palace as his bride. But things are not as they seem in the Water God's realm, and Soah finds herself falling in love with Mui, who claims to be her husband's cousin.

Bring It On!. Written and Illustrated by Baek HyeKyung. Yen Press, 2005–2008. 5 Vol. **T** Genre: Romantic Comedy.

Mi-Ha is a tomboy. In fact, she's the tomboy that all the boys at school are afraid of, thanks to her older brother's training. When a handsome new boy named Sung-Suh transfers to her school, he just might be the guy for her. However, first he's going to have to win her heart, and then he's going to have deal with her brother, and neither will be an easy task.

<u>Chocolat</u>. Written by JiSang Shin. Illustrated by Geo. Yen Press, 2005–. Ongoing Series. 7 Vol. **T** Genre: Romantic Comedy.

> Kum-Ji might be a fan of the band DDL, but she hasn't been able to join their fan club. So she comes up with a cunning plan. She'll become a member of the fan club of their main rival band, Yo-I. That way she can see DDL since the two bands seem to play at almost all of the same shows. However, pretending to be to the fan of one band when she really prefers the other may be harder than Kum-Ji expects. This series is currently on hiatus.

The Color Trilogy

<u>The Color of Earth</u>. Written and Illustrated by Kim Dong Hwa. First Second, 2009. 1 Vol. **T** Genre: Historical Fiction, Romance.

> Ehwa and her mother are the best of friends. It is just the two of them since Ehwa's father died, but they are happy together. As Ehwa grows older, she begins to feel the sparks of first love even as her mother discovers romance for the first time in years.

<u>The Color of Water</u>. Written and Illustrated by Kim Dong Hwa. First Second, 2009. 1 Vol. **T** Genre: Historical Fiction, Romance.

> As Ehwa's mother conducts her love affair, Ehwa herself begins to develop a romantic relationship of her own. For the first time Ehwa keeps secrets from her mother as she begins to take her first steps towards independence and becoming an adult.

<u>The Color of Heaven</u>. Written and Illustrated by Kim Dong Hwa. First Second, 2009. 1 Vol. **T** Genre: Historical Fiction, Romance.

> Both Ehwa and her mother wait for love to return. Ehwa waits for the return of her fiancé from his quest to earn enough money for their marriage. The trilogy draws to a close as Ehwa takes the last steps into adulthood.

<u>Comic</u>. Written and Illustrated by Ha SiHyun. Yen Press, 2006–. Ongoing Series. 8 Vol. **T** Genre: Romance.

> Alice is having quite a bit of luck lately. She just became the youngest winner of a comic contest and not only gets her own comic published, but she'll also get to work with some of the comic artists she's idolized. However, Alice may find that not everything is as she dreamed, and real life may not quite resemble what happens in a comic book.

<u>Croquis Pop</u>. Written by KwangHyun Seo. Illustrated by JinHo Ko. Yen Press, 2009–2009. 6 Vol. **T** Genre: Adventure, Supernatural.

> Da-Il's new job working for a famous comic artist would be a great opportunity except for one little problem: he has no artistic ability. However, before too long a ghost named Mu-Huk shows up. He is able take form via Da-Il's

creativity because Da-Il is a Croquer, a person with the ability to shape the stories of vengeful ghosts. Oh, and he might just be the main character in his boss's latest work.

Cynical Orange. Written and Illustrated by Yun JiUn. Yen Press, 2005–2009. 9 Vol. T Genre: Romance.

Hye-Min might be the most popular girl at her school, but that doesn't make life easier for her. While the boys all seem to love her, all the other girls are out to get her. Plus she has to hide her cynical and dark side. But when she gets rejected by the one boy she does like, Hye-Min decides that she's not playing nice any more.

Deja-Vu: Spring, Summer, Fall, Winter. Written by Youn In-wan. Illustrated by Yang Kyung-il, Yoon Seung-ki, Kim Tae-hyung, Park Sung-woo, Byun Byung-jun, and Lee Vin. Tokyopop, 2008. 1 Vol. O Genre: Romance.

Will tragic and unfulfilled love always remain so? Two lovers meet time and again, never quite managing a happy ending. Through time and space, they keep finding one another, and perhaps one time, they'll have a chance.

Demon Dairy. Written by Chi Hyong Lee (Vol. 1) and Yun Hee Lee (Vol. 2–7). Illustrated by Kara. Tokyopop, 2003–2007. 7 Vol. T Genre: Action, Adventure, Comedy, Fantasy.

Raenef is the newly appointed Demon Lord. The only problem is he just happens to be the exact opposite of what a Demon Lord should be. It is up to Eclipse, a powerful and well-known demon, to help get him ready for his duties. With Raenef, Eclipse is definitely going to have his work cut out for him.

Dokebi Bride. Written and Illustrated by Marley. Netcomics, 2006–. Ongoing Series. 6 Vol. T Genre: Drama, Romance.

Sunbi was born into a family of shamans, and like her grandmother, she can see dokebi or spirits. Her grandmother is a well-known shaman in their village and the surrounding area. But when her grandmother dies, truths that Sunbi has been protected from are revealed, and she will have to make decisions about her own path in life.

11th Cat. Written and Illustrated by MiKyung Kim. Yen Press, 2005–2008. 5 Vol. T Genre: Fantasy, Romance.

Rika is training to be a wizard. The first step is to find a magic staff. As Rika and her friend Eujen set out to do so, Rika has a chance encounter with a dark sorcerer and ends up setting off on an adventure involving a kidnapped princess. Volume 5 of this series is not numbered and is titled *11th CAT Special*.

Forest of Gray City. Written and Illustrated by Uhm JungHyun. Yen Press, 2007–2008. 2 Vol. T Genre: Romance.

Yun-Ook rents out a room to help make ends met. However, her new tenant, Bum-Moo, isn't exactly what she expected. Rather mysterious and aloof, the two of them argue most of the time. Plus there's the fact that he's only 17 and a high school dropout. But when Bum-Moo indicates he likes her, Yun-Ook finds she's not sure what to do.

Freak: Legend of the Nonblonds. Written by Yi DongEun. Illustrated by Yu Chung. Yen Press, 2006–2008. 4 Vol. **T** Genre: Action, Adventure.
Tublerun, Verna, and Lorel are the next generation of bounty hunters. Calling themselves the Nonblonds, there's nothing that these three can't or won't do for a client.

Goong. Written and Illustrated by Park So Hee. Yen Press, 2006–. Ongoing Series. 23 Vol. **T** Genre: Romantic Comedy.
Chae-Kyung is not very happy with her life. Her grandfather's friendship with the former King of Korea means she is bound to marry the current crown prince. It doesn't help that the crown prince acts likes a jerk. They are bound together despite their own wishes, and perhaps there's a chance as they get to know one another that they might find love.

Hanami: International Love Story. Written by Plus. Illustrated by Sung-Jae Park. Dark Horse, 2007–2008. 4 Vol. **T** Genre: Comedy, Romance.
Joonho was having a great day. He had just confessed to his longtime crush, Sae-un, and she agreed to go out with him. Then he learns that his family is moving to Seoul, immediately. Feeling alone in the big city, Joonho soon manages to stumble across a cute Japanese exchange student named Hanami, not to mention offend her grandfather. And that's only the beginning of his troubles.

Heavenly Executioner Chiwoo. Written by Lee HaNa. Illustrated by Park KangHo. Yen Press, 2005–2008. 5 Vol. **T** Genre: Action, Adventure.
Chiwoo has never really fit in. Rebellious and without a father, he is the town's outcast. But when his father does arrive, Chiwoo learns the secret. His father is a Mangnani, an executor who carries out God's judgment, and only his dance before a person's death tells their fate in the afterlife. However, the emperor is trying to wipe out all Mangnani, and Chiwoo's life is now in danger.

Hissing. Written by Kang EunYoung. Yen Press, 2008–2009. 6 Vol. **T** Genre: Romance.
Aspiring artist Da-Eh finds herself with two men in her life besides her father and her little brother. Sun-Nam aspires to be a tough guy while Ta-Jun is one of the best-looking guys around, even if his smile doesn't quite work on Da-Eh. She soon finds that love may not be what she expected, and all three of them are going to have to figure out their relationships.

Jack Frost. Written and Illustrated by JinHo Ko. Yen Press, 2009–. Ongoing Series. 5 Vol. **O** Genre: Action, Adventure, Comedy, Horror.
The first day at a new school can be hard for anyone. For Noh-A, her first day at Amityville High will include losing her head, literally. Noh-A is a

mirror image, a human who has died but now is immortal, and she may be in a great deal of danger as well. The mysterious Jack Frost may be the most dangerous student in the school, but he seems to be willing to help her. For now.

Kill Me, Kiss Me. **Written by Lee Young You. Tokyopop, 2004–2005. 5 Vol. O Genre: Romantic Comedy.**

When Tae Im convinces her identical cousin to trade spots with her so she can attend the same school as her favorite idol, neither of them expects to find themselves dealing with love, bullies, and some rather awkward situations.

LAON. **Written by Hyun You. Illustrated by YoungBin Kim. Yen Press, 2010–. 6 Vol. O Genre: Supernatural.**

The police discover a little boy naked and hungry. What they don't know is that he is Laon, and he really is a nine-tailed fox. Or he would be if his tails weren't missing. Laon is determined to get his tails and his powers back before anyone else gets to them.

Legend. **Written by SooJung Woo. Illustrated by Kara. Yen Press, 2008–2010. T Genre: Fantasy.**

Eun-Gyo's managed to get suspended from school for fighting. When her mom flips out because of it, she runs out. The next thing she knows, she's been kidnapped by a young man named No-Ah and whisked off to the past. Eun-Gyo is now involved with the legend of the Seven Blade Sword, and going home just yet is not an option.

Les Bijoux. **Written by Jo Eun-Ha. Illustrated by Park Sang-Sun. Tokyopop, 2004–2005. 5 Vol. O Genre: Action, Fantasy.**

In a world where the Habits rule and most must work the mines, a strange child is born. Lapis Lazuli's family are slaves, and when they are killed, Lapis vows revenge. Lapis will change the world or die in the attempt, but he won't stop until something changes.

Let Dai. **Written and Illustrated by Sooyeon Won. Netcomics, 2006–2008. 15 Vol. T Genre: Drama, Yaoi.**

Jaehee rescues a girl from a street gang and encounters Dai. Unaccountably drawn to Dai, Jaehee finds him both a friend and a tormenter, and in the end, Jaehee doesn't know if he can escape being drawn into Dai's dangerous world.

Lights Out. **Written and Illustrated by Myung-Jin Lee. Tokyopop, 2005–2008. 9 Vol. T Genre: Action, Comedy.**

Gun's a kid with a troubled past trying make a new start. He's transferred to a new school and is trying to be a good student. And he's just met a girl who has changed his life, Seung-Ah. However, a new start may not be as easy as it sounds, and the path to love is definitely rocky.

Model. Written and Illustrated by Lee So-Young. Tokyopop, 2004–2005. 7 Vol. **T** Genre: Horror, Romance, Thriller.

Jae's an aspiring art student, currently studying in Europe. When her roommate leaves a gorgeous unconscious man on the couch, her entire life changes, especially since the man then proceeds to drink her blood. However, Jae ends up striking a bargain with the man: her blood in exchange for him being her model. But is this a deal with the devil and will Jae survive it?

Moon Boy. Written and Illustrated by Lee YoungYou. Yen Press, 2006–2010. 9 Vol. **T** Genre: Action, Adventure, Fantasy, Romance.

Besides the fact that her eyes turn red at night, Myung-Ee is a pretty normal girl. When she transfers to a new school, she finds a familiar face, but Yu-Da doesn't seem to remember her at all. She has other problems as well. Myung-Ee is about to be drawn into the fight between Earth Rabbits and Moon Foxes, and it could claim her life.

Neck and Neck. Written and Illustrated by Lee Sun-Hee. Tokyopop, 2004–2007. 8 Vol. **T** Genre: Comedy, Drama.

Dabin just happens to be the daughter of Seoul's biggest crime boss, but that doesn't necessarily make things easy for her. She's got a crush on Eugene, who only thinks of her as a little sister, and the new kid in her class just happens to be the son of her father's rival. She's definitely going to have an interesting time at school, to say the least.

One. Written and Illustrated by Lee Vin. Tokyopop, 2004–2007. 11 Vol. **T** Genre: Romance.

Eumpa One is new at Daewon High School. He used to be a musical prodigy, but now he's determined to live a normal life. However, when he gets caught up in a romance involving a new teen music star, he might just end up stepping out into the spotlight again.

One Fine Day. Written and Illustrated by Sirial. Yen Press, 2010. 3 Vol. **A** Genre: Slice of Life.

Join Rang the mouse, Guru the cat, and Nanai the dog as the three of them have adventures around their home.

One Thousand and One Nights. Written by Jeon JinSeok. Illustrated by Han SeungHee. Yen Press, 2005–2010. 11 Vol. **O** Genre: Fantasy.

The tale of Shahrazad and how her stories saved her life is rather well known. However, what if she was a he? Sehara is desperate to save his sister from the sultan's harem. But can his stories save his own life or has Sehara doomed himself?

Peppermint. Written and Illustrated by Eun-Jin Seo. Tokyopop, 2006–2007. 4 Vol. **T** Genre: Romance.

Hey's got a crush on her schoolmate, the teen star EZ. However, she has horrible luck in regards to that. Not only does she end up bullied by EZ's other fans, but now some guy named EO has claimed that that she's his girlfriend. Love isn't easy, and Hey's not sure what her heart really wants.

PhD: Phantasy Degree. Written and Illustrated by Son Hee-Joon. Tokyopop, 2005–. Ongoing Series. 10 Vol. **T** Genre: Comedy, Fantasy.

Sang has decided to get herself an education at the Demon School Hades, even if means becoming a monster herself. And that will only be the beginning of her adventures. This series is currently on hiatus.

Pig Bride. Written by KookHwa Huh. Illustrated by SuJin Kim. Yen Press, 2009–2010. 5 Vol. **T** Genre: Romantic Comedy.

When he was eight years old, Si-Joon finds himself tricked into agreeing to marry Mu-Yeon, a girl who covers his face with a pig mask. Mu-Yeon tells him that they will meet again on his birthday. When that birthday finally rolls around, Mu-Yeon pops into Si-Joon's life again, and he had thought it was all a dream.

Priceless. Written and Illustrated by Young-You Lee. Tokyopop, 2006. 3 Vol. **T** Genre: Comedy, Romance.

When Lang-bee's con artist mom runs off leaving her behind, she finds herself fending for herself and trying to repay those her mom scammed. Things get even more complicated when she ends up pitted against the rich girl of her school for the heart of the same boy. What's a girl to do besides try her best?

Priest. Written and Illustrated by Min-woo Hyung. Tokyopop, 2003–2007. 16 Vol. **O** Genre: Action, Adventure, Horror, Western.

In the Wild West, minions of a fallen archangel prepare for their dark lord's return. Only one man stands in their way. The fallen priest Ivan Isaacs has sold his soul in order to put a stop to the evil that threatens humanity, and he won't stop until it is destroyed.

Raiders. Written and Illustrated by JinJun Park. Yen Press, 2009–. Ongoing Series. 6 Vol. **O** Genre: Action, Horror, Supernatural.

Irel Clark has just found the Holy Grail, and he's promptly forced to drink from it. Now he's immortal, and there seems to be a mindless horde of the undead after him in order to eat him. Immortality is certainly leaving much to be desired so far.

Real Lies. Written and Illustrated by Lee SiYoung. Yen Press, 2006. 1 Vol. **O** Genre: Science Fiction.

In three short stories, Lee SiYoung explores alternates realities and possible worlds.

Run, Bong-Gu, Run!. Written and Illustrated by Byun Byung-Jun. NBM, 2007. 1 Vol. **T** Genre: Family.

Bong-Gu and his mother arrive in Seoul in order to search for his father. With the help of an old man, they search, and they may find that new beginnings can spring from dreams unfulfilled.

Snow Drop. Written and Illustrated by Choi Kyung-Ah. Tokyopop, 2004–2006. 12 Vol. **O** Genre: Romance.

So-Na isn't exactly happy about being forced to return to school. When she meets Hae-Gi, she finds a kindred spirit. But love is not easy when both have secrets in their past that might threaten their new relationship.

Sugarholic. Written and Illustrated by Gong GooGoo. Yen Press, 2009–2010. 5 Vol. **T** Genre: Romance.

Jae-Gyu's grandmother has sent her from their small country town to the big city, and Jae-Gyu's more than a little lost. However, she quickly runs into Hee-Do, a young man she used to bully. Only now he's a rock star, and he's in the position to get some payback. But that might not be what he wants.

The Tarot Café. Written and Illustrated by Sang-Sun Park. Tokyopop, 2005–2008. 7 Vol. **T** Genre: Fantasy, Horror, Romance.

Pamela is the owner of the Tarot Café. It is after midnight when her supernatural costumers come to her for tarot card readings. From fairies to vampires to others who come to her, Pamela gives them all advice. And in payment, Pamela takes pieces of the Berial's Necklace, which she is collecting for reasons that deal with her own dark secret.

13th BOY. Written and Illustrated by SangEun Lee. Yen Press, 2009–. 12 Vol. **T** Genre: Comedy, Romance.

Hee-So really thought that Won-Jun was the one. It was love at first sight for her, and things seemed to be going well at first, but now he's dumped her. Won-Jun might have been her 12th boyfriend, but Hee-So isn't ready to move on to number 13 just yet. The real question, is can she win Won-Jun back or should she really move on to boyfriend number 13?

Totally Captivated. Written and Illustrated by Hajin Yoo. Netcomics, 2007–2009. 6 Vol. **O** Genre: Drama, Yaoi.

Ewon ends up an errand boy for a loan shark, thanks to the mafia. The gang leader in charge of him, Mookyul, can't help taking an interest in him. But Ewon also has an ex who could complicate things, and the whole situation is complicated.

Very! Very! Sweet. Written by JiSang Shin and Geo. Yen Press, 2008–2010. **T** Genre: Comedy, Romance.

As a punishment for being a spoiled brat, Tsuyoshi is told the family secret: they're Korean, not Japanese. And then his family ships him off to Korea. Coincidence has him ride in a taxi with his new next-door neighbor, Be-Ri. Sparks fly between the two of them from the start, and Tsuyoshi is going to have more than just culture shock to deal with now.

Visitor. Written and Illustrated by Yee-Jung No. Tokyopop, 2005–2007. 5 Vol. **T**
Genre: Drama, Horror.

Hyo-Bin may be the beautiful new girl at school, but she isn't all that she seems. Haunted by terrifying nightmares, she is beginning to have trouble during the daytime as well. Are her dreams going to be reality or does she really have a chance for a new start at this school?

You're So Cool. Written and Illustrated by YoungHee Lee. Yen Press, 2008–2010.
6 Vol. T Genre: Romantic Comedy.

Seung-Ha is considered the prince of the school, and just about everyone wants him or wants to be him. Nan-Woo has never really thought she had a chance with him. However, when he asks her out, it seems like a dream come true. What she doesn't expect is that outside of school, Seung-Ha's something of a jerk. Does her dream really have a chance of coming true or is Nan-Woo on the road to heartbreak?

Chapter 6

Manhua

Chinese comics or manhua (pronounced mahn-hwah) are the least well known of the three types of Asian graphic novels. The comic industry in China also is not as big as it is in Japan and Korea. Manhua are the least available Asian graphic novel form in North America, with only a very small pool of titles having been published in English. Like manga, manhua read right to left. Manhua do come from mainland China, but they often come from Taiwan or Hong Kong as well. Manhua comes in full color at times as well as in black and white. Titles in this section are simply arranged in alphabetical order and are tagged with all of the relevant genres.

Manhua

- From mainland China, Hong Kong, and Taiwan

- Read right to left

- Appear both in full color and in black and white

Chinese Hero: Tales of the Blood Sword. Written by Ding Kin Lau. Illustrated by Wing Shing Ma. DrMaster, 2007–2008. 8 Vol. **T** Genre: Martial Arts.
> When Hero was a child, his family was attacked and killed in an attempt to steal the family's heirloom, the Blood Sword. Hero has dedicated his life to mastering kung fu and protecting the sword. But when old enemies turn their attention to his new family, Hero is more than willing to take up the fight.

Crouching Tiger, Hidden Dragon. Written by Wang Du Lu. Illustrated by Andy Seto. ComicsOne, 2005–2006. 13 Vol. **T** Genre: Martial Arts, Romance.
> Martial arts masters Shu Lien and Li Mu Bai journey throughout China fighting both enemies and their own feelings.

Hero. Written by Zhang Yimou and Wing Shing Ma. Illustrated by Wing Shing Ma. ComicsOne, 2005. 1 Vol. **T** Genre: Martial Arts.

The king of Qin has just survived an assassination attempt. He has declared that no one may approach him any closer than 100 steps. However, a nameless man comes to the king with a story, and as he weaves his story, it may lead to a surprising conclusion.

The History of the West Wing. Written by Sun Jiayu. Illustrated by Guo Guo. Yen Press, 2009. 1 Vol. **T** Genre: Romance.

Lady Pianpian has fallen in love with Chen, a wandering scholar. But in his current occupation, Chen can't hope to aspire to her hand in marriage. Furthermore, her mother's approval must be won or the two lovers will be kept apart forever.

An Ideal World. Written by Weidong Chen. Illustrated by Chao Peng. Yen Press, 2009. 1 Vol. **T** Genre: Action, Adventure, Fantasy.

A You chases rabbits in his dreams, and once he wakes up, his day goes from bad to worse. However, when he spots another rabbit, following it may lead him to some of the answers A You is looking for.

Orange. Written and Illustrated by Benjamin. Tokyopop, 2009. 1 Vol. **T** Genre: Drama.

Orange doesn't think she has anything to live for. Standing on a rooftop, she meets a young man who might just change her life.

The Other Side of the Mirror. Written and Illustrated by Jo Chen. Tokyopop, 2007–2008. 2 Vol. **O** Genre: Romantic Comedy.

Both Sunny and Lou have hit low points in their lives. But their meeting one night turns into an unexpected love. Can they really manage to find a happily ever after, or is life really as dismal as it seemed when they first met?

Real/Fake Princess. Written and Illustrated by I-Haun. DrMaster, 2006–2007. 5 Vol. **A** Genre: Historical Fiction, Romance.

During the Jin Kang Rebellion, a concubine managed to smuggle Princess Yi Fu out of the palace and put her under the care of a man named Tang Hui. From there, both of the princess and her new guardian disappear. Ten years later there is peace again, and a search begins for the lost princess.

Wild Animals. Written and Illustrated by Song Yang. Yen Press, 2008–2009. 2 Vol. **O** Genre: Drama, Historical Fiction, Romance.

At age 16, Ma Xiaojun is coming of age during the Cultural Revolution. He rebels against the system with his friends, but he has a solitary side as well. As he becomes obsessed with keys and with an untouchable young woman named Mi Lan, he struggles with growing up and all that it entails, wondering if he'll ever be able to unlock the mysteries that plague him the most.

Chapter 7

Resources

There are quite a number of print resources on anime and manga available these days. They range in tone from scholarly to instructional, for those who know nothing about manga or anime. Much is available, from guides to the various formats to extensive histories of them. Unfortunately, at this point, there are no print resources for either manhwa or manhua. Entries in this section are arranged by title.

Anime: From Akira to Howl's Moving Castle. **Written by Susan J. Napier. Palgrave, 2005.**

This scholarly work on anime and Japanese culture is accessible to adult and teen audiences. There is also an earlier edition titled *Anime: From Akira to Princess Mononoke*. There are only slight differences in the two editions, and both are valuable additions to a collection.

Anime Explosion!: The What? Why? and Wow! of Japanese Animation. **Written by Patrick Drazen. Stone Bridge Press, 2003.**

Anime Explosion provides a general guide to anime. The first half of the book looks at the history, conventions, and themes in anime, while the second half focuses on specific films, TV series, and directors of anime. Material in the first half can also apply to manga as well as anime.

Anime and Manga: The Complete Guide. **Written by Wiki Editors. Transactual Systems, 2010.**

This book is a collection of Wikipedia articles relating to manga and anime. It includes information on publishing companies, biographies, and the fandom. It provides references for much of its information as well as the sources for the articles.

Manga: The Complete Guide. **Written by Jason Thompson. Del Rey, 2007.**

This book is a collection of all the reviews for manga published in North America up until the date of publication. It includes in-depth explanations of manga genres and a glossary of common anime and manga terms as well as a bibliography.

Manga: Sixty Years of Japanese Comics. **Written by Paul Gravett. Laurence King, 2004.**

> This look at the history of manga from 1945 is accessible to most adult audiences. Many visual examples are presented throughout the book.

Manga! Manga!: The World of Japanese Comics. **Written by Federik L. Schodt. Kodansha International, 1983.**

> A scholarly work on manga, this book is older and slightly out of date in some regards. However, it provides very useful information and groundwork on manga and Japanese pop culture, even if it does not cover more recent trends and series of manga. It is also one of the best early scholarly works on manga and is accessible to most audiences.

One Thousand Years of Manga. **Written by Brigitte Koyama-Richard. Flammarion, 2007.**

> Koyama-Richard looks at manga from its earliest roots in Japanese art to its current form. The book includes a glossary, timeline, chronology, bibliography, and selected interviews.

The Rough Guide to Anime: Japan's Finest from Ghibli to Gankutsuo. **Written by Simon Richmond. Rough Guides, 2008.**

> This introduction and guide to anime includes information on how anime is created and connections to manga. It also includes a glossary and a list of 50 anime.

Samurai from Outer Space: Understanding Japanese Animation. **Written by Antonia Levi. Open Court, 1996.**

> *Samurai from Outer Space* provides introduction to anime for those who are not familiar with it. While slightly dated, the book is very accessible and provides a good introduction to anime. Much of the information in the book applies to manga as well as anime.

Understanding Manga and Anime. **Written by Robin E. Brenner. Libraries Unlimited, 2007.**

> An extensive guide to anime and manga, this title provides all sorts of information from common conventions to bibliographies and program samples. It is geared for a library audience, but is accessible to a general audience as well.

Appendix

The Films of Studio Ghibli

Studio Ghibli is known for its stunning and beautiful films. Created by Hayao Miyazaki and Isao Takahata, Studio Ghibli is responsible for some of the most beloved Japanese films. The films appeal to an audience across generations. They are beautiful to watch and tell intriguing and delightful stories. Hayao Miyazaki is responsible for many of the films, either as director or screen writer, and his *Spirited Away* is the only non-American film to win an Oscar for Best Animated Feature to date. Studio Ghibli's works make for a very good introduction to some of the best of anime and provide a wonderful contribution to a library's anime collection. The annotations in this section are listed in chronological order and include the director of each film.

Princess Mononoke. **Directed by Hayao Miyazaki. Studio Ghibli, Miramax, 2000. 134 Minutes Long. 1 Disc.** T

> In the process of saving his village from an enraged boar god, Ashitaka also finds himself cursed. He is informed that his curse will kill him and soon. However, he is advised to seek out the place where the boar came from and to see with "eyes unclouded by hate." So Ashitaka sets off on a journey that that will lead him to two women clashing on opposite sides of a battle. Lady Eboshi runs Iron Town while San lives with the wolves that raised her and defends the forest from those who wish to mine the iron beneath it. Can Ashitaka forge peace between the two factions or will his curse kill him first?

Spirited Away. **Directed by Hayao Miyazaki. Studio Ghibli, Disney/Buena Vista, 2001. 125 Minutes Long. 1 Disc.** Y

> A shortcut on their way to their new home takes Chihiro and her parents to what looks like an abandoned theme park. Things get even stranger when her parents get turned into pigs. With the help of the mysterious Haku, Chihiro manages to secure work at the bathhouse from the witch Yubaba, but Chihiro has to give up her name in the process. Now known as Sen, she must try to find a way to save both herself and her parents and get the three of them home. *Spirited Away* won Best Animated Feature 2002.

Castle in the Sky. **Directed by Hayao Miyazaki. Studio Ghibli, Disney/Buena Vista, 2003. 125 Minutes Long. 2 Discs.** Y

Pazu's life changes when a girl falls out of the sky and into his arms. Her name is Sheeta, and she's being chased by both pirates and government agents. Deciding to help Sheeta pulls Pazu into an adventure like no other, as the two try to reach the mysterious castle in the sky known as Laputa before anyone else and unravel its secrets.

Kiki's Delivery Service. **Directed by Hayao Miyazaki. Studio Ghibli, Disney/Buena Vista, 2003. 103 Minutes Long. 2 Discs.** A

Finally 13 years old, it's time for Kiki to take off and leave home in order to spend a year on her own as an apprentice witch. However, Kiki finds that making a home and a place for herself is harder than she thought, especially since her only magical skill is the ability to fly. But as she makes some new friends and starts her own business, Kiki may find that her own magic is more than enough as long as she believes in herself.

The Cat Returns. **Directed by Hiroyuki Morita. Studio Ghibli, Disney/Buena Vista, 2005. 75 Minutes Long. 2 Discs.** Y

Haru's bad day culminates with her nearly getting run over in order to save a cat. When the cat actually thanks her, Haru thinks she might be delusional. But that night the King of the Cat Kingdom visits her to inform her of her reward, including that she is now to marry his son. Desperate for help, Haru turns to Baron and his friends for assistance at the Cat Bureau. Together with Baron, Haru hopes to be able to escape the fate that she accidentally brought upon herself.

My Neighbors the Yamadas. **Directed by Isao Takahata. Studio Ghibli, Disney/Buena Vista, 2005. 104 Minutes Long. 2 Discs.** Y

Even the most ordinary of life's events is always interesting with the Yamada family. Takashi, Mitsuko, Shige, Nonoko, and Noboru might not always get along, but they'll always be a family.

Nausicaä of the Valley of the Wind. **Directed by Hayao Miyazaki. Studio Ghibli, Disney/Buena Vista, 2005. 117 Minutes Long. 2 Discs.** Y

The world has become so polluted that toxic jungles cover the planet and large insects roam the world. Much of the air is filled with poisonous spores. But the Valley of the Wind is a safe haven, and its princess, Nausicaä, has a talent for understanding and empathizing with the animals of her world. When invaders from the Kingdom of Tolmekia enter her valley, Nausicaä is in a race against time to make allies, maybe forge a fragile peace, and perhaps unlock the secrets to save their world.

Pom Poko. **Directed by Isao Takahata. Studio Ghibli, Disney/Buena Vista, 2005. 119 Minutes Long. 2 Discs.** Y

When a new suburb development of Tokyo threatens the home of the Tanuki, mischievous raccoon spirits, they decide to fight back. Under the guidance of several wise old Tanuki, the young raccoons begin to learn how to transform and study the humans who threaten them. But is it a hopeless cause or can they find a place in modern Japan?

Porco Rosso. **Directed by Hayao Miyazaki. Studio Ghibli, Disney/Buena Vista, 2005. 94 Minutes Long. 2 Discs. Y**

In the skies above the Adriatic Sea, sky planes rule, and Porco Rosso is a well-known bounty hunter. Once an Italian military ace, Porco now is a man-sized pig as well as one of the best seaplane pilots in the area. He takes on jobs hunting down the pirates that plague the skies and spends his downtime either on his island or visiting the famous Hotel Adriano. When a new American ace challenges Porco, he may be in the flight of his life.

Howl's Moving Castle. **Directed by Hayao Miyazaki. Studio Ghibli, Disney/ Buena Vista, 2006. 119 Minutes Long. 2 Discs. Y**

Sophie's life working at her late father's hat shop is quite ordinary up until the day she is cursed by the Witch of the Waste. Now looking like a 90-year-old woman, Sophie sets off on her own. She finds herself in the wizard Howl's famous castle and makes a deal with the fire demon Calcifer to try and break the agreement that binds Howl and Calcifer. In return, Calcifer will break her curse. But breaking that agreement might be more difficult than Sophie expects. Nominated for Best Animated Feature 2005.

My Neighbor Totoro. **Directed by Hayao Miyazaki. Studio Ghibli, Disney/Buena Vista, 2006. 86 Minutes Long. 2 Discs. A**

Satsuki and Mei have just moved to a new home in the country. Their mother is sick in the hospital, and nothing is the same as it once was. However, when Mei stumbles across Totoro, the guardian of the forest, she makes a new friend. Totoro is large, fuzzy, and mysterious, and the girls are in for several adventures with their new friend.

Whisper of the Heart. **Directed by Yoshifumi Kondo. Studio Ghibli, Disney/ Buena Vista, 2006. 111 Minutes Long. 2 Discs. Y**

Shizuku has spent her summer reading, and she can't help but notice that every book she's checked out was previously checked out by one Seiji Amasawa. Besides this mystery, Shizuku ends up following a cat to mysterious store. The owner tells Shizuku the most interesting stories, and it is there that she actually runs to Seiji. As the two of them become friends, Seiji's determination to follow his dream inspires Shizuku to figure out what her own dreams are and follow them.

Grave of the Fireflies. **Directed by Isao Takahata. Studio Ghibli, ADV, 2009. 89 Minutes Long. 2 Discs. T**

Seita and Setsuko are a brother and sister struggling to survive during World War II in Japan. With the death of their mother and the absence of their father, the two of them struggle to find a place for themselves in the world and the means to survive. In the end, they are simply another two victims of the war.

Ponyo. **Directed by Hayao Miyazaki. Studio Ghibli, Disney/Buena Vista, 2010. 103 Minutes Long. 2 Discs.** **A**

When Sosuke finds a magical talking goldfish in the ocean near his house and names her Ponyo, a friendship will form between the two that has some unexpected consequences. Separated from Sosuke by her father, Ponyo will do just about anything to return to her new friend, including upset the balance of nature. The two friends have an interesting journey before them in order to set things right.

Tales From Earthsea. **Directed by Goro Miyazaki. Studio Ghibli, Disney/Buena Vista, 2011. 75 Minutes Long. 2 Discs.** **T**

Darkness and chaos have come to Earthsea. Something is trying to disrupt the balance of the world, and Prince Arren is caught in the middle of middle of it. He is on the run and haunted by something. However, the wizard, Sparrowhawk, takes him under his wing, and Arren begins to learn something of what is going on. But he may never be able to escape what stalks him if he does not confront it instead of running away.

Author Index

Title Index

Subject Index

Genre Index

This index covers titles that fit into a genre but are not in the genre's section in a chapter. It also covers genres that may not have their own individual sections in the book.

About the Author

ELIZABETH F. S. KALEN is a recent graduate of the University of Western Ontario's Master of Library and Information Science program. She has been an avid fan of manga and anime since middle school and continues to be one today. Elizabeth has spent time in Japan on several occasions and has worked with exchange program organizations both in Japan and the United States. She currently lives in Portland, Oregon, and is searching for her first library position. This is her first publication.